PRASHANT'S

An Incredible Life Journey !!!

Epitome of Patience, Courage and Endurance – Life of a
medico Legal case winner - straight from his father's heart

Seshadri. Mu. Ra

First published in 2020 by

Becomeshakespeare.com

Word it Content Design & Editing Services Pvt Ltd
119-123, Building No J2, Wadala Truck Terminal,
Wadala (East), Mumbai 400037, India
T: +91 8080226699

ISBN - 978-93-90040-18-6

Dedicated to

Shree Vigneshwaraya Namaha... Shree Venkateshaya Namaha
Also dedicated to the tireless efforts of dear Pavan
(the book's hero's heroic younger brother); to the heroic
mother Indira; scores of family well-wishers and friends
who stood by us like the Rock of Gibraltar.

ABOUT THE AUTHOR

Mu.Ra. Seshadri is a retired Sr. Executive from Bharat Heavy Electricals Limited, Hyderabad, India. After the death of his son in 2011, many of his friends and family requested him to bring out Prashant's story to the world to inspire people through his extraordinary life achievements under challenging circumstances.

It was a very painful exercise for him and his wife to re-live the difficult moments to compile the book. Not withstanding these difficulties the author went on to narrate the life story of his son (Late Prashant).

Prashant had definite plans to start charitable institutions for the physically challenged persons. In keeping with his last wishes the Author and his family have decided to utilise the entire sales proceedes of this book for the intended noble purpose.

FOREWORD

Respected Dr. Gururaj Karajagi Vidya-Vachaspathi Sir, It is my pleasure and our entire family's and friend's pleasure to be in contact with you, for over half a decade through your publications, pravachanas. We all stand fully benefited from your highly practical thoughts/expressions transmitted to the public through You-Tube. We are your keen followers and remain enchanted with your thoughts on Human Values and adopting such noble thoughts into our day-to-day living life and become most useful citizens of our motherland and mother globe.

In a much smaller way we have brought out this MS for Public Reading and assimilation so as to uplift, sky high, the morale of many thousands of differently abled brothers & sisters across the globe... It (the publication) is a downright practical narration of life of our very dear, very affectionate PRASHANT who went on to scale Himalayan Heights of glory and success DESPITE VERY SEVERE ENFORCED PARAPLEGIA confining him to wheel-chair life long from a sprinting, jolly, hilarious running jumping boy's stature.

Your highly thought out FOREWORD is Platinum lining for a golden book. We will be sharing our happiness as we progress towards bringing out the hard & e book copies of the biography.

Million thanks for the blessings.

IN LIEU OF A PREFACE

Truth really can be more amazing than fiction. The literature has all kinds of true stories of people rising above overwhelming odds and managing to succeed and even thrive in spite of situations that seem impossible. Learning about their experiences, we are inspired and feel more hopeful about dealing with our own life challenges.

True adversity hits hard and sometimes comes out of left field. That withstanding, I have, over a period of time, developed a mindset that *"life does not happen to you, it happens for you."*

As a religious person, I have come to terms that trials and blessings are somewhat the same thing.

I have made a conscious decision to perceive challenges as something that could make me a stronger person in the long run. With that perspective, I have been able to deal with my adversity in the most productive way. But to reiterate, it took a lot of conversations with friends and loved ones for me to arrive at this conclusion. You don't simply handle adversity. You must work through it with the support of others.

Human spirit has a remarkable ability to transcend almost anything that gets thrown at it. The strength of the human spirit is the force that guides people out of the darkness.

You don't have to be a believer to gain wisdom from this statement. With every challenge that comes our way, there is always a way out of it. That's the human spirit. The spirit comes through in the form of perseverance. Iron sharpens iron. Adversity builds character.

I can honestly tell you that not once people think about how wonderful it was that their character was being strengthened during the crisis. No sir. It sucked them completely! And it sucked for everyone! But once they were on the other side of the adversity, it is in retrospect that they saw the growth.

This became clear to me when I was reading the biography of Franklin D. Roosevelt whose life was truly a roller coaster. Franklin D. Roosevelt entered public service through politics, but as a Democrat. He won election to the New York Senate in 1910. President Wilson appointed him Assistant Secretary of the Navy, and he was the Democratic nominee for Vice President in 1920. In the summer of 1921, when he was 39, disaster hit him. He was stricken with poliomyelitis. Demonstrating indomitable courage, he fought to regain the use of his legs, particularly through swimming. At the 1924 Democratic Convention he dramatically appeared on crutches to nominate Alfred E. Smith as "the Happy Warrior." In 1928 Roosevelt became Governor of New York. He was elected President in November 1932. What a journey on the face of an adversity! Then I learnt a lesson that *"Our scars tell us where we have been in life. They do not have to define where we are going."*

All this came to my mind in a flash when I was given the soft copy of a book written by **Sri. Mu.Ra. Sheshadri** with the title, **"PRASHANT'S – An incredible journey".** This truly is a gripping story about an young man with dreams in his eyes and plenty of talents on his side was deprived of a happy and vibrant life by cruel fate and careless hands.

The story of Prashant's incredible journey touches each one of us. A very healthy boy with zest for sports and life goes on his two-wheeler to the hospital for a check for frequent fever associated with shivers and is rendered a lifelong paraplegic, is a ghastly tragedy. It is an unbelievably horrible episode. That too caused by a doctor! Medical Profession is one of the oldest professions and most humanitarian one. Doctors in India are treated as second life savers after God. The standard of care from doctors and hospital authorities is expected to be more in comparison with other cases of negligence. We go to the hospital with total trust and submit ourselves completely to the care of doctors. If that doctor does not stand up to the trust and we are let down, we lose faith in the profession itself.

When something terrible happens to the individual, it is natural that the person would fall into a depression. In other words, traumatic or difficult times in their lives lead these individuals to become depressed. Depression is insidious. It is sneaky and hard to identify. Some of them sought help and got medication prescribed to help level them out through the rough spot. Some stayed on the medication. Others stopped.

For all of them, one common denominator was the feeling of being alone in their problem. Isolation kept them from getting the help they needed, causing their situation to become worse. Whether from embarrassment, shame, stigma, or any of a host of other reasons, they turned inward and sometimes lost faith.

Fortunately, Prashant came out of the isolation and got the help he needed. Caring family members pulled him out. Prashant's younger brother, father and mother stood by him at every turn of the process in which he had to fight with his own health and also the legal battle. We know that the judicial process is irritatingly slow and expensive. Especially when this became a medico legal case, it was further complicated.

Public awareness of medical negligence in India is growing. Hospital managements are increasingly facing complaints regarding the facilities, standards of professional competence, and the appropriateness of their therapeutic and diagnostic methods. After the Consumer Protection Act, 1986, has come into force some patients have filed legal cases against doctors, have established that the doctors were negligent in their medical service, and have claimed and received compensation. The situation is not different in developed countries also. The National Health Scheme of the U.K. announced it has paid out more than £1.63 billion in damages for medical negligence in 2017/18; this is an increase from £1.08 billion in 2016/17 with the highest number of claims coming from emergency medicine.

It is truly exciting to learn from this book the gallant effort Prashant made to fight the case himself in the Supreme court. In fact, the judgement of the court makes a special mention about his poise and grace. *"Before we end, a word of appreciation for the complainant who, assisted by his father, had argued his matter. We must record that though a sense of deep injury was discernible throughout, his protracted submissions made while confined to a wheel-chair, he remained unruffled and with behaved quiet dignity, pleaded his case bereft of any rancour or invective of those who, in his perception, had harmed him"*.

That this battle took sixteen years bears testimony to the determination and perseverance of Prashant. His efforts resulted in the Highest court granting him the highest compensation in a medical case in India till then. (May 14, 2009). That is some consolation for the intense struggle that he led, though, it took away the vibrancy from his life and made him dependent always.

Though, Prashant did not live long, the saga of his life would always remain a role model and a great motivational story for any young person. I should really congratulate the entire family and particularly Sri. Sheshadri, the father of Prashant, for having withstood the agony and burden of managing the unimaginable crisis, supporting and travelling with his son everywhere, handling resources and most important, becoming a pillar of moral strength till the very end.

I have had tears in my eyes while reading a few narratives and I am sure every reader would be touched by this book. I recommend this book to every young person.

Dr. Gururaj Karajagi
18.12.2019

Chairman,
Academy for Creative Teaching, (ACT)
Bangalore - 560032

CONTENTS

INTRODUCTION

This is a narration of down to earth true facts in the life of an eminently different-from-vast-majority of youth. His life from day of birth in 1970 was simply rosy and rapturous all through; **but it was suddenly, without notice, violently shaken by a medical negligence unpardonable by any yardstick. It is beyond any sane guess.** Yes, **a blooming flower naturally beautiful and emanating fragrance was simply crushed under the thoughtless arrogant and negligent acts, all combined, of a surgeon. There was no reason or rhyme behind these life crippling surgery strikes;** and those strikes coming from a highly "a to z - MBBS; MD; Mch" qualified surgeon. This ghastly act occurred at his prime youthful age of 20+ years, but who, from his own inner strength, from his conviction, gallantry, and bravery, displayed by the youth quite out of the reach of ordinary masses, re-railed himself most admiringly

It is perhaps a paradox that people with excellent upbringing from their childhood face the challenges of life of calamities boldly, calmly and productively. The enforced damage dwarfed the mighty Himalayan mountain ranges! The wounds inflicted on him at the prime of youth cannot be equaled in depth even by Lake

PRASHANT'S-An Incredible Life Journey!!!

Baikal one of the deepest lakes on the globe. Imagine what it was to lose walking faculties at this young age when Prashant was the cynosure of all sports loving eyes!; Name a game he did not play, of course for recreation and health build up. He had learnt to swim in flowing waters at the age of Five (5) years, vocal music at the age of six years. To be felled from such a high pedestal in life and YET keep on self-boosting his morale to live life grandly despite the physically imposed handicaps required only guts of steel and he possessed this in abundance.

Although Prashant was compelled to have a break in education since 1990 to 1995 –for five crucial long years at the graduation level, he never lost his heart nor direction nor the steel will to re-rail himself on life tracks. He was most ably supported by his own live wire younger brother, who sacrificed one year of his academics to look after his needy elder brother, round the clock. Likewise, he was surrounded by a host of well-wishers who did not hesitate to take voluntary breaks even in their professional careers. **Nobility complemented nobility. Human love and affection at its zenith**. The bon-homie which he received to boost his morale that kept him moving forward, demonstrated the virtues of mankind.

The whole universe holds doctor-brethren and sister-doctors in high esteem for the noble services they render to humanity. Quite in contrast, what did, this small minority few do, to uphold the nobility of their profession? It will, certainly, go down in the history of medical attention as an incidence of shame that tarnished the name and nobility of that profession.

A fine needle piercing into the predetermined spot on Prashant's thorax apparently guided by ultrasound (or Fluoroscope guided), **certainly not requiring even local anesthesia, resulted in lifelong paraplegia. His walking faculties maimed; morning ablution activities all, totally rendered ineffective... As if these damages caused were not enough to qualify the already MD qualified medical doctor-brothers into award of higher post-doctoral faculty, they did not hesitate to cut off thoracic ribs, ligate intercostal arteries causing severe respiratory problems. To what extent** a surgeon can go to cause damage if he failed to consult with his colleagues on his proposed surgical procedure or for that matter on the treatment approach; **to what extent** he can cause damage to his patients if he did not carry out complete diagnoses duly taking advices from his colleagues for selecting such and such diagnostic procedure for pin pointedly understanding the root cause of the ailments/ diseases; **to what extent** he can cause damage to patients if he did not ascertain the risk-benefit analysis of treatment or refusing to undergo treatment. All such other issues would figure prominently in a medical treatise on Dos and Don'ts. And it all happened in the instant case of mini surgery for biopsy sake only for taking out a tiny spec of the extra grown unwanted masses!

A doctor has a special duty to the patients under his treatment to appraise them with the contours of the procedure he is contemplating, likely risks involved in the procedure, pre knowledge of handling/reversing damages if they occur.

Readers will soon learn in the pages to follow, how our country's Judiciary, non-medical, meticulously followed these basic commandments **even for hearing this very tragedy as a complaint before them** and before pronouncing their Landmark Judgment.

How Prashant, a youth well-bred since childhood in all aspects of decent living including studies, extracurricular activities like sports, music, rose like a meteor, despite having been suddenly reduced to a state of living vegetable, despite being forced to depend on daily activities totally on attendants round the clock, is now HISTORY .

IT IS NOW **ONLY** HISTORY of the PERIOD from 23rd October 1990 to 28th June 2011 AND BEYOND into ETERNITY.

And why was he pushed into this vegetative state? It would be a million-dollar question that would remain unpublished by the medical fraternity till eternity for obvious reasons; although it is not beyond a common non-medical person's comprehension after he browses through medical literature! **Even on the day of the enforced tragedy, Prashant had driven a full 40 km distance on his two-wheeler. Only a week before the tragedy, he had logged a dozen visits to the swimming pool, played cricket, tennis, tens of kilometers of jogging as part of activities additional to his mainstream of studies at college. Physio exercising at home, daily without let up, kept him fit as a fiddle. In short, there was no cause for any ill health since**

his childhood till this black day of October 23rd in the year 1990.

Prashant had very high ambitions galore to go in for higher studies and qualify himself to be Ph. D-Doctorate in Mechanical Engineering and to carry out special research later after obtaining a decade of practical experience. Alas! all these ambitions were severely crushed under the feet of the negligent doctors. With all these enforced obstacles, he went on to complete his Engineering Degree (sitting in wheelchair) with Honours; went on to acquire computer programming skills and software developments. There was no stopping him. Determination kept on elevating him professionally and landed him into lucrative jobs. He added several awards to his achievements.

Notwithstanding the physical challenges, he was deputed abroad for assignment with hard nut-to crack customers and returned to his motherland with plenty of feathers in his cap.

His achievements were not confined only to job. He had read medical literature about recovery from his enforced handicap. Although they had held hopes within the first 2 to 2 ½ years, Prashant's condition continued to be status quo as on the date of discharge way back in May 1991 and even beyond.

He enlisted the enthusiasm of his father to prepare for a legal battle. Prashant read and reread all that precious medical knowledge culled out from medical textbooks, publications and even from computer <med-line data

base> and became virtually a doctor to fight his case on equal footing with doctors who had harmed him. Whereas his father made out the strong case at the first encounter court of law namely The National Consumers Disputes Redressal Commission (abbreviated NCDRC) and won the case handsomely succeeding in that Hon'ble Court holding the doctors negligent on several counts; Prashant took upon himself to argue the case in the Highest Court of India namely the Supreme Court of India. The family was compelled to approach the Apex court on the aspect of enhancement of compensation (although we were extremely happy with the earlier Court, on the aspect of negligence). So thoroughly prepared was Prashant to argue his own case in the Apex Court that he held the Hon'ble Bench spell bound for nearly 3 days at a stretch, could convince the Hon'ble Bench of the gross negligence by the doctors and the Hospital cum Institute of Higher Learning. The court was pleased finally to dismiss the doctor's arguments and allowed Prashant's case and went on to pronounce **Their Judgment–a true Landmark indeed.**

After fighting patiently, painstakingly for nearly 16 years in the two Courts of Law of his mother land, Prashant received standing ovation in the hall of the Supreme Court of India for his acquired legal prowess, for his acquired medical knowledge in clinchingly convincing them on the damage caused to him by sheer negligence, malfeasance, misfeasance and nonfeasance.

The Judgment Order besides granting him the highest compensation in a medical case in India till then (Judgment Order dated 14th May 2009), was drafted to

record their appreciation as reproduced below: <Before We end, a word of appreciation for the complainant who, assisted by his father, had argued his matter. We must record that though a sense of deep injury was discernible throughout his protracted submissions made while confined to a wheel-chair, he remained unruffled and with behaved quiet dignity, pleaded his case bereft of any rancor or invective for those who, in his perception, had harmed him>.

PRASHANT'S-An Incredible Life Journey!!!

At Machilipatnam studying Engineering 1989

18 years Youth Prashant messing-up with food 1988

CHAPTER-I

FROM HAPPY COLLEGE DAYS TO HOSPITAL!!

It must have been around 5AM, the day dawning... Seshadri, Indira (Prashant's parents) and Pavan were still fast asleep. The main doorbell rang. "Oh, my goodness gracious, who could be knocking at the door at this angelic hour": Indira murmured.

"Who else can it be, it must be the milkman" sounded Seshadri still half asleep; prone to habit, involuntarily he got up, carried an empty vessel for receiving milk from the regular milk vendor. As soon as he opened the door, there were surprises galore! It was not the regular milk vendor; but standing at the door a tall, handsome figure smiled at him. Immediately he announced loudly: "Indira, Pavan! get up immediately and see for yourselves and experience the surprise for the day!".

It was indeed a pleasant surprise to one and all in the house. Pavan dashed down the flight of stairs **and greeted his elder brother**: "Hi, how come you at this hour and that too unannounced and returning home so soon! Is everything alright? Or is it you could not resist the temptation of mummy's yummy, yummy vegetable cutlets dipped in hot tomato sauce! We are all very curious to hear the reason for the sudden dash home more like a newly married daughter dashing to her parents at the first created opportunity".

The atmosphere at home suddenly got transformed into mirth and laughter quite akin to the rising Sun in the sky at that very fine morning moment.

Hardly had Prashant, alias Pantu, entered the house, the younger sprayed a barrage of questions at his elder; enquiring about the conditions at his newly adopted home i.e., the Machilipatnam college town: "How do you manage to get up in the morning all by yourselves? There is no daddy to sing < suprabhatam > into your ears to wake you up there!. What do you have for breakfast? Don't you miss mummy's favorite masala dosa with cocoanut chutney and mango pickles? What time do you get your bed coffee? What...What?" endless questioning!

Prashant smiled at his younger brother's anxiety. "Look, Machilipatnam cannot ever take the place of my mummy's home; I did get cold bed coffee, but good hot idli with chutni and mango pickles for breakfast. You know it is good for a student's health"; the trademark eternal smile involuntarily appeared in his face. The two brothers went on till 9 am exchanging the incidences at their respective places.

Mother would intervene, "boys now get ready for break-fast. You can continue your <parliamentary discussion > afterwards".

The two brothers soon got into wash mode and promptly appeared at the breakfast table. Favorite masala dosa was awaiting them. They enjoyed the sumptuous delicacy to their belly's content; had tea as a change and settled into the drawing room corner for continuation of their < parliamentary debating>

His chums living next door also joined them in their conversations. The usual atmosphere at home returned after a long break much to the enjoyment of their parents.

Pavan started sharing his high school 8th class anecdotes with Prashant, "Hey, look, you were not there to do my homework, I had to do it all by myself, do you guess the results! I managed to get the same grades as I used to, with your help; don't you appreciate and agree I have become wiser!"

Prashant smilingly patted him on his shoulders and said "who said you are less wise? I was confident of your level. I only used to help you so that we go out earlier to field and play cricket! Do you get me Steve? Prashant narrates his new atmosphere at college and hostel. "Hey Pavan" he continued, "There is no mummy or daddy to wake me up; But my chum Sreeram - alert and active like the traditional < Guntur mirchi> (Guntur town is famous in Andhra Pradesh, for hot variety of chillies!), would be over my bed, pouring drops of water into my ears at exactly 5:30am. I had to perforce, get up at 5:30am hesitatingly".

"I would join the long queue for bath and manage to be there before 6:30am"

Pavan had a hearty laugh at the enforced discipline

brought into his elder brother's life. "Hey boo (that is how they used to address each other jokingly); which other friend would help you to go to breakfast table". Pavan cajoled his elder. "What do you mean? I am crazy for breakfast as you know. So, I do not need anybody's help. We have many messes to choose from; we do visit all of them by turns. Food is of course good. The specialty of Machilipatnam was - there are white chutney, red chutney, grey chutney, green pickles for dosa and idli. We all thoroughly enjoyed each and every dish and side dish": Prashant mischievously declared.

The two brothers went on and on unmindful of time ticking to noon! Indira, mother of the two brothers reminded them "It is getting late for lunch"; She had already prepared special dishes for the children. All four in the family congregated for lunch and thoroughly enjoyed every delicacy served on the table. Prashant, having missed out the vegetable cutlets, would ask mummy for a second and even third helping of the delicacy.

Lunch over, both the brothers, one thought, would settle for a short nap. But the two- some apparently had other plans. Old chums descended on their sweet home. David- one of his chums was surprised to see his friend back home so soon. "What is the matter dear? How come you are here leaving the college at this time of the academic year?

"Forced holidays yaar, Mandal Commission had recommended reservations for students from backward castes. But we had all protested against the Commission on their really <backward recommendations>"; public at large and students in particular, had no objections for such reservations purely with the aim of up-lifting <backward students at studies > but class distinctions based on castes, creed, religion or gender had no place in their society. "So, We all students bunked college and as such I managed to get back home; hey, how about playing short cricket": suggested Prashant. All jumped in at the proposal and Lo! They were all soon off to cricket field. David bowled 6 balls in an over without conceding a single run, called <a maiden over> in cricket parlance.

Prashant chipped in, "hey dear chum, since when did you learn to bowl maidens over? you were simply so shy just a year back and would keep off company of girls!"

"No yaar! I have to keep pace with changing times; you see"; silently utters David. All had a hearty laugh. "It is too hot to continue playing cricket": Pavan suggested for a dash of the company to swimming pool. Soon all were in the pool waters. The two brothers displayed their prowess in free style swimming; David had specialized in butterfly strokes. Together they all swam across and along the pool several times. Tired, they all lay flat on their backs floating and deep breathing and soon regained their energy back to normal.

"I miss this sport in waters yaar; my college is still constructing the pool on the drawing board! However, Sri Ram and I would venture into the not far off sea and enjoy swimming particularly on weekends for hours on end". Prashant shared his thoughts with fellow chums. All returned home downright tired. The ever-understanding mom of the two brothers had prepared delicious dishes to appease the hungry palates of her children. Both the brothers drew their mom's attention from the front door. "Mummy we are hungry like wolves; what special delicacy you have prepared for us and for our friends?: enquired the two brothers. Lo, the two smelt from the distance itself, hot tomato soup being brought in a tray, "Here is your pet dish. Enjoy to your heart's content", so saying she placed the large tray with tomato soup and bread crumbs.

"What is next mom", demanded the two brothers is unison after gulping down two bowls of soup each. "Your next favourite is here", so saying she pushed another large tray over the table. "Hey! Look David, my mom knows your taste. Delicious hot vegetable cutlets with tomato sauce and chilli sauce are inviting you. No compromise freely enjoy as many as you want", Prashant announced to the gathering around the table. "What next?" all sang in chorus. "Let us see the famous Telugu-film <SAAGAR SANGAM > with Kamal Hassan in the male lead and the beauty queen-Jayaprada as the heroine" announced Prashant beaming his eternal smile.

Mom and dad could hear soundtracks from the bedroom at the top. Laughter, loud cheers were flying into the thin nightly air from the room at the top. "Good night children; retire to bed soon, you have to get up early" so saying the parents went off to bed.

All of a sudden parents encountered Pavan downstairs with abated breath in the middle of the night; "Mom, Prashant is shivering violently on the bed; please come up immediately". All of them ran upstairs and noticed him in total discomfort. He was having heavy rigorswith temperature.

Pavan had already called for the BHEL hospital ambulance. The ambulance had reported with a mobile doctor. He promptly examined Prashant then and there itself and advised the young student to be shifted to hospital. On arrival at the hospital, the young patient was, on examination, found to have high temperature, accompanied with shivering. The patient was administered avil injection intra-veinously and paracetamol tablet orally and kept under observation for the next hour.

This treatment appeared to have worked on him; for, we found him off to sound sleep and with temperatures recorded every half an hour, coming down to normal. He was already under the care of devoted nurses and duty doctors. Pavan and his mom retreated to their home located within walking distance from the township hospital.

Anxiety about Prashant's condition brought back Pavan and his mummy to the hospital next morning involuntarily. He was found already awake reading the morning newspaper. "Dad, Mom, Pavan do not worry, I had a good long sleep. I do not have any temperature now". Indira had brought steaming hot idlis with

Chutney. Her previous night's worries disappeared on seeing her son with the ever patent smile. "Prashant get up and break your fast". So, saying she served him a plate of idlis. "Very delicious, can I have 2 more Mom?" So saying he had a second helping.

Morning duty doctor thoroughly examined the patient and found him to be normal. Seeing this normal and stable condition, dad left for his office. Pavan left for his college. Mother, however decided to stand by and sent in her leave application to the school where she was working. It was lunch time for mom and Prashant. The two ate together and both went off on a short nap. A little while later however, Prashant woke up his mother saying, "I am feeling a bit uncomfortable with a sort of chill and shivering; give me blanket".

Mother beckoned the duty nurse "sister, please cover the patient with blanket and call the duty doctor for thorough check up immediately". It was about 3pm in the afternoon; the duty doctor visited the patient and examined him. "How are you Prashant?" enquired the doctor.

"Violent shivering and temperature bother me for a second time doctor" he replied. As a first aid, the doctor prescribed avil injection and paracetamol tablet; took leave of him to visit another patient. The medicines apparently seemed to be effective as the patient got back to normal without any shivering and any temperature.

In the evening both his dad and Pavan descended on the hospital directly from their respective workplaces.

On seeing Prashant, both enquired, "dear, how are you today?" he smilingly replied: "daddy I am fine alright. But this temperature and rigors seem to play hide and seek with me!"

Hearing this, father got a bit worried and enquired from the duty doctor, "What do you say about these symptoms of fever and rigours visiting him quite often?"

He also expressed his anxiety and plans to thoroughly investigate into these symptoms. He turned to nursing sister and advised, "take blood samples and send them to laboratory for investigation to rule in /rule out any malaria and/or typhoid because symptoms point in that direction". Sister arrived with syringe and approached Prashant. "Oh! My goodness gracious! Sister, how a sweet person like you can cause pain to me!" said he, cajoling her. "Do not worry; it is only a micro needle prick far less than a mosquito bite! so saying, the nurse gave < her patient> a big smile and drew two vials of blood samples.

Mother left for home only to prepare dinner and then return to hospital. In the meantime, Prashant's friends had come to know of his hospitalisation and they all descended into the hospital to give him company. As usual the atmosphere had been enlivened with jokes flying across freely, accompanied by bursts of laughter now and then. Young as they were, the duty nurses and doctors also joined the band wagon to share jokes.

Duty doctor: "Prashant you are alright; take good rest and if all is well, we may discharge you by the next

Evening". So, saying he bade his patient "good night". Mother had planned to give him company and therefore stayed back at the hospital. They both chatted till about 10 pm and dosed off to sleep. On her regular hourly rounds the duty nurse found him experiencing rigors at about midnight. He was found to have high temperature. The duty doctor was requested by the patient's mother to study this repeat cycle of shivering with temperature - this was the second night's observation in a row.

Seeing pulse rate, BP all normal, the doctor again prescribed the repeat medicines; patient again got back to normalcy and went off into sound sleep; The clock struck six gongs in the morning. Both mother and Prashant were awake; after exchanging morning pleasantries, he beckoned his mother for a hot cup of BOURN VITA. So far so good; "Sister, let me see the last reports on blood samples taken already". And the doctor saw the blood report as Malaria/ typhoid negative. When, for the 4th time, the rigors and fever symptoms visited him again, the entire investigating team of medical personnel got jittery.

Quite perplexed, the doctor on duty consulted with his senior colleagues about this on and off fever and rigors phenomenon. They all, this 4th time, decided to <catch these unwanted visitors by the scruff of their neck> and decided on investigation and this time, to see if it is any manifestation of possible pneumonia. A chest X-ray was ordered, and Prashant comfortably walked into X-ray room without any assistance.

To the dismay of one and all, the chest X-ray revealed

Many surprises! Bony - erosion of 2nd, 3rd and 4th ribs in the thorax, Huge masses spreading into the <posterior -mediastinal region of thorax>! The doctors at BHEL co.'s hospital went into a mini conference and decided to get the patient thoroughly investigated with CT scans and biopsy of the extra grown masses. The chief medical officer in charge of BHEL hospital had already prepared complete set of history sheets and the referral documents and sent for PRASHANT's father who was busy in a <production review> meeting at the factory premises. Within an hour, he arrived at the hospital and met his Co's Chief Medical Officer - colleague. "Doctor is everything alright with my son" enquired anxious Seshadri, PRASHANT's father.

"Nothing to worry about. But the presence of huge masses in the posterior mediastinal region having eroded 3 ribs in a row must be investigated thoroughly. So, we are referring the patient to multi-specialty Institution of Medical Sciences at Hyderabad. Ambulance and referral papers are ready; please accompany your son in the ambulance to Hyderabad city". So, saying, he handed over all papers including lab reports on blood samples, X-rays, to a junior doctor who would accompany the patient in the ambulance.

On the way to the multi-specialty hospital in Hyderabad, we reached a well-known diagnostic center for yet another scanning of the chest to ascertain the vastness of spread of the tumor masses through Computerized Tomography (CT scan). These scans also confirmed the presence of huge masses invading into the various

Structures in the posterior mediastinum, closest to the vertebral bodies.

On arrival at the IMS (Institute of Medical Sciences), chest physician specialist Dr. Ashish Bogani saw the healthy, blooming, smiling Prashant and wondered who the patient was!; he examined all the X-ray and CT scans in details, noticed the erosion of three ribs in continuous sequence clearly from CT scans and put down his understanding of the reading as < Neurofibroma > ?!

At this stage this specialist chest physician had to handover this case to his senior professional colleague in internal medicine due to his scheduled departure to USA for higher learning. **This could have been a welcome second opinion if only the internal medicine professor had taken clues from the recorded opinion of his younger colleague**. Dr. Vaidya (name changed) of the IMS, recommended FNAB/ FNAC Biopsy procedures. "We will take out tiny noninvasive samples from the biopsy procedure and ascertain the pathological nature of the tumor in the hospital's laboratory": said Dr. Vaidya to Prashant's attendants.

All including the investigation team had to wait for a full 5 days to get the result of biopsy after the mandatory 96 hours culturing period in the laboratory. Being an outpatient Prashant and his attendants went back to their routine with instructions to come back for results of biopsy after one week.

A week passed by, **Prashant** readied himself and, **hopped on to ride the two-wheeler and signaled "daddy you be**

Comfortable as pillion rider; I will drive all the way".
Father and son duo drove through thick and thin of
traffic and reached the hospital- a full 25km away from
home and immediately met Dr. Vaidya and enquired
"Doctor is the report of biopsy ready?"

"Ready alright but not conclusive" came the reply from
the Physician. Anxiety clearly discernible on his face,
Seshadri enquired back "How come no results doctor?
The tumor masses, as you have seen in CT scans and
X-rays, do exist like a monster in the chest. They appear
very much like the great Himalayas".

Dr. Vaidya replied: "I am myself baffled! Let me order a
repeat of the FNAB under fluoroscope guidance instead
of the earlier ultrasound guidance. So, saying he directed
us to the laboratory for yet another noninvasive FNAB
biopsy. The lab technician on seeing the beaming Prashant
quipped: "I am sorry, I have to push the long needle again
into your back! but I am sure you will bear this pain of
piercing again for the final time!" Prashant was all smiles
and uttered: "you can go ahead, no problem, after all I
have to be game for <WHAT CANNOT BE CURED must
BE ENDURED!>" Second week of anxiety to get at the
result also turned out to be a failure!

Unwittingly, at this diagnosis stage, wiser counsels
appeared to have let down the <men in white coat>! Or had
they stopped thinking altogether? In either case they had
allowed themselves to be carried back to "square number
one" 'WITH NO FINDINGS EVEN after 3 such FNAB/
FNAC Biopsy attempts on definitely existing unwanted

masses. THIS CERTAINLY IS a case of KIDDING against a patient who had come to the hospital for sound, well thought over, well planned histo-pathological investigations. Father of brave Prashant lamented "Oh my dear doctor of medical letters, what next ?"

"We will try the sure shot CT guided biopsy this last time" somewhat confidently announced Dr. Vaidya! And beckoned the lab-technician

"Sir, the CT guiding equipment is presently out of order" said Dr. Krishna Murthy (the attending Radiologist) and suggested that he could do biopsy <under fluoroscope guidance>.

Dr. Vaidya: "let us go ahead with the suggestion". Yes. Fluoroscope guided FNAC biopsy was done alright! But ONCE AGAIN it all turned out to be a failed procedure!

It was a crucial juncture and simply baffling and embarrassing to the medical men claiming a to z lengthy qualifications (MBBS, MD, M.Ch). Alert mother of dear Prashant, who incidentally taught Science subject to high school children within the BHEL Township, joined the team of doctors with her version /understanding of the instant situation. "Doctors, the lump/mass growth may not be ONE MASS like a sphere BUT, in all certainty, could be <inter-twined and crisscrossed like a young girl's hair plait>; the piercing needle could be missing the target and instead, entering into the empty space in between two plaits!!"

No reaction but only spell-bound faces of the attending Medical team members!!

Like a magician <producing a pigeon from nearly no-where>, Dr Vaidya darted out " IDEA! IDEA!." He prescribed an altogether new "invention!"; and this happened to be "SURGERY – called in medical parlance – Excision biopsy by thorocotomy" because, perhaps at that stage, it occurred to his cerebrum that surgical procedure was the only available method.

How rationale was this decision at this juncture will remain a subject matter for thesis /theses for all the post graduate students of medicine around the globe. These thoughts and decisions will remain questionable for the present, for the morrow and future; particularly in the backdrop of failure to detect even after 4 biopsies. After all these monstrous tumor masses existed in the patient's thoracic zone clinchingly captured both in pre diagnostic X-ray and CT scans.

A paradoxical situation prevailed. Even a non-medical person like Prashant's mother could think of the definite possibilities of the probing needle missing the target because of its scattered and clustered pattern not necessarily a single lump. But these medical experts could not exercise their minds over these possibilities.

An arrogant doctor expressed his feeling: "I am very busy; I have to attend several waiting patients. Let me adopt the sure shot, fail-safe procedure of removing the masses in their entirety. Let me thereafter study coolly in uttermost details, the nature of these masses in the laboratory". To the stressed and strained parents and Prashant included, it looked as though, as if they are planning <to remove the uterus if a lady does not want any more children!!>.

Prashant's father spoke to Dr. Vaidya "but doctor; How could you think of a major surgery for a mini – biopsy. How could you think of cure for diagnoses; how could you think of a surgical prescription without knowing the root cause of the problem?"

Dr. Vaidya: "I can understand your anxiety as father. But you must allow me to do my utmost duty in all its sincerity. After all I know, having over a century count of publications on internal medicine to my credit, what is right or what is wrong?" "The only method, the only prescription practiced all over the world, is excision biopsy by thorocotomy!" But these thoughts remained only in his cerebrum. Neither the patient under investigation nor the parents nor his affectionate brother Pavan were aware of the complicated surgical procedure but only thought it to be a simple biopsy procedure for histopathological examination.

"Prashant you get admitted for the above procedure", Dr. Vaidya gave his final verdict and walked away for his other assignments. The two brothers wanted to have their heart's content and decided "hey Pavan, let us enjoy before we get bogged down at hospital with pre-operative procedures from 19th Oct 1990 for a full 4 days!" suggested the elder Prashant.

A long list of entertainment including visits to chat masala down the hospital lane

Avenue; seeing Telugu movie at Ameerpet - not far

Away from the hospital, again were penned down. Prashant drove his younger brother on their daddy's two-wheeler and parents followed them to the hospital in an auto rickshaw. All formalities gone through and he was promptly wheeled into the private ward as inpatient on 19th Oct 1990 well before 9am that morning.

Duty nurse promptly announced, "I will be back into the private ward with sterile sets of syringes for blood sampling etc. before noon". Taking this opportunity (of 3 hours for start of investigation!) Prashant decides "Hey Pavan, let us quickly go over to that masala joint just across the hospital avenue". So, deciding the duo disappeared from the hospital and after entering the eatery ordered their favourite dish - < Bhelpuri chat masala >." Very tasty indeed", said Pavan, "shall we have one more helping"?

"Oh no, Duty sister will administer < laxatives > first instead of pricking me for blood samples!!": Cajoled Prashant with his eternal trademark smile. "Okay let us call it quits for now" so deciding, the two brothers return to hospital bed promptly before noon. Duty nurse arrived promptly with sparkling stainless-steel tray fully loaded with several sets of sterile syringes, cotton swabs denatured spirit in mini – bottles and of course at least half a dozen sterilized sealed test tubes for samples collection.

She had taken care to label all the test tubes with patient's name, his hospital inpatient No. duly bar- coded, all securely bonded with self-adhesives on to them

As she approached the bed, she saw the occupant reading newspaper. "Prashant, one moment please; let me take first two samples of your blood"; she tried to rub spirit soaked swab on his wrist; but lo!, to her surprise, she noticed Prashant had disappeared from the bed and instead noticed the younger brother Pavan reading newspaper on the bed!. Pavan instantly jumped out of bed saying "sister, you are dialing the wrong number!"

Before she recovered from her shock and gained her mental balance, she could see Prashant sprinting into the ward only to confuse her further! She stood motionless and uttered "who is the non-patient between the two of you brothers?": Prashant apologized for the confusion and mix up caused and offered his hand for the prick; duty sister finally succeeded in drawing blood from the designated patient. "Any more for the day sister?" he enquired.

"No, this is all for the day. Next prick will be tomorrow for further detailed investigations "replied the equally young sister with a mischievous smile on her face.

The two brothers turned on the room TV for watching their passion sport! Cricket; exchanged news of their respective colleges at Machilipatnam (Prashant was doing his 3rd year degree in mechanical engineering) and Hyderabad (where the younger brother was studying pre-university final). All along Prashant narrated his rendezvous and adventure in the Bengal Sea in the company of his classmates & chums SriRam, Raghuram, Venumadhav; how he daringly pulled his classmate

Out from the sea preventing a near drowning incident. "Hi Prashant, it is boring here till next morning .Let us disappear from here and watch cricket match on TV with our chums at home; Mummy will be game to keep on feeding us with our delicious eats " Pavan added.

"Then we have to take permission from the duty doctor", saying this both of them met the doctor on duty: "Hey, what are you up to? Tomorrow will be a total tests day; don't forget you are an inpatient here" cautioned the doctor smilingly.

"Doctor you also watch TV in between rounds and for the same avowed madness i.e., cricket! We will definitely report back at least an hour earlier than spelled out by you" cajoled the two brothers in reply in unison. "Okay, Okay, don't put me into disrepute, I may even be taken to task by the hospital administration. So do come back and report to me with an empty stomach before 7am tomorrow", so uttering, he signed the slip permitting them to dash home now worry free. Prashant only drove the scooter with Pavan as the pillion rider and they both reached home. Mother was saying her evening prayers and was disturbed by the call- bell at this unusual late evening hour; she stood motionless as she saw her pet children at the door, "how on earth you are back home?; what transpired between you both and the duty doctor?; you have disappeared from the ward like before!; have you at least taken permission from the duty doctor?" So poured out her mind, the affectionate mother of the duo. Not minding the unscheduled kitchen duty, Indira set herself the task of preparing delicacies of their liking.

As planned, they switched on the home TV to watch cricket. Dinner over, the two brothers bade good night to their parents and went upstairs.

Curious as always, father of the duo sneaked into their bedroom to see for himself if they are really taking rest. Lo! What did he find?; Jokes flying across and daddy hearing them talking: "Hey Pavan, what if the nurse had taken in the noon, your blood sample instead of mine because of your supine position on the patient's bed!". "No problem for us is it not? Your blood would have been declared as < O Rh +ve > and mine would have been declared as< B Rh +ve>" joked Pavan.

"You say no problem!; the whole team of doctors would have been sent into a state of utter confusion" said Prashant.

"Hey look, yesterday's duty doctor who had recorded your blood as < O Rh +ve > and today's doctor and nurse would have recorded it   as < B Rh +ve>, Ha! Ha! Ha!" laughed Pavan aloud. And finally, the two brothers appeared to have dosed off as the parents down below did not hear any more < gaffa>; it was already mid night!

Promptly the two got up early, got ready and soon were on the road driving on the scooter to hospital; timely, they remembered that Prashant should present before the duty doctor with stomach empty. They finally made it to the hospital, reported on time to the ward- doctor.

"Sister good morning! now you can try your investigations on the taller of the two brothers i.e., myself- the real patient!": Uttered Prashant giving her his patent

Smile. Sister promptly reaches the ward with syringes and this time she attended on the correct patient (the elder of the two brothers)! took two more samples of blood and left for the laboratory.

Dr. Vaidya the internal medicine expert visited his inpatient, went through the X-rays. CT scans and the previous day's reports on blood.

He talked to the patient's mother who was present there in the ward at that time and holding the X-rays in his hand he blurted out," Do you have another child?".

Somewhat perturbed, mother replied: "Yes, I have a second child"

Dr. Vaidya: "boy or girl?"

Mother: "Doctor! What does it matter to you or to the present situation? anyway, it is okay, the second child is also a boy".

Dr. Vaidya: "then you are very lucky indeed";

 To which mother shouted back "What do you want to convey through your unparliamentarily discussion?".

Dr. Vaidya: "Madam you see, I find from the X-rays and CT scans that Prashant has no hope of survival".

Mother: "Doctor, you have admitted the patient for further investigations which are just underway, how then you draw your own <celestial conclusions> only from X-rays / CT scans?".

DR. Vaidya: "You see, the X-rays & CT scans show the

Existence of huge masses in the thoracic cavity and very rarely a patient can survive in such a case".

Mother: "Mere existence of a huge mass without establishing whether it is benign or malignant has led a professor and an expert in medicine to such a damaging conclusion! Kudos to you, Professor!!"

"Four biopsies conducted earlier have not given any conclusive evidence on the histopathological nature of the tumor masses. Is it not baffling doctor, that such a huge mass, **if turning out to be malignant**, can allow a patient to live long without any symptoms as they grow from a small speck to such a big size (described as football size by CMO of BHEL hospital)?"

She went on further and loudly shouting at him asked: "If you had announced such a damaging opinion **that too, before laboratory checkup**, to an illiterate and weak minded mother of the patient under investigation, could you imagine the condition of such a mother?"

"Is it difficult for you to foresee that she would have definitely collapsed on to the floor? You have obviously transgressed all cannons of ethics in uttering /drawing without proof, such lamentable and unsubstantiated inferences / conclusions?"

Perhaps such silly thoughtless outbursts and behavior by a professor in internal medicine, could have elucidated pardon from Prashant's father, but certainly not from the life –giver i.e.; Prashant's mother. Soft spoken mother, however, took courage and questioned as to how a professor level doctor can make such inferences / Conclusions without biopsy. (It is not to suggest that juniors have permission to draw such baseless, unproven inferences) when it is universally known that<biopsying> is a mandatory diagnostic procedure for ascertaining the pathological nature of the tumor masses to rule out/or rule in the malignancy based on the biopsy results before even thinking of penning down any prescription.

This conversation apparently cockled his thinking process and that is perhaps, why he decided to recommend <excision biopsy by thorocotomy> which procedure, he went on to explain in later part of Prashant's life, meant, both as cure and diagnosis! In the meanwhile, he continued to be hale and hearty and even mercurial, as doctors were ransacking their brains for the persistently elusive pin- pointing result.

19th Sept 1990 to 18th Oct 1990 - A full one-month period was available for pre- prescription investigations- a period of time long enough to carry out all diagnostic procedures! Prashant went through this investigation period by shuttling between his residence in BHEL Hyderabad Township and multi-specialty hospital- a full 25kms distance, joyfully covered on 2 wheeler with father riding the pillion. He never lost this opportunity of frequent visits to hospital, for enjoying his avowed pastime namely visiting eateries, hotels and cinema theatres in between investigations.

Came 18th Oct 1990: Prashant visited the designated Multi specialty hospital, reported to Dr. Adimanava

- The famous CT surgeon who promptly uttered: "Prashant you get admitted tomorrow itself; we will be going ahead with further tests/checkups before the scheduled surgical procedure for biopsy sake".

Prashant's father to the designated surgeon: "Dr. how do you go about for the biopsy?"

"We are going to make a small incision into the posterior thorax to take out a micro sample of the tumor masses", said the attending designated surgeon.

"Doctor, I have plans to see cricket match at least post lunch session. So, can I be sure of being freed from the procedures within an hour?" Prashant smiled at the doctor. Patting him (his patient) on his back, Doctor assured: "do not worry. It is a small tiny procedure for taking out a tiny sample. I suppose you should be free to go back to your private ward within a matter of half to one hour".

He finally walked back to the scooter parking area, drove back home. Mother anxiously waiting at home welcomed the duo with yet another eatery delicacy.

Dawned 19th October 1990, Prashant gallantly took to the steering wheel again with his younger brother seated in front and parents seated in the back. The 4 wheel-drive lasted just an hour and all four presented before the hospital administration for allotment of private room with TV and internet facilities. The sisters lost no time in starting off with blood sampling. Junior doctor presented himself at the private ward and started checking all essential parameters:

HR (Heart Rate): 84 \ per minute (normal)

Temperature: 98.4 F (normal)

BP - - - ---------: 120/80 mms of Hg (normal)

"No h/o (history/ of): chest pain; cough; palpitation; not a known diabetic; not hypertensive

O/E (on/ examination): well built, well nourished: Not anemic, not cyanosed nor jaundiced;

: No clubbing or pedal edema

CVS: NAD (nothing abnormal detected)

Laboratory investigations revealed: HB, BUN, Creatinine; FBS, Urine all normal; No Neurological problem at the instant hour.

Between 20th October 1990 and 23 rd. October 1990: The duty doctors and the attending nursing staff carried out regular checkups to ensure that the patient was < free from any > hurdles like fever, cough, cold which would otherwise lead to postponement of the planned surgical intervention albeit for biopsy sake only.

23rd Oct 1990 SUN rose as brightly as ever! But no casting of shadow of any coming event. No indication of WHAT WAS IN STORE?

The designated surgeon visited Prashant in his private ward; the latter addressing the doctor expressed: "Doctor, I would like to brief you about my future plan, before the start of the medical procedures. I am determined to complete my BE Degree course by

March 1991 from Machilipatnam, India; go on further to complete Masters in Mechanical Engineering abroad; go further on to acquire a Doctorate in Mechanical Engineering in Design specialization; take up teaching in Universities abroad before returning home to serve my motherland. Teaching is my obsession. I take it that I am being subjected to biopsy procedures ONLY and any decision on any prescription will be only after knowing the results/findings from biopsy"

The designated surgeon's reply was in the affirmative Indicating that he was in tune with the patient's thoughts.

SO FAR SO GOOD!!

Promptly a nurse arrived to take Prashant into the Operation Theatre with a wheelchair. It was 9 'o clock in the morning. "Why wheelchair sister? I can as well, just walk into the OT myself" he smilingly addressed her.

"No Prashant, it is the hospital "diktal" please do not take it bad": replied the sister giving him a broad smile.

"Ok! It is your prerogative. Get me the chair" Prashant indicated.

Promptly he occupied the wheel chair and entered the OT after smiling at his parents, younger brother and well- wishers gathered outside the OT.

The younger brother Pavan and Anupama (god sister for both the brothers) had made it a point to wish Prashant a quick return from OT after biopsy procedure;

parents in Turn, had blessed him for safe return from the operation theatre with the biopsy results coming out uneventful and insignificant.

"I will be back perhaps within an hour": so, saying he smiled at all and passed through the widely flung open OT door. With Prashant inside the OT, all his Kith and Kin and friends started a lengthy discussion on the possible outcome of biopsy.

Pavan remarked "Let us all go out for the matinee show along with my elder brother who will, in any way come back by 10AM i.e., just within an hour."

"No yaar": uttered David (PRASHANT's chum and classmate) "Prashant liked to eat out at hotel Sarovar, we will all drive after matinee show"; discussions continuing endlessly, plans for outing poured from each one of PRASHANT's company gathered at the hospital.

The clock struck 10 gongs; an hour had already elapsed. David told everyone present "Now Prashant will come out of the theatre, giving us all his customary trademark smile".

The waiting period got transformed into lively joking session.

Krishnan burst out with laughter when Pavan cracked his elder brother's pet joke on the Indian flying - Sikh

- Milka Singh <overtaking the thief instead of catching him!!>; hospital ambience had been turned into a gay atmosphere.

Even the on lookers and waiting- ins of other patients joined in to make the atmosphere even more lively. As the clock was ticking fast towards 12 noon, parents in particular were lost in chanting prayers for uneventful results of biopsy.

****

Even the on lookers and waiting- ins of other patients joined in to make the atmosphere even more lively. As the clock was ticking fast towards 12 noon, parents in particular were lost in chanting prayers for uneventful results of biopsy.

CHAPTER- II

BLACKEST DAY IN PRASHANT's LIFE

Time was ticking fast it was already 12:30 noon. Everybody present, started to look towards the OT door in expectation of Prashant walking out a free man.

Doctors were seen walking out of the OT door. Even as a wheelchair appeared at the door exiting, Pavan rushed to the doctors asking "How is Prashant, is he coming out next? wait a minute doctor, some wheelchair is coming…"

On noticing a different patient in the wheelchair, Pavan's anxiety grew deeper. Doctors left for their wards without answering him. Queries, Curiosity, anxiety only seemed to multiply.

Parents, Pavan and friends started looking at all trolleys being wheeled, after surgical procedures, out of OT for being kept under post-surgery observation prior to discharge.

Prashant's mother filled to the brim with anxiety expressed to her husband "trolleys after trolleys have been wheeled out of the OT complex and yet no sign of Prashant's trolley!"; yet another doctor came out of the

OT door, Indira rushed to him and enquired "How is Prashant? It is already 3hours since he entered the OT; it was planned to bring him (the patient) out within a half to one hour. Why don't you tell us?"

Doctor replied: "Inside the OT complex I operated upon another patient by name George, please wait for your doctor to come out and apprise you of the outcome", so saying he paced away.

Yet another trolley appeared at the exit door, David rushed to the trolley only to get disappointed in not spotting his chum coming out. All of a sudden but only after 3 full and a good half hour later, he noticed yet another trolley and shouted.

"At last it is Prashant's trolley being wheeled out".

Everybody rushed towards the trolley and in one voice addressed "Prashant, how are you?"

No response! but the trolley was being wheeled towards intensive care unit (ICU). The sister pushing the trolley was asked! "Where are you taking our Prashant after biopsy? Is it not for giving him a small rest in a general ward before discharging him?"

< Prashant will be under observation in the ICU > replied sister.

"But why ICU? Sister", shot back Prashant's father. "The procedure was only for biopsy".

However, the sister stopped the trolley for the patient's attendants to have a look at him. On getting no response from Prashant the nurse explained. "Patient continues to be under the influence of General Anesthesia, he will undergo intensive care".

"But sister! sister! where is the concerned surgeon who performed the surgical procedure? And why admit him into ICU?", demanded the anxious father and mother in one voice. "I have no idea where the surgeon is?", so replying, she continued her trolley- pushing forward to ICU. The situation was quite embarrassing and questionable for, nowhere in the world, the operating surgeon failed to turn up at least after the surgery to briefly brief the anxious attendants of the patients about the outcome of the procedure within the OT

No sight of the concerned surgeon, no sight of his assistants either, despite three crucial hours post operatively; and this sent shock waves into the assembled crowd of attendants and well-wishers. They started debating amongst themselves.

Suddenly they all found the patient's father darting towards the lift which had carried away his dear son to ICU.

"No time to wait for the lift" so uttering to himself he darted towards the staircase and literally started to fly down the flight of stairs, sometimes skipping a step and another time hopping into the 3rd step. Somehow, within a matter of minutes he had to reach the ground floor; reach the ground floor he did alright; but hectic efforts to locate either Dr. Adimanov or the neurosurgeon (who had been invited into the OT by the operating CT surgeon) failed to locate either of them.

They apparently had disappeared into thin air without having the courtesy and also without performing the primary duty to inform the attendants about what transpired inside. What stood out predominantly was the inaction on the part of operating surgeon to brief the attendants about the outcome of medical procedure. Anxious mother of Prashant also uttered: "how can the two fail in their duty to meet the anxiously waiting attendants and brief them; why they chose to disappear into thin air without using the front door at which location all the attendants were waiting anxiously with abated breath".

Prashant's father and Pavan concluded with tension gripping their minds: "Most probably the surgeon must have caused some serious damage during the biopsy procedure itself."

Anupama was at her wits end and exclaimed "how can a small biopsy procedure, admittedly needing administration of General Anesthesia to enable painless incision into the thorax, go on for < hours on end > uncle?: he must have caused some big damage and that is why the doctor appeared to have fled the scene "so saying she also darted down the flight of stairs.

Pavan obviously under melancholy reverberated "how can my dear brother continue to remain under the influence of GA even three hours after cessation of mini surgical procedure, consented to, only for biopsy purpose?". These two vital thoughts continued to haunt every one of the gallant Prashant's attendants.

They scattered themselves in all directions to locate the perpetrator of the anxiety i.e., the great Dr. Adimanava; but he was not traceable even after ransacking several possible locations – the OPD consultation wards, post recovery wards, his office, the hospital library.

"Where could he have gone? Or is it that he has taken up yet another surgery" pondered one and all in attendance. Answer to the instant anxiety had to be found; Prashant's father repeatedly knocked at the ICU doors.

Nursing sisters did answer the door knocks by saying: "patient is under close observation, do not disturb" such replies could only increase the blood pressure of one and all of the attendants; suddenly to the surprise of all present, we found our dear Prashant being wheeled out of the ICU doors towards Radiology!!. On being questioned again, the nurse replied: "we are taking Prashant for MRI scanning".

"But sister, why is he being taken to MRI scanning now, that too after a mini surgical procedure for biopsy" demanded his father.

"The operating surgeon and the duty doctor in ICU will explain soon"; so, saying the nurse quickly guided the wheeled stretcher to radiology Centre.

Lo! yet another anxiety created in the minds of all the attendants.

The patient was wheeled back into the ICU after an hour.

Waiting from the reasonably expected 10, O' clock in the morning to 6pm in the evening was much too large a pressure to withstand. Everyone was literally dancing up and down; Prashant's father had gone down to Dr. Adimanov's office room at least half a dozen times!!. When he returned to ICU doors after the sixth futile attempt to locate Dr. Adimanov, the ICU door gently opened, the duty doctor put out his head and called for Prashant's father; soon both the parents rushed towards the door. The duty doctor literally prevented the patient's mother from entering the ICU ward but wanted only the patient's father to get in. At this juncture his mother shouted back "why are you preventing me- Prashant's life giver?; why are you insisting on father only?; I feel strongly that something terrible must have happened inside the OT; what is wrong if both parents see the patient together?"; the duty doctor pleaded for entry of one person only at a time and literally physically held her back .

Not wasting any further time, his father consoled his better half and rushed inside.

Each and every step towards the patient was as heavy as the rock of Gibraltar; the twenty and odd steps to the patient's bed appeared to be infinite on time horizon. Finally father did encounter his dear son and found him sleeping; looked around for the duty doctor but found him standing remotely; On enquiry as to what had happened, the doctor came out with a heavy heart and announced "sir, Prashant has just now recovered from GA"

"But doctor what is all this GA business at this late hour? After all he entered the OT at 9am in the morning and now it is well half past six pm in the evening!"

"Doctor please tell me all without mincing words. We were waiting from reasonable 10am in the morning".

"No briefing by the operating Dr. Adimanav or his assistant ; the patient was taken to ICU instead of the expected general recovery room; he was wheeled out to Radiology dept several hours later; Now you are saying he has just come out of GA -nearly 8 hours after administering the first GA!!!! around 10.00 clock prior to surgery and at least 6 hours after the patient was wheeled out of the OT into the ICU!!!. Does it mean that he was under anesthesia for hours on end that too long after surgical biopsy procedure!".

Prashant's father anxiously fired the salvo of questions, but the duty doctor appeared to be expressionless. Deep inside he also must have been shaken beyond belief about what had transpired since morning.

Gently holding father's both hands the doctor finally announced "your son dear Prashant is alright but however he has been rendered paraplegic from chest level and below; he will be confined to wheel chair life-long."

On hearing this shocking news, Prashant's father sprayed barrage of questions at the doctor demanding "where is that criminal surgeon Dr. Adimanav?; we have been looking out for him since morning; has he disappeared?; how has all this tragedy been allowed to happen?"

The doctor on duty remorsefully replied: "sir, I was not present in the morning in the OT. I was on evening duty in the ICU; unfortunately, I do not know how it all happened in the morning"

The father totally crestfallen, had to take courage, had to alter his countenance to get ready to meet his dear son for the first time since morning.

He slowly approached Prashant's bed, who beckoned to his father as usual beaming his trademark smile!

He uttered to himself "what an intriguing situation! he is smiling!; perhaps he may not be aware of what has befallen him"; so thinking, controlling his emotions and demeanour, he enquired "Pantu dear , how are you feeling ?"; to which he replied: "I am fine but I am experiencing a strange feeling; whenever I want to turn sides only the chest and upper portion swing along but the lower portion appears weighed down heavily and therefore unable to turn at all"; it was an enough pointer to the tragedy that had struck our dear Prashant, it was a tragic and dramatic situation inside the ICU and the father found himself in a crisscross situation where he could neither console his son nor did he have the courage to announce this news to his beloved better half-waiting trembling and anxiously at the ICU door step .

He however mustered semblance of some courage, stepped ahead and embraced him with a heavy heart but maintaining outward calm excused himself to go out to bring in his anxiously waiting mother and Pavan; but nevertheless in a hurry to take <head on> that criminal surgeon wherever on earth he may be absconding. He flung the ICU door open and rushed towards the stair case, unmindful of the presence of dear Indira right at the ICU door entrance itself; started literally jumping down the stair case sometimes skipping one step and sometimes 2 to 3 steps at a time in order to reach the devil of surgeon down below. Prashant's mother, so far totally oblivious of the situation, strongly suspected some tragedy and involuntarily started following her husband down the flight of stairs screaming: "tell me what happened to our dear son? is he alive?". Prashant's father replied as he continued running down the flight of stairs: "our family boat is sunk; he is there alive but as good as not".

By now Seshadri had already descended to the ground floor and on seeing no surgeon, no director in the immediate vicinity, made anxious enquiries on the where-about of the irresponsible surgeon and equally irresponsible Director of the medical hospital. Medical personnel, however, confided that the <two great performers> had retreated into their cozy residences. It was an uphill task to get at the contact telephone numbers of these two negligent doctors. As Prashant 's mother finally reached ground level she saw to her agony and astonishment that her husband was having heated exchange of talks with the Director, whose residence phone number he had successfully managed to ascertain. It was only on overhearing this heated conversation with the Director, she came to know of the real tragedy that had befallen her family.

****

Patient's father Seshadri: "Mr. Director of the institute of Medical Sciences! Are you aware of what tragedy was created inside the OT this morning, in the name of a simple mini surgical procedure only for biopsy sake?"

Director: "I am aware of it".

Seshadri: "You are aware of it!; already 10 hours have passed and you have not bothered to contact us ; not bothered to explain to us about the outcome. There are a million of enquiries to be answered; what efforts were made to (even attempt to) reverse the tragedy?; where Is that criminal Dr. Adimanav?; where has he escaped without even talking to the patient's attendants ? ; has he performed <a minor surgical procedure for biopsy?> or <a major butchery of the multimillion dollar spinal cord?>".

Director: "I was invited into the OT only after the operating CT surgeon caused this neurological damage."

Seshadri: "is it not all the more important for you, as the Director of a renowned medical hospital and Institute of Higher learning, to have, firstly, come to know of it immediately after the tragedy at the least?; and secondly, was it not your duty to have gone immediately into a conference of all specialists including neuro physicians-all available by dozen counts, under the same roof, to discuss ways and means to restore normalcy, to reverse the tragedy?". "And now, without any further procrastination you present yourself along with that butcher doctor Adimanov for a one to one discussion on how to go about further?".

Director: "We will be there within an hour". It was only on overhearing her husband's heated conversation as above, Prashant's mother came to know of the real tragedy–that is paraplegia manifesting itself as total loss of mobility and confinement to wheel- chair lifelong; instantly she went into a state of shock and collapsed on to the floor.

By now all the attendants had descended to the ground floor in search of Prashant's anxious parents.

On hearing the shocking news, her elder brother, normally strong willed, also went into a state of shock and collapsed on to the floor. Krishna, her elder brother had come down to attend to and assist his most affectionate and loving sister but was himself shocked and went into a state of unconsciousness.

The Director of the Institute of Medical Sciences and the <Great butcher> arrived late in the night- a full ten hours after causing the tragedy.

The patient's father: "you both were ordained to visit the patient's attendants in the morning immediately after surgery. What prompted you both to run away from the scene?. Anyway there will be no use discussing the past but we should and must discuss, even at this late stage, as to how best to stabilize the criminally disabled patient? ; as to ascertain from experts in the neurology field, what procedures can be attempted to restore normalcy?"

Both the men belonging to the noble profession

apparently had no solution to offer as can be inferred from their <heads- bent demeanor>.

Seshadri: "For heaven's sake wake up and speak; if necessary we can even arrange to fly the patient to USA, UK or other major hospital destinations of repute for treatment either within or outside the country".

The culprits could only murmur with heads bent "nothing can be done at this stage, it is irreversible".

Seshadri: "Ah!, what an answer from great professionals in medicine? why did not both of you, call for an emergency session with luminaries, available under the same hospital roof, for eliciting second, third opinions (of other brains as well) to determine ways and means to reverse the tragedy that has been criminally enforced on the brilliant young engineering student?"; the duo doctors could only stand like statues with their heads bowed like criminals!!.

He continued: "If causing life-long irreversible damage is negligence, carelessness and deficiency in service of Himalayan mountain proportions; not caring to go into emergency session within hours of the tragedy, to chalk out ways and means to at least attempt to reverse the damage caused, constitutes a still greater magnitude of negligence raised to the power of infinity. No one in the society, including us i.e., the affected family, denies that you belong to a highly noble, revered, respected and honored category of professionals for the noble health restoring services they selflessly offer; but what is the situation like now?, dear expert in neurosurgery! and professor emeritus expert in cardio thoracic surgery!?"

The duo doctors: "we understand you and your family's agony; unfortunately, it is the rarest of rare cases where… err .err".

"Quite obvious indeed!! - where from will you have words to continue!".

Patient's father: "What is your next step? In what way help can be rendered to this brilliant young boy felled by the surgeon's scalpel? why don't we call the hospital's neuro physicist/ expert as the first step to ascertain the extent of damage?".

The duo (doctors): "We had sought his opinion in the morning immediately after surgery and his expert advice- to immediately scan his spinal cord through MRI (Magnetic Resonance Imaging) which was done".

Patient's father: "Ah! what a great thought process!? < Allow the boiling milk to spill over to the floor and then, only later, weep over the spilt milk?>. Why was MRI scanning not done pre- operatively during the diagnostic stage itself? We, as common men, with very little knowledge of diagnostic and treatment medical procedures, know that X-Ray; CT scan; MRI scan are all universally accepted and practiced tools for diagnosis; is it not a clear case of <putting the horse before the cart>!. Kudos! our country's Government should recommend your <noble> act to the Swedish Nobel Committee to award the Swedish <not Nobel but noble> prize in medicine posthumously… sorry, I beg your pardon, post-operatively". With silence from the defaulting duo in white coat continued, patient's father suggested to requisition the expert opinion of a renowned neuro expert from Bombay- a Doctor-Professor-as suggested by the chief of his employer's medical hospital.

All members and well-wishers of the family took turns to visit Prashant. Indira -Prashant's mother, who had already recovered from the shock, suggested: "let no one of us disclose the tragedy when we meet him; Prashant is soft spoken , we have to only carefully and intelligently disclose the tragic news after weighing his reactions lest, any sudden announcement, should cause shocks in him". Leading the way Indira slowly and surely approached the ICU door and lo! What did she see there? A few nursing sisters and duty doctors were in a shocked state of melancholy and were seen even bitterly weeping over the tragedy that had befallen the upcoming bright engineering student.

Indira requested: "How is my son inside? I want you sisters and doctors on duty to advise me the correct approach and stance to disclose this news to my dear young son".

One of the sister's present, softly replied:" Madam, this news has already been disclosed to him as soon as he opened his eyes after recovery from GA".

Indira: "Oh! My god, how did he react?"

Yet another nurse from those gathered outside the ICU, seen wiping her tears rolling down her cheeks, held Indira firmly and uttered: "do you know, aunty, how Prashant reacted on hearing the shocking news?; we were all trembling and shaking within ourselves, when the duty doctor, loaded with injectable calmpose sedative (to meet the possible and expected impulsive outburst) announced to the patient: "you have come out of GA, now please take it calmly; unfortunately the morning surgeon has committed a grave negligent act during the surgical procedure": so saying he stood silently in expectation of reply from Prashant.

Prashant (the patient): "what has happened? Please let me know."

The duty doctor noticed the same beaming smile on his face; took courage and began uttering: "Dear Prashant , you have been rendered paraplegic which means you're walking faculties have been grossly interfered with and you will be confined to wheel chair lifelong"; he the duty doctor, announced the unpleasant news alright, but could not control his emotional tears flowing down his cheeks like the eternal Ganga from the Himalayas !

Narrating the episode that had transpired between Prashant and the duty doctor inside, to the patient's mother –Indira, the nurses broke down completely shedding tears.

Prashant's mother trembling, sobbing, entreatingly requested the nurse: "how did my dear son react on hearing the terribly tragic news; did he break down? did he shout? did he attack the duty doctor?"

"No, no, no such wild reaction dear aunty!; on the other hand, we were all surprised and wonder struck to see him close his eyes for a moment and opening them and calmly uttering: "I will face this calamity boldly in life like the great Christopher Reeves and none the less great British physicist Dr. Stephen Hawking, whose life stories, I had read with great enthusiasm in my college days"

The nurses were awe struck at this response from a permanently incapacitated youth!.

The nurse said to Prashant's mother: "aunty, your son is not an ordinary person; only, perhaps one in a million nay, one in a billion only can withstand such a big shock in this way; he is a yogi, a sage, a saint; he is calm in the midst of adversities; he is not Prashant; he is Prashanth-Mahasagar very much like the great ocean traversed by hundreds of merchant ships carrying megatons of merchandise - the Pacific Ocean , but no ripples"; she continued sobbing "I have never seen a boy like him nor will I ever see such a person in my life".

Indira finally took courage to meet eye to eye her dear son inside. She slowly opened the ICU door and walked to Prashant's bed as beckoned by the nurse who accompanied her.

What a meeting of the four eyes!; mother's two eyes attempting continuously to control her tears; and her dear son's two eyes as usual bright, big and dark shining and extending his forearms to greet his dearest on earth -his mother; she had gathered enough courage and ran towards his extended arms and got into blissful eternal embrace; from the four eyes flowed uncontrolled at that, tears of joy of meeting as if years had passed!

No wonder every moment from the time she entered the OT till this stage was a vast expanse of time counted

Not just in hours but each second elapsing timelessly like a year! Finally, uttered mother to her dear son: "We are all there with you. Your papa and mummy (I) will be your two legs all the time. you can criss-cross, traverse the whole universe and achieve laurels beyond compare ; your younger brother Pavan, will be your back bone; your maternal uncle and his family – affectionate Jaya aunty, dear Kavitha and dear Sirisha will be your stepping stones and will stand by you as the great rock of Gibraltar; Bhat uncle and Nirmala aunty with their sweet daughter - the incomparable Anupama and son- the dynamic Ashok; as also a-z NSLN Murthy uncle and Saroja aunty and the famous triumvirate - Asha, Shubha and Raghu and well-wishers and all friends will ,always be around you like <a pride of lions> to enable you to face life boldly and smilingly". (all these 3 families lived as neighbors for over a decade, AS ONE SINGLE CLOSE KNITTED FAMILY).

It was noble on the part of the mother to have uttered such words and assurances; Prashant in turn giving his involuntary beaming smile, remarked: "Mummy!, with you and papa around me round the clock; with Pavan hopping into our place of abode despite his future planned foreign jaunts for higher studies, I feel fully secured and assured in life. I will traverse the life journey boldly leaving no stone unturned to come up trumps, notwithstanding the physically imposed challenge". What a dramatic transformation this bold and courageous attitude of dear Prashant brought in his parents!; they had entered the ICU with full knowledge of the tragedy and its after effects lifelong; but came out in deep admiration of their gallant- soldier son's bravery and determination to face all odds with just positive frame of mind.

Yes!, dear readers, no evil, no devil of a storm can conquer the brave and the gritty very much like the great Prashant who went on to practically demonstrate and lived life with purpose.

****

CHAPTER- III

PRASHANT's CHILDHOOD

Prashant was born to peace loving, god loving Spiritually inclined parents who believed strongly in the worthiness of God gifted life by living it with purpose, by spreading love and affection amongst the fellow beings, by constantly endeavoring to give something much more to the society than that unflaggingly given, by the latter and utilized by them. This spirit was the adrenalin flow in Prashant as well. Whatever he saw he grasped, whatever he learnt he comprehended and digested after due filtration promptly and timely guided by his parents. So much so at the young age of 3 years he would recall the entire sacred Ramayana episode in all its minutest details painstakingly narrated to him by his parents. Guess why? Guess What for at this juvenile age?! He was more inclined to look for things around, play with things around than to allow his dear mother or even father to appease his hunger and thirst. It had become, by consideration of parental desire to make him a strong boy in mind and body, a religious routine, he was a poor eater of general food. Lo! the parents did meet with early success in identifying the procedure for feeding him. It was such a routine that had to be repeated into minutest details that there was no room

For plus or minus deviations in the sequence. Would you like to hear on the effect of deviations?!; just to quote an example: - Try narrating the incidence when Jatayu - the Eagle bird God tried to protect Goddess mother Sita from the clutches of the devilish Ravenna by substituting Jatayu with Sampathi; he would promptly retort saying it was not Sampathi who tried first to save mother Sita but it was Jatayu.

It was indeed prodigal for a 4-year old child to narrate <the whole sacred Ramayana>, non-stop for 6 hours without break and most astoundingly, without missing out even a single incident AND without missing the sequence!

He would, however, not require any story telling for gulping down Coco cola and munching Cadbury's chocolate. He had meticulously watched his father leave home for office/factory. He would also collect some handily available book, shove it under his armpit, kiss his mummy good bye and would straight away venture into school classrooms just two cross roads away from our residence; he would enter classrooms for seniors and lo!, the entire classroom would become alive with Pantu's (Prashant's household nick-name) pranks and all students mimicking along with him. There was so much of noise created that the neighboring class teacher would rush to find out what had happened. He loved going to school from young age so much so when we really decided to send him to pre nursery, he would get ready by 7 in the morning with a book shoved under his armpit and with his shoes on. Prashant was only enthusiastic and ready to leave for school from day 1. He went on and on in studies overflowing with enthusiasm. He would never be second to any one in extracurricular activities as well. He had developed, as a 15day old child, good ear for music. The Young mother had no difficulty in silencing the young boy if at all he cried by switching on music. This virtuous habit turned out to be very handy later in his life. It had been groomed into him from young age, to always do right things and those right things in full measure. He picked up this healthy trait and his living life became worthy example to others. His playmates would seek his company, his classmates would emulate him to grasp what the teacher taught in the classroom in one go and would answer any question put to the class with accuracy and simultaneous drawing of admiration from the teachers. He always wanted to be class topper and he achieved his desire in fine style: once in the sports competition organized regularly by school management, he decided to get the first prize in slow cycling race. He had practiced for weeks and months both forms of racing, be it the slow or the fast version. "He cajoled most competitors to go past him and in the heat of the moment they would unwittingly oblige him and speed away and this little Prashant would find himself with only one or two in the fray left behind. When he found only he and his best classmate and friend were left in the race, he offered to give his friend a chance to enjoy the pleasure of securing the first prize for the first time and he would oblige him by speeding away". Whether it was cycling, cricket, kabaddi, table tennis, football, swimming he was there participating in all sports activities. One fine day as a small boy he entered a tennis court with his father's tennis racket. Much to his amusement he was welcomed by all his father's tennis teammates. And that was the <Shree Ganesh> (beginning) for his pursuing the field tennis sports career as well. Debating skills, poem writing, and mathematics quiz competition were all added to the kitty of his extracurricular activities. He liked to read books and became a voracious reader and would visit library regularly. Prashant maintained this healthy strain of life activities throughout his middle school, high school and Pre-University levels so much so he had easy entrance into the field of Engineering at the end of his XII standard pass out. Life for him was going on pleasantly with continued excellence in studies and all extracurricular activities.

****

9 year young & Mischivous

PRASHANT'S-An Incredible Life Journey!!!

Waiting to join cycle racing 12 years young

CHAPTER- IV

PROGNOSIS BEGINS –

The blackest day had set in Prashant's life. He lay prostrate on the bed totally oblivious of the future series of religiously rigorous schedule he had to mandatorily undergo to come back to semblance of normal. None of us including him had any idea he would have to continue in the hospital for long periods for physiotherapy rehabilitation alone, not to speak of other post-damage treatments. He lay on bed displaying his trade mark smile Did he know subconsciously, that a terrible tragedy had struck him? and yet, maintained his composure as was cultivated in him since birth? Let us read on to get the answers to this one-in-a billion exemplary cool reaction to a tragedy.

The next day 24th Oct 1990, started with calmer counsels leading to thought of consulting the chief medical officer of BHEL (his father's employing company). The latter came forward readily to invite an eminent neuro- specialist Dr. Singhal from Bombay to obtain < second opinion> for going about further. He arrived promptly and went ahead with examining the patient .He was shocked beyond belief, to notice that dear PRASHANT's spinal cord had been severely tampered with, during the unwanted enforced surgery in place of simple fine needle aspiration biopsy (FNAB) under CT guidance. Unfortunately, he noticed that wiser counsels had not prevailed during the diagnostic stage. He expressed shock as to how and why the fail- proof, the sure- shot MRI scanning was not deployed as a fundamental pre- prescription diagnostic procedure leaving the FNAB under CT guidance as only the next in line procedure? He also concluded that the spinal cord had been needlessly tampered with, both directly, through application of traction and indirectly, through interference with collateral stroma (blood supply supplemented through intercostal arterial branches). The irreversible damage caused stared directly into his eyes, involuntarily shed tears and with a heavy heart, he disclosed this information to the shock- struck parents. He opined that Prashant being quite young, there were some chances of <collateral blood supply> being established in the immediate future AND went on to propose <immediate rigorous physiotherapeutic exercising> as THE REAL and PARAMOUNTLY NECESSARY rehabilitation solution. So opining, he left with a heavy heart.

As continued efforts to <leaving no stone unturned>, a third opinion from a family doctor-neurosurgeon was also sought. He opined that under the obtaining and created conditions, there should have been an attempt to <reconnect the ligated intercostal arteries> (as had been admitted by the perpetrators of the ghastly damage during the unwanted surgery in their Operation Nothings)

The two, second and third opinion expressing experts as can be seen, did a noble service befitting their noble chosen profession more dutifully and as a matter-of-factly than the two perpetrators of the ghastly crime brought on the brilliant young student of engineering on 23rd oct1990.

Parents, friends, well-wishers continued in a state of shock for days on end; blind-folded submitted themselves to rigorous physiotherapy exercising as the only left-over procedure to minimize the impact of the imposed life- long suffering. Deep, however, in their hearts the parents were at a loss to fathom the depth of feelings within Prashant's magnificent physiological structure. His smiling demeanor could not reveal the real feeling deep in his mind to the outside world (not even to the psychologist who later attempted to help him). There was, undoubtedly a time bomb implanted into him through this tragedy. This time bomb could explode any moment, any day, soon. Each one present at the occasion, seeing the calmness in his face and in particular the doctors and nurses wondered whether they were seeing a yogi, a saint in dear Prashant; nursing sisters in particular, gave expression to their motherhood feelings, through incessant flow of tears; male doctors, after all being humans and humane, also could not hold back their tears like their feminine counter-parts. Yet another demonstration of the nobility of medical profession!. That was the situation obtaining then and god only knew what the mental situation within the mental frames of the duo doctors was – culprits who quietly slipped out of the ghostly scene into their cozy residences! And it is left to the readers to figure out the situation in the minds of Prashant's parents, kith and kin and well-wishers; perhaps only a Sherlock Holmes could bring out the mental situation more precisely and realistically.

With each day passing curiosity, to get to know the reasons for the damage that had been caused, grew to mountain proportions. All members of the family were restless. As a firsthand information it was imperative to interrogate the designated surgeon, the surgeon who had caused all this misery.

Parents gate crashed into his OPD consultation room and forced him out from there for detailed discussions.

Prashant's agitated mother: "Dear doctor, you have caused irreparable, irreversible damage on my dear son and never bothered to meet us. Instead, you have run away from the OT leaving us gasping every second Is this the international practice? is it ethical on your part and on your profession?". There was response through eerie silence; he only stood like a statue with head bowed.

Prashant's agitated father stepped in and questioned him: "Dear doctor, you were entrusted with responsibility to diagnose firstly, to diagnose secondly, **to diagnose completely before even prescribing any major surgery**. The agreed procedure, following failure of 4 attempts at fine needle aspiratory biopsy/ cytology, was a microsurgery with the expressed aim of taking out a speck of the extra grown masses for histopathological examination in the same hospital's laboratory"

Doctor's reply: "I agree with you that the procedure adopted was for diagnostic purposes to start with. "

Prashant's father: "Although, I am a non-medical person, it is common knowledge of common practice anywhere on earth, to takeout only a tiny sample, perhaps, less than a maize corn size for biopsy sake. Where was the question of taking out such huge masses (as to fill a larger than liter capacity kidney tray) solely for biopsy purpose?".

DOCTOR: "We have followed the international procedure; the procedure adopted was meant both for curing and diagnosing. Even the internal medicine expert Dr. Vaidya shares these thoughts".

Prashant's father: "Oh! I see, this, you claim as the international procedure! <Remove 'ALL' for curing and send 'SMALL' for biopsy> i.e.; you have <PUT THE curing - HORSE BEFORE THE Diagnosing - CART>. Out standing achievement in the field of Medicine this!" .

The doctor suddenly fell silent!; perhaps indicative that silence is the golden answer!

Prashant's father: "To take out a small spec it was sufficient to make only a button- hole incision of the thorax poster-laterally. Is this not the national, international, global procedure? ; why did you cut open the entire hemi thorax postero- laterally and in case of our dear Prashant who had a 42 inch chest, the incision appeared to be no less than 21 inches long!!"

Doctor: "I took the decision to remove/excise out the whole mass as I found the growth was highly extensive across the ribs in the thorax and it could turn malignant in future. In order to avoid repeat major surgery later, I did the major surgery now itself to help him".

Prashant's father: "Kudos to you doctor. You should be awarded <Padma Vibhushan>, only to be upgraded to <Bharat Ratnam> for the immediately next repetition of curing first and diagnosis next! **Don't you realize you have made <Prashant a living vegetable now to save him from imaginary cancer later>?**

Doctor: "I can understand your agony. But. err .err

Prashant's father: "sorry for the interruption doctor. How can you think of prescription **(let alone cure)** before diagnosing? What you prescribe for treatment and cure-are they not dictated by the findings of biopsy?"

Doctor: "Since huge lobulated masses had grown extensively to the point of applying constant pressure <On adjacent structure> and started eroding even the ribs, I took a decision to remove them once for all.

Prashant's father: "First of all please let us know whether you correctly understood the biopsy result".

Doctor: "Although the biopsy result came out as nonmalignant, I took the decision to excise out".

Prashant's father: "what a decision?; All around the

globe, admittedly, there is urgency for careful removal of malignant tumors; but where was the urgency for excising out a benign tumor without discussing

a) With other doctors and

b) With the parents

c) and mandatorily with the patient himself

Doctor: "My intention was only to avoid a second time this large incision which was anyway necessary in the immediate future".

Prashant's father: "you also came to know from the biopsy result, that the tumor masses were neurological in nature. Had you any doubt at this stage about the vastness of these extra grown masses of neurological origin?"Doctor: "The result came clearly as nonmalignant and plexiform neuro fibromatosis".

Prashant's father: "How did you think that there was urgency and that you, as a CT surgeon ,were competent and not a neurosurgeon!; why did you not even at this belated stage 1) Close the incision wound ?; 2)Allow the patient to come out of GA ?; 3) Immediately call for a conference of a neurologist, a neurosurgeon?; 4) Also call, in view of erosion of three consecutive (2nd, 3rd and 4th) bony ribs, an orthopedic surgeon for consultations as second, third opinion before applying your treasured possession i.e; the scalpel on our dear Prashant's thorax?"

Doctor:"I did invite neurosurgeon who is also the Director of the hospital institution into the OT".

Father: "A neurosurgeon inside the OT! and ascertained the pathological nature as plexin-form neuro fibromatosis!

Father : "And yet you, the <Bharat Ratnam> CT surgeon performing neurosurgeon's duty! what a thoughtful, brainy decision!"

Doctor: "I was the leading surgeon, on noticing blood oozing out from a hole in vertebral body at T4 level, I invited the neurosurgical specialist".

Father: "you had to wait for the neurological damage to occur and then call a neuro expert inside the OT!

Was it not mandatory on your part to have involved these experts (neuro and ortho) at the pre operation stage itself particularly when three consecutive T2, T3, T4 level vertebral bodies were involved?"Doctor: "Since the growth was in the thoracic region, I only was competent to perform the surgery."

Father: "Oh! My Goodness Gracious!; do you want me to believe that there are organs and structures concerning ONLY a thoracic surgeon in the thorax?; Do you want to dismiss my acquired knowledge that there are 12 thoracic vertebrae, there is the dorsal spine running through these 12 thoracic vertebrae: there are 11 inter vertebrate foramina in this span (of 12 vertebrae) plus one each ivf on far sides of T1 and T12; there are 2 lobes of lungs; and many other adjacent organs concerning other specialties as well?"Doctor: "I appreciate your acquired knowledge. but you see, the starting surgeon for any surgery in the thoracic cavity must necessarily be a CT surgeon."

Father: "I do agree with you doctor, that one of the team of doctors must necessarily be a CT surgeon. But how did you start off without any neurosurgeon, particularly when you received the biopsy report, during the procedure itself, confirming the pathological nature as non-malignant and most importantly, as neurological in nature?":

"Earlier you have averred that you did invite a neurosurgeon. Most evidently after causing the neurological deficit; is it not?!!"

Doctor: "You see! Err….

Father: "Knowledge is GOLD .Do you think that anatomical knowledge cannot be acquired by non-medical humans?; With local anesthesia, may be General Anesthesia, You could have made a small incision into the thorax (posteriorly); then slightly held apart the cut open skin with a forceps and after seeing the huge lobulated masses with your naked eyes (naked because no microscope was required); the same FINE NEEDLE of 22G/24G thickness, could have brought out the micro sized sample for being sent to laboratory for histopathological analysis. Have I displayed any superhuman intellect in making this statement? Of course I am no Einstein; but I do know that this procedure (of taking out a micro sample) is simple and not requiring an Einstein brain either!!"

"What was the exact role played by the neurosurgeon (also the Director of the Medical Institute) when once he was requested by you into the OT?"

Doctor: "He helped me in arresting the oozing of blood from a hole at T4 level of vertebral body; then we closed the wound in layers with gel foam; he opined that his intervention was not needed at< that stage>".

Father: "That meant you have already inflicted a serious NEUROLOGICAL damage! Being horrified within yourself, you have invited a neurosurgeon post damage. What an expertise displayed!! by a highly qualified doctor with Mch PDF Honours !

****

CHAPTER- V
START OF THE INEVITABLE

Damage had been caused; not reversible at that. Therefore, simply there is no room for brooding over the tragic past; we have to muster courage and move forward in life. More than parents and dear brother, Prashant himself took the lead.

The Neuro experts from within the hospital faculty and from outside were clear in their minds when they advised physiotherapy as the best next course mandatorily to be adhered to, in order to stabilize the patient and rehabilitate him. The two experts also emphasized the paramount need to keep continuously cheering the patient and upping his morale incessantly. Friends, relatives and family members specially the younger brother, took on these responsibilities as sacred duty smilingly. With grit and determination Prashant made things easier for all the medical attendants with his characteristic positive attitude to life and continuously kept the attendants smiling and cheerful instead of the other way around.

Then started physiotherapy exercising in the private ward itself. There was no scope for taking Prashant to physiotherapy unit; he had to be stabilized in his sitting position first, before making any attempt to take him out of the private ward itself. The physiotherapy master would arrive promptly at 9am every morning. It was Prashant who would smilingly welcome him but not without mischief! Guess what? "What a pleasure it is for you to touch my feet! You see! I am no God!"

Physio: "Do not worry!; I always treat my patients as second gods because I love serving them most faithfully. <Service to patients is service to god>". So replying equally jocularly, he would start with exercising the lower paralysed parts!

Promptly arrived PRASHANT'S maternal uncle known for his witty conversations and joined the younger brother Pavan.

Physio: "Dear Krishna, as I pull the right leg to extreme right to exercise the hip joint, the left leg is also accompanying!". All present had a hearty laugh! Pavan quipped: "Doctor you see the right and left legs are so friendly like me and my brother. They cannot live without each other!"

Again, laughter in the room! Krishna mama jumped into the fray with his characteristic smile "Sreeman Pavanji, hold one chacobar in your hand and show it to the left leg, it automatically gets attracted to the delicacy and stays away from the right leg. And when the physio exercises the left leg, shift the chacobar to the other hand and show it to the right leg. Simple solution! You see!"

Now started Exercise no.3 i.e.; training his physique to

Sitting position. This of course required help from Pavan & Krishna mama on both sides; and for back supporting, Prashant's dear mother at the back. The physio would be in front pulling the two outstretched hands to bring him to sitting position.

Prashant would quip: "you see, four of you put together are struggling to bring me to sitting position; see my strength!"

Krishna remarked: "you are my able-bodied pupil – see how nicely I had trained you during the yesteryears. Keep it up, my dear Bala Bheemasena- the mythological moving tower of strength !"

The physio would enter the room somewhat in a sympathetic mood, but on finding the hilarious atmosphere created around Prashant in the room, he would carry out his exercising rig-morale joyfully and would leave the room in ecstasy, admiring within himself the positive attitude of the whole family including the charming Prashant.

This, he had noticed how all the members of the family had come together with sole intention of keeping him always cheerful notwithstanding the harsh reality of suffering enforced.

Day after day, his admiration and praise for the gallant fighter rose and in less than a week's time, he had become his close friend and well-wisher. Every morning, Prashant would wait anxiously for the jolly exercising hour. The neurology specialist Dr. Murthy had made it a point to visit his fan at least once daily; had amply

Clearly emphasized the importance of taking extreme precautions of the immobilized hips, knees and ankles contracting the dreaded bedsores due to skin breakdown as a result of continuous pressure. He recommended a simple solution to prevent bed sores - resting these parts on very soft bedspreads. These bedspreads can be improvised at home itself by stitching together several silk sarees in layers. However for long duration of supine positions (sleeping lying down) the most effective would be the use of Alpha beds/water beds. Lo!, listing of recommendations by the neurologist had hardly been completed, when family well wishing friends joined in queue to prepare the soft cushions from silk sarees. Saroja Murthy would collect half a dozen of her silk sarees; neatly stitch them into thick cushions from several layers. And as if not to be left behind, Nirmala Bhat would collect all her old sarees and neatly stitch them together in layers.

The next morning, the two angels came to the hospital with smart presentation packs and cheered him saying: "Dear sonny, here are anti-bedsore cushions for you."

Time moved on. It was the 10th post-operative day. Duty doctors promptly arrived to remove the old bandages and got ready to remove the stitches. Prashant's mother silently observing the procedure noticed that the incision wound had not healed at all. She enquired: "Doctor, I see that the incision wound has not healed at all. Why don't we leave it undisturbed for another 2-3 days or until the wound is completely healed whichever is later."

-ARRIVED 10th POST-OPERATIVE DAY

"Madame" replied the duty doctor: "It is the universal procedure to remove the stitches at least on the 10th day and not later".

"But doctor" said Indira interrupting him: "The procedure of stitches' removal is definitely dictated by the condition of the wound on that day. In the instant case, it can be seen very vividly, that wound still appears reddish indicating incomplete healing. "And", she goes on to add," Prashant had been administered 8 hourly decodran injections. It is clear from medical literature, that decodran, administered to highly effectively restore normal blood flow, has a negative side- effect of slowing down the healing process. Consequently, is it not prudent to wait for a few more days?"

Doctor: "But you see madam, there will be complications if we leave the stitches for too long. So it is our duty to remove them instantly. It is also the considered opinion of my senior doctors".

Indira: "Looking into the realistic unhealed condition (of the incision wound), at least you try to remove only alternate stitches".

But this appeal appeared to have fallen only on deaf ears; for, the duty doctor started to remove them one by one and ended with removing all in one go!.

The expected horror was there for everybody present to see. Lo!, the wound started opening out like a spring and to her horror, Prashant's mother, could see the inside

Parts of the thorax!; This scene sent shock waves into her; screaming aloud, she rushed out in search of the doctor. Seeing him attending to another patient, Indira shouted to him: "Doctor you never cared to listen to the pleadings of the patient's mother. Now go and see the patient's thorax; you will definitely recapitulate your college days' knowledge of anatomy of thorax. The thorax has sprung open exposing vertebrae, ribs, the heart beating rhythmically, the lungs bellowing. Oh! My god, what the hell you have done to my angel-son?". "Surely un-pardonable, judged by any law of the globe".

Doctor coolly replied: "Madam, you have not seen bigger incisions, bigger wounds; please do not panic"

Aghast at the duty doctor's insensitivities to the realities of the medical condition of her dear son, she spontaneously, involuntarily held his collar by the scruff of his neck, pulled him towards the ward where Prashant was resting unaware of yet another imposed tragedy!

"Even, at this late stage" Indira shouted, "for heaven's sake, put secondary sutures immediately".

Doctor saw the patient's condition alright; yet, such anxiety did not seem to cut ice with such stiff brained gladiator. "What the hell you have done to my dear son?", reacted the non-plussed mother. He chose to disappear perhaps, to have a second opinion or to consult with and take approval from his boss!. There was no trace of any nursing activity till late evening. The sprung open wound had been left open for a full 8-10 hours period without applying secondary sutures; and worse still, without covering the incision in the torso with at least sterile pads.

Prashant's parents, attendants and well-wishers all, could not take these medical misadventures light heartedly; in fact, no human being on earth can sit back at such a situation. After all, Prashant was second to none before. But here he is lying in bed helplessly.

The hospital realized much too late, by which time heavy infection of the blood had already set in. No amount of delayed secondary suturing could prevent <septicemia- a dangerous, nearly fatal infection of the entire blood circulatory system> from brain to ankle and feet i.e.; from top to toes!!. The patient had developed high temperature.

Mother to father: "I have checked the body temperature after I felt his body unusually hot, the mercury having touched 106.8 degrees Fahrenheit".

Father: "We have heard of 104–105 degrees F temperatures. Let us call the nurse for ascertaining its correctness with a brand new thermometer"; within a few moments nurse was called in; she checked the temperature with not one, but with 2-3 thermometers and confirmed, to her horror and to the parents' panicking, that the recording was really correct.

Out she rushed to the duty doctor; and simultaneously, to get ice cubes, having understood the seriousness of the moment, parents also rushed to different wards to get bucketsful of ice cubes having realized that <application of cold packs on forehead, chest and in fact, all over

the body>, could only bring the situation under control only as a first-aid; the duty doctor was yet to arrive; Prashant's father rushed out to the nursing station and finding the duty doctor listening to music on the radio channel pulled him out:

"Doctor, why no response to emergency call? The patient is running 106.8 degrees F temperature!"

Doctor: "I will be there right now" so uttering he finally arrived at the patient's bed and was shocked to record 106 degrees F temperature of his body!; immediately he consulted with his seniors and made arrangements to administer general purpose antibiotic <Fortum> injection.

Father waited patiently for the injection to be administered expectedly after giving a test dose; with the help of attending nurse, the Fortum injection was finally administered.

Doctor to sister: "you immediately take blood samples and send them to laboratory for ascertaining the type of infection and suitable antibiotic <after 96 hours of blood culturing>"

Remaining calm till the blood samples were taken and sent to laboratory for culturing, Prashant's father engaged the doctor on duty for a discussion: "Doctor, from the morning the thorax incision wound had been left open after premature removal of the stitches. The hospital had not taken precautions even to apply secondary sutures and/or sterile dressing. As a layman, I could comprehend this situation to be responsible for high fever. How did it not occur to your brains as the most definite cause of severe infection?"

"Now suddenly you all wake up and administer this broad spectrum <fortum> antibiotic. How is it that the full dose has been given without a test dose? are you sure the patient's biological system would accept the heavy dose straightaway?".

Conversation was still on! **duty sister rushed to the doctor to announce complications galore**.

Evidently the heavy dose had been outrightly rejected by Prashant's bodily system as obvious from the resulting multiple side reactions!

Mother was aghast with series of side reactions; one side of PRASHANT's body turning pale; non coherence in talk/speech; clenching of teeth- all took place within matter of a few minutes after the first injection **without test dose**.

She rushed out again to catch the duty doctor by the scruff of his neck and shouted at him: "without observing the reaction of the administered heavy dose of antibiotic (which is only broad spectrum and not yet confirmed by blood culturing reports), how could you leave the patient's bedside? You people had left the patient in the morning without applying secondary sutures. And now in the evening, you have left the patient's bedside without observing the side reaction of a non-tested full dose of fortum!".

Doctor : "Do not worry madam!; it is a broad spectrum antibiotic which is generally given pending laboratory precise indicating reports which come only after 4 days of culturing".

He arrived at the bedside and noticed for himself, the series of violent side-reactions.

Mother: "doctor, how do you explain these fast appearing side reactions?; what is next now?".

Doctor: "Madam, I can understand you parents; but pending laboratory test report we have to continue with this broad spectrum antibiotic to bring down the high temperature":

So saying, he ordered nursing sisters to transfer the patient immediately from private ward to the intensive care center (ICU) - A clear case of continued deficiency of medical attention!

Patient had been administered the second 8 - hourly dose inside the ICU. When the parents visited him in the early morning hours, to their surprise, they observed that their dear son did not display his trademark captivating smile!. Surprised at this unusual development mother quipped: "did you sleep alright in the night?".

There simply was no answer, no smile either!. But he signalled through his hands, that he had become voiceless!

Mother to the duty doctor in the ICU: "You have already given the 2nd 8-hourly dose; complications are piling up; he cannot even give us his traditional morning smile;

he has lost his speech; his hands have become pale white; temperature remains at the high level of 106 deg. F!!".

"What have you done to my son?; Will you please stop this <frightening fortum> and perhaps, **try** after consulting with your colleagues, **some other broad spectrum antibiotic drug and that too only after duly finding its acceptance   by the patient's biological system, with a test does without fail?"**.

All these advices and thoughts' sharing appeared, for the second time, to fall on deaf ears because the duty doctor not only went on to justify the injection of fortum drug but had fortified his mind into continuing with the subsequent doses 8- hourly. As any dutiful mother would be, Indira visited her hapless son lying on bed (she had never seen him in this condition for the 20 years of his life so far) only to notice that, in such a short time of ten days from enforced surgery, Prashant had developed even more nasty surprises that went on unfolding despite the tall claims by the medical staff about intensive caring.

Carelessness appeared to be the <mantra> (i.e; the solution!) for the medical staff attending on him even in the intensive care unit; they all seemed to be lacking in the knowledge of the consequences of a violently reacting drug; the attending duty doctor including the internal medicine doctor Vaidya, who started it all with his thoughtless advices, had obviously no clue; no knowledge of the violent reactions taking place one after another with each subsequent dose.

Despite Prashant's mother's outbursts and questioning, the doctors continued treatment with the ineffective and even negative fortum; even the fourth 8- hourly dose had not steadied the temperature raise; it remained at the horrifying level of 106deg F.

The treating doctors apparently did not take cognizance of these side reactions seriously. For, they continued with the fourth 8- hourly dose unmindful of further side reactions. Lo!!, as expected by the anxious parents, yet another tormenting side reaction followed!

Could you guess what it was? already pale like a white lily; already clenching his teeth; already voiceless; our dear Prashant had been visited by an entirely new reaction i.e.; loss of swallowing capacity which mother detected when she tried to feed him.

Like magicians, the doctors would attempt to solve this new problem by fixing the Ryle's tube and start feeding; next comes the fifth dose given as per their schedule!

But with what result?; yet another side reaction; this time he had <difficulty in breathing>!; the treatment mill continues to run!

Doctor: "Nurse, fix the oxygen mask and monitor heart rate/pulse rate".

Mother: "doctor why are you not able to control these side reactions? why **are you not able to bring** the temperature **even a wee-bit down from the 106.8 degF high mark? Even at this late stage why don't you stop further doses of fortum?"**

Doctor: "prepare the patient for the sixth dose of Fortum", he so ordered the nursing sisters.

Dutifully (or shall we say brainlessly, thoughtlessly) the sixth dose did not stop playing havoc on the patient through yet another in a row, side reaction.

This time the patient's left half of the body started shaking violently; so violent were the tremours that even the cot started shaking violently!

A leading hospital (or should we christen it as a "ghost-hospital"!) **goes ahead with the seventh dose** (they were, as yet, waiting for the 4 days culturing report from the laboratory) **and as if not to lag behind the dosage count, the side reaction count also moved upwards**.

This time our dear Prashant went into a state of delirium and started violently attacking the medical attending staff and parents (not distinguished)!!

Parents and attendants including Prashant's dear younger brother had been left in a state of continuous shock with these side reactions occurring galore.

Mother took courage and gate crashed into the hospital institution's Director's office and ordered him to visit her son immediately.

The Director did visit the patient but remained motionless, speechless!

Prashant's father: "Dear doctor Director! what is going on in this leading hospital? Do the treating doctors have any <ulterior motive> to keep the patient continuously on the decline, by administering the same, not only ineffective, but also negatively effective, widely reacting drug to possibly escape responsibility?"

Visiting Director (doctor): "you see in the absence of final laboratory 96 hrs- culturing report, we have no option but to continue with this broad spectrum antibiotic drug".

Prashant's father: "Director, do you want to make a statement here <what cannot be cured must be endured!>. How does the hospital fail to connect the nexus between violent side effects and so called broad spectrum antibiotic drug? Why did you doctors not try out OTHER BROAD SPECTRUM DRUGS after testing IN MINI DOSES on the patient?". We are damned sure that these violent reactions are only due to fortum".

Director evidently had no answer!. But he managed to murmur:| "We will however investigate these side reactions and negative results in our attempts at bringing down the temperature even after 7 doses".

The situation obtaining at the present moment can best be explained as a case that had gone too far for any living being to digest the treatments given.

Panic stricken, the attending medical staff including the doctors wanted a CT scan of the brain. Promptly it was done to rule out / rule in brain disorder!!. Where from this thought?, this ailment?;Or induced and imposed undoubtedly!

Not finding any clue of brain disturbances, the eighth dose of fortum was finally decided to be given!.

Doctors relied on CT scanning at this late stage, the parents and family members relied on their fervent prayers to god.

Call it a miracle or call it a message from the skies above or call it a grace of god, the godly mother of dear Prashant went into deep meditation seeking HIS DIVINE HELP readily available for all His ardent seekers; she continued her prayers totally lost from the outside world; she did seem to get the answer!

Guess what was the D I V I N E ANSWER?

She saw a million Suns' bright light continuously flashing across; she heard words of advice <stop fortum, stop fortum, fortum, for t u m m m!>

This was sufficient for the anxious mother to wake up from her meditation in the special private ward on the 4th floor of the hospital. It was already 2pm in the afternoon; she rang up her husband waiting on the patient in the ICU at the 2nd floor uttering: "please ensure to stop all further doses. I am dashing to the ICU ward"

 Prashant's father (responding to the phone call): "Dear what happened?"

Prashant's mother: "Just you please stop the medical personnel from giving any further doses!". So saying, she darted down the flight of stairs without waiting for the electric lift to take her down; In her natural anxiety, she ignored all safety norms!; was noticed to be jumping two steps at a time. Staircase users passing by her, were shocked to see this acrobatic dash down the stairs of an elderly lady!; they did enquire whether "anything is amiss"? Maintaining her speed, she managed safely to reach the ICU doors and to gate crash into the ICU ward. What did she find inside?!; a syringe already loaded with the EIGHTH DOSE of the frightening fortum; was being readied to be injected. As is the usual procedure, the air was being pushed out of the syringe barrel till a mini drop of the drug fell on the floor; Indira rushed to the doctor and uttered: "doctor, all these days as a mother I appealed to you and your assisting medical staff to STOP this ghastly ineffective frightening fortum drug; now after prayers, I have got the clear celestial message: "these reactions are only due to fortum, fortum, fo..r..t… u…m; do not dare to inject this readied dose".

Doctor Adimanov, the root -causer-surgeon of this tragedy and who happened to be visiting his patient by chance, did not heed to the mother's utterances and got ready to push the eighth dose into Prashant's torso saying "this is very costly broad spectrum drug that cannot be wasted";

Indira retorted like an iron -lady: "If it is costly, please push it into your torso; if even a drop is pushed into Prashant's, we will seek criminal action against you and your hospital institution"; so saying, she stepped forward, held Dr. Adimanov's collar, snatched the fully loaded syringe and dashed it against the floor"

All medical staff including the great Dr. Adimanav remained motionless and spell bound; from the environs of the ICU ward, clapping sounds were heard emanating from nursing sisters as if to appreciate mother's courage to save her son from further tragedy.

Later, it was understood that the attending doctors had definite plans to get rid of this case by shifting the patient to near- by mental hospital on grounds of derilious   state of Patient's mind; the sisters clapping their hands in appreciation of the boldness of the patient's mother, conveyed in no unambiguous terms, the pre-planned efforts <to get rid> of the patient to save their skins from all criminal charges of negligence.

Dear readers this is no story- telling!.

It is an absolute narration of things and events that went on unfolding each day with each dose of treatment.

Readers can ponder over and gauge for themselves, the mental and physical sufferings dear Prashant was forced to undergo besides the mental agony for his parents and attending kith and kin; and no less for his dearest own younger brother (strongly bonded to his elder, since childhood). What a situation that has been brought about!!. The "patient" had been taken inside the OT for biopsy procedure through minor surgery, predominantly, to take out a <micro sized> sample of the unwanted masses but factually turned out to be a <body destroying> major surgery that rendered the patient, <not only paraplegic from chest and below down to toes on both left and right sides of his body> but, also pushing him to a state of delirium and many other complications. This is the fittest and the most apt case for study/publishing thesis for all medical researchers across the globe.

****

CHAPTER- VI

THE MAGIC WAND CONTINUED

What cannot be cured must be endured appeared to be an honest message from the attending nuero-physician of the same hospital institution. He is the same neuro expert who **was called** by the damage causing cardio thoracic surgeon **into the OT, after the damage, for his opinion post-surgery, on that fateful 23rd October instant.**

Mincing no words this neuro physician had unambiguously declared the ischemic damage caused to the spinal cord **as substantiated, unfortunately, by MRI scanning post-surgery**. Having understood the seriousness of the avoidable damage he had chosen to help out our dear Prashant with rehabilitation procedures to bring back semblance of normalcy.

First morning knock on Prashant's private ward door!. Father of Prashant quietly opened the door only to be pleasantly surprised to see Dr JMK Murthy. "come on in doctor" , greeted Indira - Prashant's mother .

"Would both of you parents mind coming out of the ward; I would like to thoroughly examine the patient"; so uttering he, the doctor, straight away walked to

Prashant's bed, greeted him "good morning Prashant. How are you? You look cheerful".

That was half the battle won? Today is the festival of harvesting and post harvesting, rejoicing. Happy Sankranti to you, dear Prashant".

Prashant was quick to beam his customary smile and extend his hand to shake the outstretched hands of the neuro expert. "Good morning doctor!; I am looking forward to great rehabilitation exercising this morning".

"Yes of course, of course. I have come to start you off with that" uttered Dr Murthy trying to wipe off tears from the corners of his eyes; the junior doctors accompanying their senior however, could not hold back their tears as successfully.

They stepped aside and burst into severe sobs uncontrollable at that. Prashant's father stepped aside and comforted these young doctors. What a scenario?

Parents of Prashant had also cultivated will of steel to face this situation.

Dr Murthy quipped to Prashant: "did you see on your TV on DD channel a young man climbing mountain?"

Prashant was quick to respond: "doctor with your help and encouragement I would like to be that mountaineer myself one day"

"Three cheers to you, did you carefully observe that climber dear Prashant?", Dr. Murthy smilingly enquired.

Prashant who had watched the mountain climber most

Minutely replied "I salute that person's valour and determination although he too like me is physically challenged"

Dr. Murthy and his younger colleagues were pleasantly surprised at PRASHANT's resolve to conquer the mountains. These noble men from the noble profession were even more determined to help Prashant achieve his goal.

With parents', friends', well-wishers' and the ever effervescent younger brother's smiling assistance, Prashant took upon himself to learn, practice, master various challenges posed before his life

Dr. Murthy called Prashant's parents out for a brief discussion. Mother expressing her anxiety to Dr. Murthy, "when can we expect him to walk again".

"Frankly speaking madame, MRI scan of the dorsal spine conveys to me that he has suffered ischemic damage at the T2, T3, T4 levels of spinal cord".

"Since the boy is very young, there is a possibility of his regaining some of the lost walking faculties through what is called in medical parlance <establishment of collateral blood supply>"; "but however", he went on to add, "more importantly, he should undergo physio-exercising strictly every morning, and during the day and every evening for days/weeks/months/and years on end".

"You should also take care to prevent contracting bed sores by turning him on, from one supine to other supine positions every hour and put him on alpha bed cushion during mid-night hours. None the less importantly, extreme care should be taken to keep the atmosphere around always cheerful lest he should go into depression sooner than later.

Mother to doctor: "we will devote our remaining life to take care of him; to keep on attempting continuously, to bring him back to normalcy"

Doctor displaying his happiness remarked: "half the battle is won with all of you around Prashant displaying exemplary calmness and continuously cheering him, boosting his morale and always keeping it at our Great Himalayan mountain heights".

"What a common person with good health and all faculties intact can achieve, will be easily surpassed by such encouragement and morale boosting to Prashant through all your noble gestures. Please keep it up uninterrupted. He, as I can see, from all your right thinking and efforts, will never ever go to depression; not allowing him to go into depression, is the crux and heart of the physiotherapic activities".

"Physio exercising also profoundly assists in preventing <wastages in muscles> which, a physically challenged person is highly prone and vulnerable to".

Parents assured the visiting neuro specialist: "we will sincerely and strictly implement all your advices. It is our aim that our life's purpose is best served by attending to his paramount needs; service to him now, when he needs it most, is no less service to the creator Almighty Himself".

"I am very much overwhelmed with your (attendants' and family members') thoughts and inclinations and firm resolve to handle this difficult situation".

So uttering, the doctor prepared to leave for the day not without wiping tears from the corners of his eyes.

The doctor left behind a team of nurses and physiotherapists to start Prashant on the important mandatory exercising of his paralysed as well as active parts of the body.

Prashant having been rendered paraplegic was vulnerable to pressure sores particularly in supine positions either for resting or for exercising. Abundant precautions taken to avoid pressure sores, by changing the patient's position every hour, by applying talcum powder at the pressure sore points had paid rich dividends as long as he was under the family attendants' care in the private ward. Compulsions to shift him to ICU ward in view of high temperatures, brought unfortunately a series of setbacks. As already explained, it was mandatory to prevent pressure sores; but the attending nurses in ICU totally neglected these preventive measures. Within a matter of a few days, the dreaded bed sores had set in. During the permitted visiting hours into the ICU, the vigilant mother noticed blackening of the skin at the <greater trochanter> region of Prashant's thighs; she beckoned the attending duty doctor: "Doctor, what do I see?, what is that blackened mark on his thighs?"

The doctor on duty examined the patient carefully and murmured "oh my goodness, he has contracted the dreaded bedsores due to pressure being applied by the protruding boni- portions on the thigh in the supine position".

Mother hit back at the attending medical staff in the ICU: "all of us knew very well that paralysed patients should be very well protected against possible bed sores by turning such patients from time to time from one supine to other supine positions in addition to putting such patients on Alpha beds; we thought that this aspect of care is also taken notice of; but our Prashant has contracted the dreaded bedsore within one night". She went on: "Your carelessness has caused this dreaded damage. You medical staff, do not require to be told about the mandate of placing paraplegic patients on Alpha beds".

The medical staff could not respond to our queries obviously because of their grossly evident negligence.

Another night passed. Anxious parents entered the ICU to enquire about the condition of their dear son. Lo!, to their surprise, they noticed appearance of yet another bed sore; this time in the sacrum region!".

The duty doctor was called by the angry parents to Prashant's bedside. "Look what is the result of yourself proclaimed intensive care? Prashant has contracted a second pressure sore!. Who the hell is responsible for this!; why did you not think of placing him on Alpha bed from the first hour in ICU?; why have your nurses not kept on turning him to different supine positions?".

"This is the degree of care and caution in an ICU in a leading super specialty hospital! What a mockery!!"

We the parents decided to take care of Prashant's needs inside the ICU to prevent development of further pressure points. Although the hospital was reluctant to allow us in, we parents, by turns, gate crashed into the ICU but fully prepared like the duty personnel; yes we donned the white apron, the surgeon's cap on the head and the mandatory mask and took turns to keep on turning him from one supine to other supine positions religiously promptly, every hour.

Prashant's father had spoken earlier to the medical superintendent to arrange for Alpha cushioned bed without any further delay. Although everything was in position from the third night, the parents had to continue daily, Aseptic dressing (ASD- in medical parlance) of these two bedsore wounds; guess, How long these two dreaded pressure sores continued to torture Prashant and his attendants? Fifteen years!, which could have been easily avoided if only proper care had been taken from day No. ONE of imposition of paraplegia on our dear son.

This is the most elementary decision for any hospital not requiring any specialist consultations either.

In fact it is universally practised that a paralysed patient has to be protected by placing him/her on Alpha cushioned beds/on water beds for supine positions and Alpha seat cushions for sitting positions.

But here it was, in the instant case, Prashant was enforced through sheer carelessness and callousness, to suffer with bed sores for 15 long years with no abating/cure even after attempts <to turn the flap> a plastic surgery procedure.

Highly thought over and planned intervention by a skillful plastic surgeon at Bangalore city's <Jain Hospital>, saw the end of suffering on this account as lately as the year 2005 .

Recollecting the enforced damage, God only knew why it took the leading hospital a whopping 40 days of treatment in ICU to bring down the temperature to normal. Although this tardy involvement of the medical personnel deserved to be condemned by seeking discharge from their hospital, we the patient and attendants displayed extra-ordinary patience in dealing with the situation strongly influenced by the universal adage: <A bird in hand is worth two in a bush>. We had no confidence, in this critical situation, that a different hospital would create magic to reverse the calamity enforced.

At long last he was shifted back to private ward. Now was the time to start without any further delay, rehabilitation of our dear Prashant.

****

CHAPTER- VII

PHYSIO-EXERCISING –THE MAGIC WAND

Prashant had been reduced, in activities, to a physical state akin to a 3 months old child or a bird with wings chopped off!. Paralysed joints below T4 level of thorax had to be physically handled as they could not take part, by themselves, in any exercising activity. Even turning from one supine to other supine positions required helping! what to speak of efforts at making him sit up. There was no semblance of balance of the torso, even to sit with back support

His parents and attendants had to bring all the reserves of their tolerance and energy into play in order to get on with the mandatory physio exercising. There was no room to think otherwise; no room to brood over the tragedy; what could be the mental strength of the 20+ years old Prashant to undergo all these rigorous exercising? This was yet another food for thought for a psychiatrist consultant.

Physio therapist Dr. Subhash, promptly arrived at the patient's bed, greeted him: "Good morning dear Prashant, you are already aware that physio exercising is the real rehabilitation mandate under the enforced circumstances Be ready with light breakfast by 8 AM from tomorrow on wards".

Prashant nodded his head in response and assured him: "I would be ready at the stroke of 8 in the morning".

Subhash: "Dear, these are few of the simple pre-exercises: stretching both the legs apart; loosening the individual toes of both legs; rotating the ankles; rotating about the knees; I will be demonstrating to you and your attendants. These should be repeated every hour even in the private ward apart from regular exercising in the dedicated physio therapy centre downstairs".

Pavan entered the ward after his college hours. Prashant was eagerly waiting for him; smilingly he beckoned to Pavan: "Now come here and start your service"

Pavan quipped: "what is this service that is new to me?"

Prashant "I am your elder, so respect me by holding my feet & legs!"

Pavan: "Darling, I have no hesitation in respecting you; okay here I am", so saying he promptly held both his legs together.

Prashant: "It is not just holding dear!; you have to station one leg and pull the other leg away to exercise my hip joint". Both had a hearty laugh before Pavan announcing: "Hey look, your left leg is so friendly with its right counterpart. As I pull away the left, the right also follows suit!".

Prashant: "Exercising, dear, is not like eating ice cream; you should think and manage to keep one leg stable as you exercise its counterpart".

Pavan: "let me think deeply, but where from you got these ideas?"

Prashant: "the hospital physio had visited me this morning and announced serious physio exercising from tomorrow onwards".

Meanwhile he demonstrated several pre exercising at the ward itself which have to be done, as a matter of factly, every hour.

Pavan: "whenever needed I will enlist the support from daddy, mummy and Krishna mama. And, I will not hesitate to involve your visitors either! ; everybody visiting you has to pay the toll tax!!"

The two brothers had a hearty laugh!.

Sun was shining brightly the next morning. Pavan entered the ward with breakfast pack ready to offer to his elder. But surprisingly he saw him already ready to go down- stairs for physio exercising schedule.

"Hey dear!; you have outsmarted all of us . I was thinking you are still in bed!. That is simply wonderful. Here is the breakfast affectionately packed for you by our neighbour".

Pantu snatched the breakfast pack and while opening it he smelt of his familiar dish. "Ah!, I can now guess easily it must be our neighbours- the affectionate Deshmukh uncle & aunty"; and happily started munching.

 Break- fast over, the ward boy arrived with wheel chair ready to take him to physio centre down below.

Pavan helped his daddy to shift him from bed to wheel chair.

Prashant quipped in: "daddy, since when have you acquired weight- lifting skills?".

Pavan replied: "long before we were born and of course before his marriage to dear mother, father had practised weight lifting in the then USSR where he had gone as a young bachelor for Heavy Electrical power equipment factory/ plant building training!!". Laughter all around!

Wheel-chair transferred into, Prashant was wheeled away from the ward towards the lift to take him down stairs; promptly reported to the physio centre at 8 am; Subhash- the physio expert was at the door entrance .Promptness in reporting and the jovial beaming faces of both the brothers brought surprise to Subhash who murmured within himself: "Such a huge tragedy has befallen them but everyone around him are displaying positive frame of mind!!". He wondered within himself: "who is sustaining their high morale? Could there be any divine propping up?".

He did not fail to draw clear inference: "how happier the entire family would have been, before this tragedy!"

At this juncture, Prashant's and Pavan's darling- Krishna mama arrived straight into physio-centre.

He knew from this day onwards, his nephew would undergo rhythmic physio therapy and quite rigorously at that .Krishna mama had endeared himself to both the brothers ever since Prashant and family had moved over to Hyderabad from Delhi.

Krishna and his better half Jayaprada and their sweet offsprings- Kavitha and Sirisha had decided to fully devote their time to rehabilitation of their dear Prashant.

He drew closer to the two brothers and whispered something into their ears!. Lo!, the two brothers got lost in uncontrolled laughter!.

Parents looking on started to guess what Krishna uncle could have whispered into the two brothers' ears!! It was a trademark of Krishna mama and of his nephews as well. After all, the trio had always cultivated <laughter as the best medicine> during their earlier days!

The burst of laughter of these trio sent epidemic waves into the gathering at the physio-center!. All inmates including reluctant patients and physio assistants had been electrified with instant laughter.

Prashant had been waiting for the word <go> with exercises. Transferring him from wheel chair to rolling mat on to the floor itself required special skill and training. Subhash took the lead with Pavan and his daddy supporting him from under his arms and gently lifting him and the master holding his two legs.

The trio successfully transferred the VIP patient on to the rolling mat. Prashant quipped: "Why have you put me on the <mat>? I hope it is not a wrestling competition between me and the physio!"

Subhash looking through the corner of his eyes smilingly announced: "this is going to be the order of the day for coming months".

"Oh!, then I have to double my breakfast intake from tomorrow onwards!" Prashant butted in.

"It is high time you doubled your food intake so that you don't drop me during transferring exercises, be they from wheel chair to bed or from bed to chair" Krishna mama chipped in with his witty jaunts. "Pavan, it is not only you but I also, should henceforth, start visiting Akhadas (wrestling clubs) to strengthen our muscles!". W i t h such conversations the whole atmosphere was rendered jolly and lively. Patients who were wailing and refusing to start exercises due to inevitable unbearable initial pains all took their front seats in this newly enlivened atmosphere- thanks to Prashant and company.

With Prashant already waiting on the mat, Subhash announced: "I will now teach you rolling on your sides; you have to be lying straight flat on your back keeping your both hands close to your body".

So announcing, the physio master turned him to his side slowly and gently, laid him in that position from 1-2-3-4 -10 counts and slowly brought him back to flat lying position. It was not an easy task even for the physio master alone; therefore he looks around, sideways, for Pavan to assist him. What did he see?!. Pavan having vanished from the scene all together, Subhash beckoned to his father: "uncle please look out for Pavan"; his father correctly guessed and found him wiping tears from the Corner of his eye!; hugging him affectionately he brought him (Pavan) to the <wrestling arena>.

Tears gone, Pavan got into jovial mood and started off with his elder. For the first day exercising was limited to rolling 10 times from left and 10 times from right sides.

Subhash introduced one by one all the participants to Prashant. He had noticed dramatic transformation in these participants from hesitation to enthusiasm; from lethargy to energy; from melancholy of painful exercising to readiness to go ahead with exercises!. Oh, what a change that has been brought about!

"Thank you Prashant, thank you Pavan and you all, you have all brought life into this platform /arena enlivened the whole atmosphere". Subhash the physio master and his assistants did not fail to so describe this electrified atmosphere brought about with the arrival of Prashant and his company of attendants.

Day number 2, was even more lively at the exercising arena!. Before start of rolling exercise, Prashant noticed Ravi - the 6years old boy; he had no control over gripping things with his hands since birth; the exercise suggested to him was to slowly grip the ball and throw it as far away as he could.

Subhash tried a few times to help Ravi to grip the large sized ball; but he was unable to grasp it, as it invariably caused unbearable pain whenever he attempted to do so.

Prashant, watching this scenario excused himself from his own schedule for the moment and beckoned to Ravi:

"Ravi let us play together; you throw the ball to me; I will, in my supine position throw it back at you for one -love score. It will become one- all if you throw it back to me. Okay dear!"

Lo! this mini conversation appeared to have had immediate effect .

Gripping difficulty forgotten, Ravi started in right earnest, out of sheer enthusiasm to out- score, he threw the ball back at Prashant; there were loud clapping all around. Subhash became the instant local referee and announced the score as "one- all"; at the end of six exchanges the score was "3- all!". Before calling it a day, Ravi went near Prashant and requested him: "Anna! (meaning elder brother), you come at the same time everyday and we will play the game regularly to score "15- all!" and restart with <love all !!!>

Ravi the little master with only 6 summers and 6 winters in his kitty of age (when two Russian friends miss each other and meet after a long time, they generally greet each other: "oh!, after how many winters and how many summers! We are meeting") had unwittingly and involuntarily left his own impression on the elder Prashant.

Prashant would have mastered the rolling exercises within 5-6days but was really inhibited by the unpleasant pressure sores that had been gifted by the negligent medical attendants in ICU, where earlier, he had had to spend, compulsorily, over 40days at a stretch.

Despite all these pressure sores, he went on to master the

Skills in rolling exercises within a month's time. Subhash went ahead with series number 2 exercises i.e <sitting on knees>

This required yet another series of pre- exercises. From the position of <lying on his back> Prashant was slowly lifted to sitting position <with legs remaining stretched> by clasping his two hands by two attendants and with yet another, the third attendant, gradually supporting his back (to prevent him from falling back); all in the family joined this exercising brigade, fully motivated, Prashant mastered this technique also smilingly within matter of 2-3weeks.

Series number 3exercises, happened to be even tougher than the previous 2 series, as it involved <balancing his body about vertical and horizontal axes>: 1) Prashant had to be transferred from wheel chair sitting position to lying flat- on- his back position; 2) next he had to be rolled over from <flat-on-back> to <flat- on- stomach> position; 3)Next his <2hands had to be stretched beyond his head full straight>; these stages had to be gone through as pre-exercises before crossing into another series! in the same vein!

Guess what was the ambience at this stage? Prashant would quip: "Hey Pavan, do not come in front of my head lest I should pull your legs so hard as to make you also join my flattening exercise!!"

Smiling, Pavan brought a wooden stool, placed it at the end of his elder brother's out stretched hands and instructed him: "hey dear, now instead of my legs, move your forearms one by one, towards your shoulders, inch by inch till the arms and forearms are positioned at right angles to each other; this is possible since your upper chest is normal. At this position your whole body weight is taken by the two elbows.

Next with father and younger brother pulling your body about the waist from both right and left sides and simultaneously with the physio master pulling you up holding your waist belt, you take the position of <sitting on your knees> with the upper body positioned at right angles to the out stretched legs; At this stage you hold the stool with both palms. This position would exercise almost all parts of the upper body, waist and the knee joints besides giving you stable kneeling position, of course with the trio continuing to support from all the 3 sides and the wooden stool taking care of front support. This rigorously positioning exercising, he could do only for a few counts not exceeding 10.

"Don't worry dear Prashant, today you have done a great job for about 10 counts. Gradually as days of exercising pass by you will stabilize for longer periods". So advising, the physio -master slowly and steadily brought him back to lying position (prostate position). The daredevilry in the gallant soldier Prashant had set in already. He along with his younger brother would take all these rigorous exercising happily in his stride and would even share jokes between themselves. This tonic was most essential to pursue these <herculean effort exercising schedule> and it was a matter of pride at this crucial juncture that he lived up fully to the expectations of the physio master.

As the team assembled for the next day's session, all attendants had kept their fingers crossed about the attitude and frame of mood of Prashant to take on these rigorous schedules.

Lo, he was the first to command his father and brother to position him on the floor mat in <lying –on- stomach> position with hands outstretched!. Next he would instruct the trio, to take up their designated positions at the waist and in no time he would have himself positioned his body on the two elbows!; Other stages followed one after another so swiftly that, he had already taken the kneeling position asking for the wooden stool to support himself with his palms!

Round of applause from the attendants; from the nursing sisters present in the physiotherapy centre. The other inmates who had come down to the centre for their predetermined exercising did not lag behind in applauding the bravery and enthusiasm in one who had lost all his movements from chest and below.

Subhash, the physio master, as a matter of fact had no words in praise of Prashant for his gallantry, exemplary courage and positive attitude which, he went on displaying at every step, at every session.

Not a single day, not a single moment could anybody present in the hospital environ including the attending physio master, see him morose or crest fallen unlike majority in similar situations.

Always bold and smiling was the countenance of our dear Prashant. Friends and relatives who would visit him regularly with heavy hearts and expecting to see him in a depressed mood, would get into a state of pleasant shock and surprise to see him smiling, joking and at his physio exercising best.

By now the physio master had been transformed into a great chum and a frantically mad fan. Likewise all inmates of the centre got <encouragement aplenty> and started to follow the fine imprints left by Prashant; so much so the entire physio therapy center had got itself transformed into a lively recreation center.

While this was the ambience at the physio centre at Hyderabad, PRASHANT'S college Management Authorities at Machilipatnam (in the state of Andhra Pradesh) had come to know of the tragedy to their very popular student and went on to reciprocate their gesture by declaring one day holiday in solidarity.

Taking this opportunity, college mates (situated about 400 kilometers away from Hyderabad city) descended on Hyderabad in large numbers to enquire about their dear classmate and college mate's health.

Many were shocked in disbelief to see him smiling, joking despite the tragedy that had been forced on him (perforce made to descend); his chum and class mate SriRam went on to remark: "Prashant is shining and beaming like the Sun as usual; what a tragedy to befall? But admiringly what a personality he turned out to be! for all his classmates and college mates!".

It would require a William Shakespeare or a William

Wordsworth, to bring out vividly, the mental make-up of this great warrior under any situation since his childhood days. What a fine personality he had been developing into, all through his youthful years!. Perhaps it was the fine tuning aspects in his younger days that fitted him into the proverbial <child is the father of man> undoubtedly for that matter.

Where million others would have descended on the negligent doctors and the hospital with cudgels, bullets and mortar fire; Prashant remained, all through, a cool guy as cool as the turbulence- free <Prashant Mahasagar> - the pseudo name for the gigantic but peaceful Pacific Ocean.

For that gallant boy, it had been a routine schedule to exercise his body parts on spread out mattresses under the watchful eyes of his most loving dear younger brother Pavan, who had assumed Herculean responsibilities to attempt, continuously, to bring back his elder brother to near normalcy.

He left no stone unturned to keep the divine smile on his elder's face-tragedy notwithstanding.

Yes, for this noble act, he had to sacrifice, at his young age of 16 years (Pavan was born 4 years later than Prashant was born), all his young countenances, deeds and heroics from a state where he used to spend all his off-school hours with friends and elder brother in playing and fun making. Now he had assumed the serious role to assist his elder, in his massive and timeless physio- exercising compulsions; so professional was the younger's devotion to the elder, that the entire environment, whether it was in ward room or physiotherapy center, always was electrified with joy and fun.

What a transformation of the otherwise serious, monotonous ambience encompassing all inmates of the physio centre!?

Such was the influence and contribution from Prashant and his dutiful younger brother!. The grit and determination displayed smilingly even under strict and mandatory schedules of rigorous exercising and quite often painful at that, served as a fine example of <leading from the front>

The mandate for physio exercising for all the handicapped and the physically challenged, cannot be expressed in simple black and white. It has to be either experienced or seen to be believed!. The rigorous schedule called for belittling all other activities whether it is food or responding to incessant flow of visitors.

It required grit apart, super natural power to undergo these strict regimes. His childhood obsession for music listening came in very handy at these critical junctions; the physio master would start with "one, two, three, four", simultaneously, Prashant would switch on his hand held recorded music box and music noble as it is, did assist him in grossly lightening the burden.

He had become the darling of everyone around him so much so each and every attending staff was ever ready and in fact anxiously waiting to serve him at just a beck and call.

PRASHANT'S-An Incredible Life Journey!!!

He had been demonstrating practically <what it takes to succeed in life despite Himalayan proportion obstacles>, quite in contrast to easy living for a sportive person well-bred and well nurtured since childhood.

Time ticked heavily from hours to days and months; and, at the end of five months, Prashant had graduated from assisted, padded sitting stance to self-sitting position with far less support albeit for just half an hour; Self-pride in this achievement, self-cheering for this progress however small it was!!.

****

CHAPTER- VIII

Acupuncture

Prashant, his parents and the attendants including his dear younger brother and dear Krishna mama however, would want faster recovery and therefore started to put in incessant efforts for newer and more procedures to supplement the physio exercising discipline.

These efforts did start yielding some tangible results. Krishna mama appeared in the physio exercising center; waiting patiently for the routine exercising to be over, seeing Prashant relaxed a bit, thereafter he announced "hey look, I have come to know from my friend Naveen Prasad that he is feeling quite relaxed and improved after undergoing the <Acupuncture>"

Poor mama had to face a barrage of questions from each one of the attendants present in the gathering. "What is this Acupuncture? Does it involve acute puncturing of the poor patient's body? Who is this bold and gallant Naveen Prasad who had allowed his body to be punctured?"

Krishna mama smilingly replied: "oh my god!, your highly anxious enquiries have punctured my body alright!. Let me explain what<Acupuncture> is all about. Acupuncture is an ancient Chinese form of medicinal treatment which uses needles, on the patient's body pricked at predetermined points".

"Oh no!, Enough is enough, Prashant is tortured already with the 4-6 hours of rigorous exercising, I cannot see any more stressing and straining of my dear son "quietly responded Prashant's mother.

Pavan added further: "For this pricking of needles into the human torso, does it require local anesthesia at each and every prick point?; how long does each session last?". Sri Ram- PRASHANT's college mate present in the gathering chipped in: "Prashant be careful, your mama and company are proposing an organized attack on your body by needle pricking in the name of recovery".

"Let Mr. Naveen Prasad come down and present himself before us. Let us all see him without any bandages on the pricked points!!!. Then we can think of and take suitable treatment; till then, no extraneous treatment/decision for our Prashant"; whole gathering had a hearty laugh and looked at Prashant's parents who were silently enjoying the <parliamentary debate> on Acu-puncture.

His father: "Dear Krishna, please tell the whole gathering about the authenticity of this Acu-puncture treatment, the success rate of this treatment; whether it is practiced only in China or throughout the world".

Krishna mama took the center stage again and explained: "Acu- puncture, as already explained, has been practised since ages in China as a sure and helpful treatment to give appreciable relief and even total elimination of any disturbance in the health of a person".

He went on to state: "it is a form of medical treatment which uses medicated needles to prick at predetermined points so as to manipulate the <life energy> within the patient's body, thereby curing the ailment; This is accomplished by using needles to <redistribute excess prana> (referred to as 'ki' in Chinese) in the patient's body to the affected part. Congested <prana>, in the diseased part, is redistributed to other parts of the body; Blocked meridians or bio-plasmic channels are cleaned or opened by directing 'ki' to them". I have quoted this procedure from a well-known practising doctor. All in the family gathering agreed to give it a fair trial.

Parents in particular, did not want to keep the present hospital's treating doctors in the dark.

On being approached, the helpful hospital doctors opined: "we have heard a lot about this form of treatment particularly on physically challenged persons; It is quite harmless and without any side effects. It is worthy of being given a trial on our dear Prashant as an out-patient visitor to the Acupuncture center and return to the hospital as continued inpatient; we will chip into these additional efforts through arranging transport to and from the Acupuncture center back to hospital" so happily announced the physio master consulting with hospital medical superintendant.

Pavan to Prashant: "Are you ready for this trial?".

Prashant nodded his head in approval: "we shall plan after the regular physio exercising. I have also read books on Acu puncture and they base their treatment on <redirecting energy flow in human body; such a dynamism in humans (and certainly animals also) is not possible without energy at various control points in the body physique>".

As planned, visit to Acupuncture center was accompanied by Pavan, both parents and the dynamic Krishna mama.

"The new environment appeared positive and pleasant". Prashant told his younger brother. "I am sure", said Pavan replying "you will enliven the atmosphere here also".

The Acupuncture expert welcomed Prashant for the treatment session. "Look dear, we will not give you any anaesthesia but will be simply pricking tiny needles into the skin at selected points. The pricks will not at all be painful. Are you ready"?

"just prick me once . Let me experience and then take a decision!" Joked Prashant to the Acupuncture expert.

The expert skillfully pushed a few needles from ankles to knees from waist to abdomen and enquired: "Prashant do you feel any pain?";

"Go ahead" replied Prashant, "because you have selected the least sensory points!!; I am paralysed from chest and below down to ankles and feet !!".

"Oh my God!, I had overlooked for a moment, this de-sensitized zone !; however that area is equally important to be Acu punctured" The expert continued <his mission>: "Prashant now we will start from your palm, forearms, hands and shoulders; oh yes, a few pricks on chest also!"; he looked at Prashant enquiringly "And how do you feel now?"

Prashant: "Oh, much heavier pricks I have withstood 8 - Hourly for days and weeks and months!!. These pricks are only feelers from antennae of the biological insect-species called Ants! you can go ahead".

By that time Pavan saw another patient undergoing similar treatment. Each prick produced different sounds somewhere mimicking a parrot, a cuckoo, a nightingale or even a cock!; poor fellow must have been experiencing pain but the congregation went into bouts of laughter every time that patient produced chirping sounds, feeling as if, they have all suddenly landed in <a bird-park>!

"Hey Prashant, do you recognize that patient producing chirping sounds!?". He had a second look and exclaimed: "Hey Pavan, this is Naveen Prasad of <All India fame>". He is highly popular as a comedian on the Telugu screen; Prashant in the company of his younger brother and friends had routinely, in the yester-years, always enjoyed his jokes.

Krishna mama was pleasantly surprised to see his close friend Naveen Prasad; instantly he introduced Prashant and company to him.

Pavan: "see how much deeply involved he is, in his acting field!; By force of habit and practice he seems to continue his screen acting on the real stage also!"

Naveen Prasad: "Oh come on friends, that expert-"Acute" puncturist is pushing needles after needles into my body, believe me!; it is no acting in the hospital premises; it simply causes pain, pain!, do you get me – my newly acquainted friends!!?".

He turned around, and not failing to interrogate Prashant: "How come you are not acting, beg your pardon not reacting at each prick? How come you are so cool?". Prashant smiled at him and instantly they became fast friends. The expert pricked both the patients and the duo happily went on recapturing jokes from the comedian's plethora of films, unmindful of the treatment.

The whole atmosphere was charged with mirth and laughter; all inmates and doctors joined the joyful bandwagon.

The treatment prolonged for over 8 weeks on the trot, Naveen Prasad did get immense relief; whereas Prashant was not fortunate to experience any relief. Medical fraternity at the Acu- puncture center analysed the non-effect of treatment on him. They could conclude that the neurological damage caused earlier to his spinal cord was permanent; as the criminal doctors at the IMS hospital had caused <ischemic damage> as admitted in their own medical records; and as confirmed by post damage MRI scan of the dorsal spine.

Prashant returned from Acu puncture centre devoid of any improvement but was gifted with friendship of a VIP comedian who went on to become his admirer, well-wisher and friend life-long. Naveen made it a habit to keep on enquiring about his progress in rehabilitation and would visit him also now and then.

Yet another 10 weeks passed by, beyond the first five months. It was quite unheard of in medical treatment history that a patient, either after botched up or normal surgery had to remain in hospital as an inpatient all through this period continuously.

It was 31st December 1990 evening; when the whole world would congregate at their chosen premises to usher in the New Year. But it was quite a different moment for Prashant's parents, Pavan, Krishna mama and devoted friends; they were all, instead, engaged in giving company to Prashant at the hospital. There was no remorse or bitterness or impatience however, around and anywhere around Prashant!. **Human Virtues displayed at their – best !;** He continued his heroic fight against the imposed handicap , thrust on him and that which had taken away his all, walking faculty included, for the rest of his life.

Young Pavan had taken life as it presented itself in its own shape and form ungrudgingly without any rancour or bitterness. He also, like his elder, added music, mirth and masala (energy) to the life of his family and fraternity and made it look heavenly on the earth itself.

Dear Readers!, Is it not humanity at it's A P E X ; humanity at its Z E N I T H ?

Needless therefore, to emphasize how the duo got into the gallant mood to fight various odds as they kept on occurring from time to time!

Compulsions had dictated the otherwise calm and serene life in the family. Life had been torn asunder and topsy-turvy. No one in the family could think of re-establishing the pre-tragedy status of life. All were kept busy, both in mind and body, for carrying on with the day's activities; no time to think of the morrow; the present had <occupied> all their time and energy. **At this crucial juncture, intimate and close well-wishers stepped in to protect the affected family members like a fortress.**

Apart from the mandatory necessities of keeping Prashant's morale very high, lot of physical efforts had to be put in daily, hourly. Parents and Pavan had taken over the compulsory duty of attending to his morning ablutions Aseptic dressing of bed sore wounds, giving sponge bath on the bed itself, physio- exercising his lower paralysed limbs on the bed itself; and scores of other duties. They could not concentrate on meeting other requirements such as food, clothes, medicines, etc.

The ever agile and helpful Krishna mama sacrificing his all, did a gallant soldier's duty from morning to midnight; whether it is bringing deliciously freshly cooked lunch for all the four; and/or bringing not easily available medicines from far off <24hours- open> chemist's shop; and/or doing night attendant's duty at hospital.

This duty, he performed religiously regularly, for a continuous period of over thirty weeks at a stretch- A feat performed only out of love and affection; he would motor down to his residence from hospital 10 kilometers away; his dear better-half Jayaprada would have prepared hot delicacies to PRASHANT's taste and choice to be delivered at the hospital (10 km away), then attend to his factory work along with his wife!.

The couple had been blessed with 2 smart and beautiful daughters – Kavitha & Sirisha. They too contributed their mite towards caring and attending to, Prashant.

Jayaprada's sister RajLakshmi and her husband Sharma also chipped in along with their dear son Sudhakar in the service of dear Prashant.

Sharma's elder son Madhusudan had been physically challenged; required round the clock attention from his parents. Not with standing this major responsibility, the Sharmas selflessly served dear Prashant as first priority. What a sacrifice?!. What a source of strength and morale boosting for dear Prashant!. This was not all. Our family's extra ordinary well wishing friend, NSLN Murthy, chipped in with his whole family. Wife Saroja, son Raghu, daughters Asha and Shubha in supplying home readied dinner and also visiting the hospital to keep company for young Prashant.

Yet another family well-wisher, PV Bhat with his better half Nirmala Bhat, son Ashok and daughter Anupama took on the responsibility of keeping company for Prashant in the hospital, besides caring for younger brother Pavan at their home. Although Pavan spent his day time with his elder, it was planned, mandatorily, to continue with his academic career /study activities as nearly normal as possible. Towards this end, Pavan was taken care of, in the evening and night sessions, at their residence by the Bhat's family.

The care and affection bestowed on younger Pavan, was even more than that shown to their own children - Ashok and Anupama. Anupama, the daughter of Bhats was only a school going girl and innocently complained to her parents: "This Pavan has scored over me. I have become a second citizen in my own family. I get only scant attention!".

Her mother Nirmala would pacify: "Dear Anu, Pavan's parents have been kept busy looking after Prashant and paying round the clock attention on him in the hospital. Now it is the sacred duty of all of us together, to look after Pavan as our own son. Do you see the point now dear?".

Jokes apart, Anu was the first member of Bhat's family to shower even greater attention on Pavan ; with hot hot coffee in the tray she would visit Pavan's cot:

"Hey Pavan!, good morning, get up coffee is waiting for you".

Ashok, sleeping by his bedside would also share coffee with him. In fact, Ashok also would shower his full affection on their young guest. Such was the bon–homie meted out to Pavan by the Bhat's family!.

Such noble gestures from near and dear ones, took away the worries of parents on their compulsions of reduced care and attention to the younger son.

Prashant thus, was always surrounded round the clock, by caring and loving ones which provided the platform for him to spring to lively and meaningful life of achievements galore that went on to stand him out in a crowded mass even above normals.

Not one moment in his life thus far, did he look back on what had transpired but only looked, thought and acted ahead to achieve name, fame and laurels.

Acu puncture was tried out but was not productive on our dear Prashant ; the only backbone - physio exercising continuously, to bring in greater stability in sitting and various positions for exercising, was rigorously followed.

 <Never give up> was the adrenalin flow in dear Prashant and his attendants. **Psychological counseling**, as yet another effort, was given a trial to help relieve Prashant from his many **hidden** worries.

Mr. Srinivas was our new help in attempting to restore normalcy; when he arrived in our midst in the hospital premises, he had decided already to interview Prashant; "I am your friend and well-wisher Srinivas; You can bank on me for getting rid of worries if at all you have any! How are you feeling now?".

"Glad to meet you Mr Srinivas, I am thankful for your visit. But I think you will be disappointed with me because I just do not have any worries!", quipped Prashant

"On meeting you with your beaming smile, I could figure out very well that you are a gallant soldier having kept all worries away from you; not giving them a chance to even stroll near your vicinity".

"Your observations are apt; you see, my parents have given me such fine upbringing since my childhood days"."Prashant you like sharing your childhood days with me I suppose?".

"Oh surely why not": He pointed out towards Pavan, standing next to his mother: "that young boy teasing his mother is my younger, born 4 years later than me".

"Oh I see, you were never alone in your childhood days. That is really fine; a mischievous younger always influences the elder; can I conclude that your younger is really dangerously mischievous?"

"Your guess is not at all incorrect!; he is mischievous alright but is my best friend indeed. <A friend in need is a friend indeed>. In today's situation he is my back bone" replied Prashant.

"Prashant, can you throw some light on your parents?"

"Surely, my first best friends are my parents; they never ever dictated anything to me in all my life thus far. But, on the other hand, they have only enabled me always to learn about things in life as a matter- of -factly .Whether it was in studies or at play, I had always the freedom to do whatever I chose in that field".

"I can surely make out you are a self-made man whether it was achievements in studies or sports or extra-curricular activities"

"I had drawn inspiration from my parents <who were never also "rans">, but who achieved sound levels in studies and other activities of their lives".

Prashant's mother promptly introduced both her

children to the psychiatrist: "Prashant as a child would always run faster than others; would climb the stairs as first to reach the top floor; He was over inquisitive always, to know things around him in detail; whether it was studies or sports activities or other extra-curricular activities such as debating, essay writing, participating in quiz competitions; Besides, he had shown love for music as an infant; as a child he liked to read books and listen to stories of heroes; Epics like the Ramayana and the Mahabharatha interested him profoundly which he cultivated by listening to graphic animated narrations from both of us.

Srinivas to Prashant's mother: "Madam, your narration of Prashant's childhood evokes keen interest in me; I can make out he has been brought up from childhood very finely. I have a few questions to you also please".

"Please go ahead".

"How is his temperament at the present?"

"From childhood he is very calm and quiet but silently always active; even at this stage, he is maintaining the same coolness despite his heavy dependence on attendants for day to day activities".

"Do you mean to say he does not frown on the attendants if they do not come immediately on his call; or if he does not get breakfast in time or help to washing his hands in time?"

"No, there is not an iota of impatience in him; if I were busy in preparing for his next activity and would delay in attending to his hand washing needs, he would quip "mummy are you bringing the lunch also for me so that I am spared washing my hands two times!!; but my stomach is not ready for immediate lunch!"

"Does he get irritated now and then?".

"There is no chance for that either; in fact Prashant would crack jokes whenever there was delay in starting his routine exercising schedule; he would quip: "Pavan must be doing pre-exercising himself to handle my stiff legs".

"I can easily make out that Prashant is head and shoulders above many normals. I am amazed at his positive frame of mind in the midst of adversities".

"FRANKLY madam, I expected to see him (Prashant) always losing his tempers; disliking any questions hurled at him; showing extreme anger at doctors and medical attending staff; throwing things away; on his own showing his resentment against doctor Adimanov and doctor Vaidya who were the main actors in tragic negligent surgery that had brought him to this stage of total dependence on others. But, as a psychiatrist I have no words to express my marvel at this extra ordinary cool and calm conduct through all activities of daily life. He has, by virtue of his exemplary conduct throughout the daily regimes, made my profession look redundant!".

"I will be failing in my duty if I do not express my appreciation of you parents, of his dear younger brother, his dear mama and hosts of well-wishers and friends who are standing by him like a fortress. In fact what is being meted out to him lovingly, affectionately by you all is the best psychological treatment possible anywhere on the globe".

He did not mince words in his paying eloquent tributes to Prashant's greatness: "He, certainly is not a normal ordinary person but must have been created by god from celestial fibre and super human at that"; to which his mother replied with pride and smile: "yes, our Prashant is simply extra ordinary".

So expressing his opinion, Srinivas took leave of us wishing Prashant and all of us grand success in our Herculean efforts to rehabilitate the handsome gallant personality.

Pavan did not fail to notice him taking out handkerchief from his pocket and wiping the tears as he walked away from us.

****

CHAPTER-IX

CHAND BHAI – UNANI TREATMENT

Not a day passed without vomiting even water that was attempted to be taken; definitely attributable to consumption of "lorry loads" of antibiotics for a long time during his protracted stay in the hospital continuously for SEVEN MONTHS; evidently dullness of the liver had set in which was duly substantiated by frequent Liver Functioning Test (LFT). This additional health problem cropped up besides the previous challenges of disability, bedsores, UTI.-enough to send chills down the spines of parents and kith and kin.

But some divine intervention appeared on the scenario from nowhere. An Unani medicine practicing hakim – noble intended Janab Chand Bhai landed in our midst. He had, to his credit a success story of raising to his feet, an accident victim with spinal cord injured seriously. We the parents and Prashant's dear uncle made enquiries with him on the prospects of recovery of the patient. He readily agreed to visit us from the remotest corner of Hyderabad city. He was highly confident of success in this case also.

Thus began yet another form of treatment in fond hope of recovery.

Treatment had to be for a continuous duration of 5-6 hours daily and involved massaging the entire body with special massaging oils and oral medicines meticulously prepared by the hakim himself.

The duo of devotion and thoughtful treatment had their salutary effect on the patient's general health. Vomiting sensation frequently tormenting the hapless Prashant vanished within 3 months. This improvement astounded even the specialist from other medical Practices. Toxic effects of heavy anti-biotic medicines administered so far, started to disappear and patient's appetite returned to normal. He regained his general health although neurologically there were no visible improvements. However this Unani treatment brought cheers to one and all when paraplegia affected skin surfaces started to perspire!. The hakim was all enthusiasm and concentration throughout the continuous 18 months' of treatment. At the end of it all, hard devoted efforts put in by the noble intentioned hakim did benefit our dear Prashant in restoring his general health although neurologically there was status-quo.

Every contribution to his health improvements had to be given a trial optimistically.

Never to give up, parents continued with enquiry for possible improvements from other medical treatment practices. They landed in <Acu-pressure> (as different from Acu- Puncture narrated in previous pages.) This method of treatment has been known to cure many an ailment since centuries in ancient India and China. After all each and every form of medicinal practices do recognize nodal points in the body influencing health. If those nodal points are activated by external stimulation through applying pressure on pre-determined nerve endings, expecting success is within the realms of hope; this was tried on Prashant for nearly sixty sessions over a period of 2 months. Although there was no tangible improvement he was game for the trial and never lost his heart despite no improvements.

HYPER BARIC OXYGEN THERAPHY –Also TRIED

From amongst the continuous flow of visitors to the hospital, a suggestion was made to try out a very new and highly effective treatment to bring back neurological normalcy of Prashant. Parents, ever alert to cash in on new possible remedial treatments, made detailed enquiries about this new treatment called <Hyper Baric Oxygen- (HBO) therapy>.

This suggestion came from an air force officer related to PRASHANT'S school mate. This facility was available only at a military Air Force base camp located about 50km away from Hyderabad city.

Prashant's father lost no time in visiting this camp and met the Officer-Commanding this air force hospital center.

He was introduced to one Wing Commander Dr. Ratan (in charge of the hospital) whom he approached: "Dear commander Dr. Ratanji, I understand your hospital has a facility called Hyper Baric Oxygen Therapy. My son Prashant is rendered paraplegic from chest and below in an unfortunate ill - advised surgery at the Hyderabad city medical Institute hospital". So starting the conversation, he handed over to him complete medical papers including pre-operative X- rays, CT scans and post-operative MRI scans of the relevant chest regions of his dear son.

Wing commander after going through all medical records, X-rays, CT scans and MRI scans was aghast at the severity of neurological damage caused on the young and otherwise healthy patient.

It was clear to him, the wing commander ranked Doctor-in- charge, that it was a case of spinal cord physical damage and interfering with spinal vasculature.

He sighed out and addressing Prashant's father said: "the neurological damage is quite extensive. As MRI scan clearly spells out, the city hospital surgeon has definitely caused reduced flow of blood to spinal cord functioning .In our medical parlance, it is referred to as <Ischemic Myelopathy of dorsal spine>. Our facility here is pretty well-known to re-establish, reactivate affected organs of human body. Here, We allow the patients under treatment, to inhale oxygen at hyper baric pressure level. The inhaling is organized at a slightly higher than normal atmospheric pressure to ensure that both inside and outside of the patient's body is balanced at the slightly higher level. At this stage father intervened and requesed the Wing Commander: "Please let us know, if this treatment has been given to any civilian; If yes, what was the ailment of that patient?".

The wing commander patiently explained the whole

background of this therapeutic procedure: "Here OXYGEN under higher than normal atmospheric pressure is administered into the patient; is known to have excellent properties for prognosis basically reactivating/re- establishing blocked blood vessels" .

He went on to add: "we regularly adopt this procedure on our flying personnel who are subject to sudden pressure variations on their bodies while flying at different altitudes in the air or on seamen while under water deep sea diving. Both extremes in air and sea have detrimental effect on blood supply in those personnel".

Prashant's father showing keen interest enquired: "Doctor wing commander, the procedure seems to be very interesting. I would be glad if you could narrate to us similar instances, if not identical cases, being treated with this HBO therapy".

"Oh surely, Over there, can you see that elderly person (a civilian) walking up and down? Before entering the pressurized chamber for the first time, he was brought on a stretched already with one leg amputated (because of his highly diabetic condition) but to prevent second leg also from being amputated, he is being tried with this HBO –therapy".

Father expressing his curiosity enquired: "Dr. How many sitting he had had to undergo? Please tell all"

"He was treated for a continuous period of 15 days at the rate of 90 minutes per session per day. Lo! You can clearly see him walking normal; he has definitely avoided amputation in his second leg after this therapy. We are all proud of this success".

Prashant and his attendants felt that this therapy can be tried confidently and with plenty of hope, they readily consented for this treatment.

The wing commander- doctor himself took the initiative and clarified to Prashant: "Dear sunny, you may have to <hide yourself away from your attendants>, in this miracle chamber for about an hour and half each day and go on like this for about sixty sittings. Are you game to play hide and seek?", bringing humour involuntarily!

Promptly came the reply from Prashant: "I am game for this doctor; and my father also will join me in the chamber, your hospital rules permitting".

"Your father or younger brother will be permitted to accompany you into the pressured chamber. Guess what for? It will immensely hasten the process of hyper baric healing, if, simultaneously, your paralysed legs are exercised inside the chamber as the patient inhales oxygen through the mask at a slightly higher than atmospheric pressure (of course your attendant inside the cabin also has to wear the breathing mask)" .

All agreed and consented to for the treatment from the next day itself. Father had to drive Prashant the full 50 km -one way from his township residence to air force hospital each day, expected to last for a period over 2 months. After all, the efforts would be well worth the results expected.

As father was driving all the way to the HBO therapy medical center, Prashant and company (of Pavan and mother) would ponder over the therapy procedure!; Prashant would say "Hey Bhoo (that was how he addressed his younger whenever he wanted to pull his legs!) You are going to breathe oxygen at higher pressure continuously for 90 minutes per sitting. Are you ready? It may make you more active than your normal level which by itself is very high; OMG!, I wonder what will happen to you inside?!."

Pavan would retort back in the same humour –coin: "why, it is only me?; same thing will happen to you also, is it not?"

We reached the Air Force medical center promptly by 10 o'clock in the morning

The Wing Commander welcomed the team directly into the chamber!, instructing; "Let us start off straight away; Do normal breathing; do exercise your legs and hands ; your father and your brother would assist you inside. So bye bye!, have a jolly good time for 90 minutes!!"

The chamber door closed and pressurization of the chamber started promptly

Prashant inside, to Pavan: "Hey, what is this feeling light as I breathe oxygen through the mask. Are we up in space?"

"Yes indeed !!, ha, ha, I also feel very light. See, we are already at 3000 feet attitude in air!": hilariously expressed Pavan.

In less than 10 minutes the desired pressure level inside the chamber had been established and Pavan promptly started exercising his brother's paralysed legs and kept on going for a full hour on the trot, as practiced at home and/ or hospital

At the end of 90 minutes we all got out of the chamber fresh and relaxed. All thanked the Wing Commander for the day and promising to report the next day in time, drove off home ward. Prashant would stop the car for having a bite at his obsession, namely hot hot samosa with chutney and kachori!. Mother seated by the side would shed tears of joy at the sportive ambience despite rigorous schedule.

This schedule was strictly adhered to, day after day and at the end of 4 weeks, Prashant had wittingly, under gone 25 sitting inside the chamber!

The Wing Commander-doctor was all appreciation for the tireless efforts being put in by all in the family. He suggested to Prashant's father "I invite you all as my guests at the Air Force guest house.

"Although this guest house is meant exclusively for Air Force staff, as a gesture of appreciation for the efforts being put in by one and all of you foursome, we invite you to stay at our guest house as our <personal guests>.

Prashant profusely thanking the Wing Commander: "We are grateful for you kind gesture and would utilize your loving invitation particularly as it would reduce heavy strain on my parents".

Next day the whole family moved into the Air Force

guest house with bag and baggage and THAT extra medical attention paraphernalia mandatorily required daily for Prashant's care.

Both the brothers enjoyed the highly disciplined atmosphere in the air force camp. In their leisure time both the brothers would play chess (which sport was not new to them); parents would spend their leisure time mostly in the hospital library in search of some medical break-through solution leading to Prashant's total recovery, besides the HBO therapy.

Life went on for all the four of us for another one month. Prashant's general health had improved vastly. But, quite contrary to expectations, no neurological recovery was discernible.

At the end of 60 sittings the Wing Commander, in great melancholy, suggested to Prashant's father: "we are very sorry the expected turn-around did not happen; we all as a team and panel of military doctors, did go into reasons for nil progress; the damage caused during ill- advised, ill- planned surgery at the city hospital months ago, most definitely has had a negative effect. It (the damage to the spinal cord) appears to be too severe to show any tangible recovery."

"But, please do keep up the high morale and strong determination being displayed by you all in no less measure than a highly devoted and gallant Airman. After all, success never eludes the bold and the brave which is the hall mark of this gallant, fighter in

PRASHANT. We, the Airmen, have no hesitation in proclaiming that the young Prashant is second to none in his bravery!. We all wish him great achievements, name and fame".

Prashant's father, beaming happily at the superlative impressions left by his dear son on <Our Nation's decorated soldiers> had this to say: "We just do not have words enough, to profoundly thank you all for all the love, affection and concern showered on us. You have all tried your utmost best. The results are left to His Almighty God. Million thanks once again".

So exchanging pleasantries, We, the four-some, bade good–bye to the benevolent Wing Commander -doctor and his staff and drove back home.

****

CHAPTER- X

RAY OF HOPE: SECOND OPINION

PRASHANT's father consulted a number of neuro specialists/anatomists after he himself burnt mid night oil in going through volumes of medical literature in incessant search of some silver lining for hope of recovery. He could go into great depths in his discussions with experts based on his medical library acquired knowledge.

One such specialist Dr. Rama Murthy who had attained professional name and fame as a neurosurgeon and honoured with title "Father of Neurosurgery" "by his colleagues, was consulted at his hospital in Chennai (Tamil naadu state).

Prashant's father: "Dr, you have seen the medical records of Prashant; you have seen him also; what do you think of his recovery to normalcy, near normalcy? How much efforts are needed? How much time would elapse?".

The neuro –specialist Doctor (Father of neurology): "The boy is young; there are known cases recovering through <establishing of collateral blood supply > within about 24- 30 months".

"We are ready for submitting ourselves to any schedule of rehabilitation/treatment as prescribed by your esteemed hospital": father submitted.

Dr. Rama Murthy: "Apart from continuing the most productive physio exercising of all paralysed joints and healthy upper parts to make him stable, we would try to close the 2 bedsore wounds (one at the sacrum and another at the greater trochanter region)".

This team of doctors relentlessly attempted several procedures for a period of twelve days at a stretch.

Father: "Dr, what about eliminating bedsores?".

Dr. Rama Murthy: "We could help in getting rid of bedsores through plastic surgery at our hospital, or you could get it done at your home town itself leisurely.

Father thanked the Doctor, for the efforts put in by him and his team for rehabilitating Prashant.

Dr. Rama Murthy: "we feel sorry we could not show tangible results. The damage caused to spinal cord is irreversible and is heavy. But please keep up physio exercising; we would revert back to you in future if implants- procedures- under trials everywhere, get established".

Dr. Rama Murthy and his team in their farewell to Prashant paid eloquent tributes to the high morale sustained all through.

Having exhausted all these recovery attempts, we decided to pay full attention towards easing economic strangulation; by claiming compensation on expenses imposed for life on dear Prashant for no fault of his, but for sheer negligence of medical men. With all hopes of recovery dashed to pieces and giving place only to despair, recourse to legal action was contemplated,

Thus began our journey into medical literature, books, journals and periodicals. The knowledge being sought to understand the how, the why, the why not, how of the medical misadventure, had to be authentic.

There was no room for half knowledge of the damage enforced; was it avoidable or unavoidable? was there any urgency or could it have been deferred; if the biopsy investigations had revealed malignancy, then at what stage of malignancy was it; could it have been treated with non-invasive procedures! so on and so forth. Scores of such enquires had to be addressed and answers found.

However much father tried to elicit experts' opinion on the damages caused, he would return empty handed for obvious reasons of their not speaking against their own medical fraternity!. Undaunted, however, he went ahead with <operation Search>; there was no dearth of comprehension and knowledge as he turned page after page of Thomas Gray's Anatomy with specific reference to <growth of neurological tumours in the mediastinsal zones of thorax>.

He stumbled across precious information on the involvement of the invading tumuors masses with adjacent structures in the posterior mediastinum; the care and caution to be exercised while proceeding to remove such invading masses without interfering with blood supply.

With such fine leads into the causes of damage appearing in bold print, he decided to consult with Anatomy experts.

Dr. Krishna Rao, a professor in Anatomy, also a good family friend, was approached to help the former to understand the whole anatomy of spinal cord and its functioning, its malfunctioning, its misfunctioning, its nonfunctioning and such other parameters.

Welcoming Prashant's father, Dr. Rao had this to say: "I had heard about this tragic case of damage to spinal cord of Prashant; whom I had interacted with earlier and found him to be a highly promising master of studies and extra-curricular activities."

Father of Prashant replied: "Our dear Prashant has been and will always, remain a great fighter. We would all like to join together to rehabilitate him and see him march forward in life boldly"

Dr. Rao: "I shall do my bit towards this noble goal".

PRASHANT's father: "I would request your enlightened opinion as to how this damage has occurred particularly from the human anatomy point of view".

Dr. Rao: "I appreciate your inquisitiveness as a non-medical man; you see Mr. Seshadri, spinal cord functioning is the most important of all body functions". Although encased inside the hard boni vertebral column, it is vulnerable to damage if it is physically tampered with; a possibility of damaging the central nervous system because it can be accessed through the hole in between two adjacent vertebrates ; this hole/opening is referred to, in medical parlance, as Inter Vertebrate Foramin (abbreviated IVF).

"The damage to spinal cord", he went on to explain further: "can also be caused by interfering with supplementary blood supplying arteries that enter into spinal cord through the IVFs".

Prashant's father: "Professor, you have explained so clearly enabling this non-medical me, to comprehend the anatomy of spinal cord functions; could you please suggest what books periodicals, journals I should refer to, in order that I bring out clearly to non-medical Judicial Authorities, the avoidable damages caused in the instant case".

Dr. Rao: Do I see that you are wanting to file a case in the courts of law?"

Father: "With mountains of expenditure on medicines and medical services required constantly lifelong, we have to receive at least adequate monetary compensation from the perpetrators of this tragedy- doctors and the hospital included .We do know, that the present day level of medical advancements cannot help our dear Prashant to recover his walking faculties".

"Even implants cannot help him; perhaps we may have to wait for decades to see any such medical inventions coming to the rescue of such physically challenged persons".

"But we have to get on in life courageously, boldly, bravely. Huge monetary support is definitely required. Under the circumstances we have resolved to file a case of gross negligence, criminal negligence, gross deficiency of service against doctors and the hospital in Consumer Forums for Justice and Equanimity".

"Although, obviously, the doctors are squarely responsible for this tragedy, we are aware that the onus of responsibility of proving their negligence is on us - the Petitioners".

"Therefore respected Professor, we seek your help in making us understand the various aspects of functioning of the multi-million dollar worth spinal cord".

Dr. Rao: "I see your, genuine point. I do not hesitate to transmit the required knowledge to you through charts and medical reference books. So saying he went on to state: "you see, the spinal cord emanates from the brain and traverses through the cervical, Thoracic, Lumbar and sacral sections of the back bone. It has 33 different sections in all: 7 in the cervical zone; 12 in the Dorsal zone; 5 each in the Lumbar and sacral regions and 4- all fused together as coccyx at the termination of the back bone"

"From damage prevention point of view, the highly sensitive spinal cord is safely housed inside the vertebral column and with provision for the nerves to branch out to various organs outside of the vertebral column and with provision for entry and exit of arteries and veins carrying fresh blood to, and impure blood away from, the spinal cord; is it very heavy for you to grasp Mr. Seshadri" enquired the professor midway through.

PRASHANT's father promptly repeated all that he had attentively listened to, from the Professor and expressed his profound admiration for the clarity in the professor's knowledge transmitting skills and requested him: "Go ahead professor!. I can take in more without any difficulty".

Dr. Rao: "I can see an excellent student in you, ever hungry for acquiring new knowledge although you are at age of 57 years, generally considered old enough to be "slow learner!"; the Professor went on: "the spinal cord and brain together, carry out all the functions of the body through a network of sensory and motor nerves spread all across the length and breadth of the human body from head to toes".

"I do salute the creator Almighty for creating and sustaining this magnificent machine; and you Professor, for having so clearly explained the anatomical functions" intervened Seshadri.

The Professor continued: "And this network of central and peripheral nerves functions with blood and oxygen supplied to the brain and the spinal cord through intricate network of arteries & veins".

"And the most relevant point to be noted is that the spinal cord receives large share of requirements of blood through the arteries running vertically, all along the spinal column canal but the spinal vasculature also comprises of supplementary blood supply through intercostal arteries running all along the intercostal ribcage"

"And at this crucial level it is important to know that any disturbance to the supplementary blood supply to the spinal cord through intercostal space can cause irreparable damage to the spinal cord!.

I would recommend to you, Seshadri, to read the <spinal vasculature> Chapter from <Anatomy>; An enlightened rendering of human body functions by the father of Anatomy Dr. Gray".

The Professor went on to highly appreciate the anxious listener's inquisitiveness in acquiring knowledge of human anatomy and ended: "I wish you all success in your mission. Do not hesitate to seek any further clarifications any time".

The entire family profusely thanked the Professor for the knowledge sharing- totally pertinent to the instant case.

From that moment of bidding adieu to the Professor, Prashant's father started chalking out a detailed programme to visit medical college libraries for acquiring the desired medical knowledge; to get to know first-hand, what really went wrong; how it went wrong; and what would have happened if medical procedure of the instant case had not been attempted and such allied enquiries.

Answers had to be found first hand, from publications by leading luminaries in the field of medicine and medical practices speedily without any further delay. The case of gross negligence, criminal negligence had to be filed in the consumer forum for deliverance of Justice by the law courts:

-For getting adequate monetary compensation to get on in life decently meeting all the enforced expenditure lifelong.

-Factors like retirement of Prashant's father from service; day by day increasing monetary strangulations; foremost urgency to hire the services of a legal expert/a luminary in law to fight our case etc. fully kept the family busy.

ENGAGING SERVICES of LEGAL ADVISER

A senior advocate practicing in the Supreme Court of India came forward and gladly accepted to advise us and file the necessary Petitions/Appeals before the First court of law.

Prashant's father: "I thank you very much for the concern shown by you. I shall visit Bangalore at the earliest".

Legal Adviser: "Ananda murthy, your brother-in-law has briefed me already; accompanied by my daughter-lawyer, I will be right there at your Hyderabad residence by next day morning. You don't have to take troubles coming to Bangalore"

Next morning the duo accompanied by Ananda Murthy arrived promptly from Bangalore.

Ananda Murthy introduced our guests: "this is Mr. Seshagiri Rao- a leading senior advocate of the Supreme Court of India and this is Nagini his daughter also practicing law in Karnataka High Court .They both are keen to help you in arguing the case in the courts of law".

Prashant's father welcoming the father- daughter legal experts duo, discussed in details as to how go about.

Seshagiri Rao advised: "since the matter has to come up for early Judgment and since the costs of litigation have to be kept in mind, I would recommend filing the case in the Consumer Forum instead of Civil Court".

The young daughter- lawyer took over the responsibility of making notes of all discussions.

Prashant's father explained to the legal adviser: "we want monetary compensation to get on in life decently; we are not interested in seeking any sentencing punishments on the damage causers; expenses on medicines and medical services have been thrust upon us with no way to defraying them. The paramount requirements are speedy Justice and speedy compensation.

The lawyers- got into study the whole situation so has to have the feel of the gravity of the hardships imposed.

Prashant's father got a call from inside for starting physio exercising schedule; he promptly excused himself from the discussions and took the duo to Prashant's resting room who instantly greeted his guests with his trademark broad smile! "welcome to our midst Mr. Seshagiri Rao and Ms.Nagini; what has happened to me without notice should never happen to any human being ,and for that matter even to any living being on this globe". "But, the important thing is to get on in life as smoothly and as decently as possible without brooding over the past; my father has less than a year from reaching the age of superannuation; my mother has totally devoted her time to look after my compulsory needs which has resulted in her quitting a decent earning job; My younger brother's academic career is grossly interrupted. We therefore need expeditious Justice from the Courts of law through adequate monetary compensation".

"We are here to fight and get you Justice; you please rest peacefully assured": so assuring, the lawyers- duo took leave of Prashant to enable his father to start with physio theraupic exercising on him .

Mother took the guests to guest room to continue briefing them on tragic happenings and attendant compulsions enforced thereof.

****

CHAPTER- XI

PRELUDE TO RESTART OF EDUCATION

AS FOR Prashant, life had to be sustained for all its worthiness. After all, since childhood he had demonstrated his strong desire to take up Teaching; Education was the first choice to stabilize in his Life.

Being subjected to an all together different daily routine, Prashant had reservations about his capacity to resume studies that too, after a full 5 years break!.

But mother, knowing the brilliant Prashant as he was ever, assured him that his mental faculties have not been, providentially disturbed, and therefore, determined efforts would easily restore him to pre-eminent status- undoubtedly,

Thus began his <project- rediscovery>; Big Role played by his Mother!. After all, all Mothers on earth are simply DIVINE.

Prashant's Mother sitting beside him, one day suggested to him patting him affectionately on his back: "dear, your health is on the <upward recovery> slope; this is the right time to seriously plan out continuation of your studies".

Prashant looked to his mother and in a low voice responded: "Mummy, five years is too long a gap to remember anything I had read in my college".

Mother assuringly suggested: "your mental faculties including memory power are simply, to say the least, Sharp even to this day; you had always been a class topper since childhood".

Prashant replied: "mummy! It is nice to remember those happy days but how now…!"

Mother: "Then or now, it is all the same for a brilliant boy like you. Let us start off at home itself; we will provide the college environment at home itself. Do not forget your plans to complete a doctorate in engineering in the USA; your 12th standard qualification is like a black hole in your radiant sky. Surely I cannot take this and I am pretty sure you also cannot take it either."

Mother could not hold back her tears; perhaps these tears from her eyes transformed his mind set; instantly he called out: "mummy, you are perfectly right. I am game for all your suggestions. Let us start off from today itself".

Mother, father and younger brother Pavan all were overwhelmed with joy at his determination and decisions. Already loaded with the tight schedule of physio exercising, medical attentions etc, this learning schedule had to be fitted into the time frame.

Next day morning Prashant took the lead: "Mummy give me that red and yellow bound text book on <thermo dynamics>. That happened to be my pet subject at college".

Mother was only too pleased to express her happiness; she simply jumped in great excitement with joy and in no time searched the <red and yellow bound book>; handed it over to him and blessed him: "Dear Pantu, [that was Prashant's pet name], You simply start and success will be at your door, at your beck and command".

Living him alone for some time, mother - Indira resumed her kitchen duties. He started browsing page after page, chapter after chapter but could not concentrate. His father passing by, could notice Pantu unable to proceed but found him staring into the sky. Indira also arrived and noticed that he is stuck at the same page and looking at the sky!.

Deciding to adopt novel methods to spur him into study mood, she brought all her teaching skills into play. (Indira had been a good teacher in <science> subject at private school with nearly decades of teaching experience) and approaching him started off: "Pantu, you read a page and brief me about that subject; in turn, I will read the page and you will explain what you have gathered".

This way the <reading & explaining> exercise went on for several pages, day in and day out spread over a week.

Prashant's mother, would have unwittingly jotted down all the explanations coming from him; would have prepared a mini- question paper for testing his memory at the end of each week.

She quipped: "dear, one week is over; let us revise the 15 and odd pages we have covered under the

Thermodynamics subject last week. Could you narrate in your own words?"

As Prashant started explaining all that he had read, parents and all sitting clustered around him, were baffled beyond belief, how he recapitulated the subject matter the teacher- mother had discussed in particular, to finest details

Thus this reading and listening exercises between mother and son continued relentlessly, punctuated now and then with clarifications from mother and astounding explanation from Pantu, over a period of 6 months.

At the end of it all, it transpired that the young student had, admiringly, not lost any memory and instead, found himself growing in confidence from strength to strength, day by day.

This study exercise had rekindled enthusiasm in him to complete his examinations at the earliest. To give further phillip and hasten the target of completing education it was felt necessary, by one and all, Prashant included, to shift to the friendly college library atmosphere. Plans were immediately drawn to shift the entire company to his college town –Machilipatnam, located 400km away from his residing town of Hyderabad.

Prashant readily joining the think tank, laughed loudly and quipped: "Daddy you can possibly carry me with my wheel chair alright!; But how about the paraphernalia presently occupying a full room of our house!. Is it possible to carry this whole house hold to Machilipatnam!!?".

Pavan quipped in reply: "dear bhoo, if we can carry you; Houseful load/luggage is no problem at all!".

Prashant: "do you suggest that I am heavy & fatty to relegate the great wrestler kingkong to insignificance!!".

Pavan: "dear, I only cajoled; let us prepare the check list :-

1   Prashant- the VIP

2   Your wheel chair.

3   Your left side supporting pillows- numbering half a dozen!

4   Your right side-all around supporting cushions exceeding a dozen!

5   Back rest, physio - exercising paraphernalia not excluded, and medical kit,

6   Predominating mobile library of books, not to be left out from the checklist!.

7   To appease your palate, mummy has to carry to Machilipatnam, your favourite bread toaster, etc etc. And your biceps exercising 1-kg, 2-kg dumb-bell weights…; look! Dear, the list is growing endless and the luggage - a full truck load!!

Prashant's father: "Dear sunnies, this truck load does not matter and worth the efforts for the noble target of education completion!; And don't worry, we can present this bill to that butcher-doctor when we drag him and the negligent hospital into court-litigations sooner than later!"

All sang in chorus: "Three cheers to Prashant!"

"We have listed out in details, all household including kitchen equipment. Let me talk to Prashant's chum-Subramanyam's father who had been native of college town-Machilipatanam, for decades"; So uttering Seshadri instantly made a call to the college –town. The call did get through and on the other side Mr. Bhiksham (Subramanyam's father) started listening to the long list!!.

Bhiksham responded: "it is our pleasure to partake in the noble activity of Prashant's resuming his studies. You simply drive in, and we are all here to welcome you into a <ready- to- use> house equipped with all facilities." Overwhelmed at the happy welcome extended, Indira felt kilotonnes of energy being pumped into our family for fulfilling the noble task.

Preparations for the journey reached their climax .Our car, all though very much short of medieval age!, was selflessly certified to be good enough to withstand the 500 and odd kilometres journey!.

Like any long journey imposing necessary check-ups, our "lady-love" (the road- king) was given to a mechanic for thorough servicing and if necessary for replacing vital parts.

Prashant's father had great love for the old car and like an upright English man, would not think of replacing it, but always managed to keep it in fine running and service condition with periodic maintenance.

Came next week, the charming road king was aligned inside the large compound of our residence.

Pavan, his mother and neighbours who were only glad to participate in this noble venture, had painstakingly brought out the entire house hold nearer to the road king for ease of loading!

Promptly arrived in our midst, our family well-wishing friend Mohan Ram. He had been standing like a rock by our side all these difficult days. Voluntarily he jumped into the fray; smilingly passed orders in his inimitable air-force style: "Look dears all, you civilians just do not have the know-how to pack truck load on your "Road king" top; you simply leave it to me; after all I am an Air Force jawan by profession and I am used to loading a truck on top of an army jeep!."

So uttering, he jumped on to the car roof top and signaled to by- standers:" come on man; pass on to me heavy things first".

"Yes give me the back rest first……."

"Why uncle? you have not even seriously started loading but already wanting to rest your back?!!", so mischievously Pavan pulls his dear uncle's legs. "Oh! you mischievous lad!, I will respond to you later and take away your share of omlette from your mummy, but for now, pass on!". One by one the luggage went up and Mohan ram meticulously tied them to the luggage-carrier with string of knots magically formed; deftly he handled twists, turning the heavy rope round and around luggage articles.

There was no room for any looseness in passing rope through thick and thin of luggage .It had to be firm to prevent articles from diving on to the road in the event of sudden braking or climbing deep slope up the hill or down the hill sliding!!.

The car had unwittingly become a Double Decker!!, sending all bye- standers into bouts of laughter, standing simply amazed at the air force jawan's skills!!!.

All luggages loaded, the car went for a trial run with the air force "jawan" himself taking over control of the wheels.

Hardly had he completed to deftly take the car out of the compound wall, he had to brake suddenly to allow an on-the-road vehicle to pass through; lo!, What did he experience!!! He strongly felt as if the whole car is transformed into a heavily loaded mini- truck. He took a decision to drive the "mini truck" by himself all through the journey route.

The brave jawan's courage had to be encouraged; so we all discussed and decided that he only drove all through the 500km journey.

 Friends, neighbours- always loving and well-wishing, had gathered by the dozens to wish their <young matinee idol PRASHANT>, a very, very happy journey into life for the brave fight and success and glory for his infinite mental strength.

Finally the car (mini truck!) left for its destination –not simply an earthly destination but big leap forward in life despite great odds.

As the car moved on the high- way swerving to the left for giving way to speedier traffic or to the right for over taking slower moving vehicles, our <esteemed chauffeur> had to negotiate very carefully because of the double decked load over the car roof top!..

Prashant cajoled at Mohan ram: "I am safe in this mini truck with Air Force skill at command of the wheel".

Mohan ram: "Yes, you're surely under safe hands"; twisting and twirling his moustache he asserted: "after all I have driven fully loaded rocket launcher carriers. This mini truck is no big thing for me".

By the afternoon we had cleared well over 100km and approaching the 2nd largest city of Andhra Pradesh.

Prashant beckoned to Mohan ram "I am feeling pretty hungry and surely all the rest of our caravan also!; why not we all ,uncle, break for launch?".

As Mohan ram steered the car aside near a good high-way restaurant, everybody felt our pretty "lady-love" could be landing on its side!!. Sensing the apprehension of the inmates, Mohan ram quipped: "after all, you are having free jolly truck drive in a car, you see!".

The <caravan> took off for onward journey after heavy sumptuous Andhra meals. By evening, we finally entered the coastal town of Machilipatanam, where Prashant had spent 3+years as a <happy go sportive> student prior to this tragic medical misadventure. The town had special affection and love for him; here, he had achieved the distinction as an outstanding student both on and off the college premises.

The bon homie he had created here, came in handy now, a full five years later; the entire town college mates, college teaching staff, private mess mates (where he used to take his meals regularly) had turned up to receive their hero.

As they saw their dear mate being shifted from car to wheel chair aided by his experienced parents, the assembled multitude were noticed wiping tears as they went on to behold their favourite, in this physically challenged condition.

After all they had seen him as a live wire sporting personality who had endeared himself to one and all with his multi-disciplined activities; "Uncle, aunty, you please take rest, you are tired after a long journey". So saying they all immediately swung into action for shifting all luggages into the new residence from car.

"Prashant, now you are our town's/our home guest. We are here to take care of all your needs. Do not hesitate to call us any time.

Bhiksham had painstakingly and meticulously organized the <home–away- from> home. The entire host party arrived in our midst to welcome us. Once inside the new home we were completely taken aback at the excellent arrangements inside.

Everything was spic and span. Drawing room had been meticulously arranged with sofa, chairs, side tables; the bedroom with cots and mattresses, bed side book shelves. Kitchen had been so beautifully and fully established as to gladden the heart of Prashant's mother. She was quick to thank, profusely, Bhiksham saying: "I feel my

Hyderabad residence kitchen has been transported en-masse!. Nothing is left to be desired!: micro oven, gas stove, refrigerator, grinder, all vessels neatly stacked in cupboard- you name the kitchen equipment/facility and it was there !.

Mother added further: "Dear Bhiksham, so lovingly and caringly you have created <a 5- star residence facility> for us; we just do not have words to thank you".

"Madam my service is only too small and pales into insignificance at the mighty task you madam, your husband and dear Pavan are performing day in day out. After all, Prashant had spent lively days in our town. He was undoubtedly the cynosure of all eyes that beheld him. He would make friends with anyone whom he came across, at the "first sight" itself." Bhiksham said

He took care to inform: "Madam, please do not worry about anything. Kitchen help, housemaid all have been arranged; and they will all be reporting to you for duties at allotted hours in the day".

So saying, he bade good bye for the day. Parents of Prashant could instantly see the benevolent blessings of their Almighty through such noble men with such noble gestures, with self-less voluntary service. We had no difficulty in immediately adjusting to the new environment.

The next day dawned; Prashant enquired: "Uncle Bhikshim, I know, all my classmates would have left to other towns in search of their professional carriers. But

I wonder whether a few of them would have taken up teaching jobs in this college itself".

Bhiksham was quick to recollect and reply: "yes, yes, your's and Subramanian's batch mate Suresh babu- that was how he was nick-named and addressed by you all; Mohan Kumar and Christopher (nick named <globe trotter> in your college days) have taken up teachings assignments in your college itself".

Hardly had he completed his narration, there were knocks on the door!; "Guess, who could be knocking" Bhiksham to Prashant.

The three "musketeers" along with group of their bright and sportive students gate crashed into the drawing room.

Prashant was pleasantly surprised, thrilled, over whelmed with joy at meeting his old classmates.

They all embraced him and introduced their students to him. "What a surprise, Babu, to meet you and your students! and you Mohan, do you continue to ask questions in the class room at every stroke of the gong, as you were used to? Do you remember we had nick-named you "question mark?!"

"And you dear Christopher!, What more of America you have discovered which your great grand dad- the legendary Columbus had left out?!"

The three musketeers were thrilled to see their old mate at his glorious best, reminiscent of his earlier college days; but were simultaneously overtaken with grief at the tragic physical state, which the negligent men in white coat and stethoscope in hand (a physical description of a doctor) physically had driven their chum into; wiping off tears away from their eyes, they all pounced upon Prashant, embracing, hugging him passionately.

Prashant's mother and father did not fail to notice the friends' warmth and love towards their son; mother uttering in her choked voice had this to say to her husband: "Oh dear!, What a scene to witness!; Our Prashant has been showered with so much of love and affection as to carry him forward boldly in restarting his college career with effortless ease".

New younger students who had accompanied their teachers greeted Prashant with confidence and smile. "We have heard a good lot about you, your passion for studies and other activities as well". Prashant mischievously smiled: "Oh friends!, I hope you are not dragging my feet into <other activities, arena with a totally different connotation>".

"No, no, we just have been hearing in our classrooms about your extra achievements in swimming, playing cricket and tennis with college mates, teachers and professors with equal ease! They all have paid eloquent tributes for your talents. We are here to arouse the old fire in your belly once again! : so reverberated all the young visitors in unison.

Prashant thanking them all quipped: "although I cannot play tennis and cricket anymore, I am here to make our academic career very professional through exchange of knowledge"; initial introductions completed, all left for their homes.

Daily rigorous activities were already awaiting Prashant. Mother beckoned to him to <hurry up slowly!>.

Prashant's father was waiting to start off with the mandatory physio exercising as the first morning activity; "one –two-three, here we go sonny…."

Exercising the paralysed joints and the healthy joints not to be left out, he completed his first duty within the scheduled hour.

Prashant's efforts and his father's were 50:50 in this rigorous schedule!.

His mother would chip in soon to exercise the upper portions of his body that would take yet another 30-40 minutes. She would, later, switch over to her other designated activities: including giving him sponge bath on the bed itself and readying him for dress up and breakfast.

Connoisseur of the palate as he had always been, he would ask: "mummy, what is there for breaking my fast this morning?"

"With what else you can break your fast? Certainly not with <hardened rock like idlis> of the benami Udupi hotel!. But here you go! hot, steaming hot <upma> laced with almonds, cashew nuts and tomoto chuntney." cajoled his dear mummy

"Oh you are so sweet and considerate mummy. Give the plate, I will enjoy".

Within the next half hour, Prashant would be be readied to shift to wheel chair. Magnanimous- hearted lecturers had drawn up plans to help Prashant pursue his studies from his living room itself. They had promptly arrived to start their self-imposed duty time- table.

 Prashant in wheel chair smilingly would welcome them all: "Good Morning sirs, let us start with my obsession i.e.; <thermo dynamics> subject."

"Don't be surprised about the drastic changes that have been brought into effect with introduction of new- syllabus"

"Sir, no problem at all. I am as good as a new student in view of the medically enforced long break; I am game for the changes".

Appreciations and admirations galore at Prashant's positive attitude, the teachers had chalked out a new pattern to impart learning of the old unchanged syllabus as well as new changed syllabus.

The devoted student went on to read the subjects and prepare set of Questions and doubts for getting answers and clarifications from his room- visiting Professors. Their visits were obviously only after college hours and were consistently regular like the clock.

The Questions and answers; the doubts and clarifications- methods, were highly productive; the visiting Professors noticed their special student growing more and more confident day by day. With the ever increasing concentration on studies on the part of Prashant, the Teaching fraternity could not have looked for better process of knowledge- sharing with the VIP student and knowledge- gaining by the VIP student. They were all overwhelmed at this established process of learning which, in fact, had been drafted by his teacher-mother at their Hyderabad home. This learning exercise went on uninterruptedly for over a fortnight.

All in the fray, including the learned Professors had detailed discussions as to how further speed up/ accelerate the process of knowledge gaining preferably away from room confinement.

Prashant's mother suggested: "why not we all go over to the college premises even if it meant sitting in college library".

Prashant: "mummy, how can I go to college in this condition and that too in wheel chair".

Mother trying to "sell" her suggestion: "Dear, don't you think the atmosphere within the college premises is far more congenial to studies than the 4 walled room environment with only mother, father around you and of course the Professors who are magnanimous to visit you in your room? You will be surrounded with tens and hundreds of books for referral/cross referencing in the library besides other students visiting also for referencing; that would create a benign environment for serious studies. Further, it would be far far convenient for your Lecturers/Professors to help you clear your doubts then and there itself, during their inter- lecture -leisure hours".

Always game for new thoughts and new suggestions, the young aspirant and knowledge seeker agreed to give it a fair trial.

As the noble mission progressed, a totally new development unfolded much to the embarrassment of the steadfast and gallant Prashant!; sounded nearly impossible and unheard of and unethical on the part of a sacred institution primarily engaged to imparting universal knowledge to aspiring students to become useful future citizens!!. Such topsy-turvy happenings are certainly beyond the imagination of readers.

Now read on what really transpired.

Seshadri (father) called Bhiksham on phone and requested his company to go to the college principal for discussing with the latter, the subject matter of re-admission of Prashant into the college after a long medically enforced break. Bhiksham promptly arrived to accompany him to the principal's office room.

"Good morning sir" father so addressing entered the Principal's room with his permission.

Principal enquired: "what can I do? In what connection you are here?"

"I am Seshadri- father of your yester years' college student seeking re-admission after an unfortunate medically enforced break in his student career".

Principal: "Oh! Yes, I have heard of this student and the tragedy that has befallen him at the Hyderabad city"; "But" he continued: "you please forget his readmission at this late stage of the academic year, since it is already December now and hardly 3 months away from the Annual examinations".

Seshadri and Bhiskam both parents of two brilliant students of the college submitted: "sir, tragedy apart, enforced hospitalization continuously for three and plus years, further period of stabilization for another 2 years have all added up to 5 years of discontinuation. But the brightening aspect is that Prashant has resolutely decided to continue his education to complete the BE Degree course and that is why we are here".

Principal: "I have already told you clearly that I cannot entertain any readmission at this late academic year stage. He will have only 20% attendance against the required minimum of 75%".

Seshadri submitting in reply: "sir, it is a question of fulfilling the student's strong determination to complete studies even after such a long break- as long as 5 years. First and foremostly the young Prashant wanted the college environment for attending to classes with other students so as to forget his past and move forward in life".

Principal repeating his stoic stand: "I just cannot readmit him; whatever be the explanations from your side". So blurting out, he got up from his seat and walked away!.

Seshadri's and Bhiksham's pleadings to him (the principal) to refer the attendance shortage problem to the University Authorities for their consideration and permission as a special case on medical background, vanished into thin air behind the retreating principal.

Seshadri running behind the principal, pleaded: "you please admit him, we will submit an application for the condonation of attendance shortage, to the Vice -Chancellor of the University through you- the principal".

Principal retorted and shouted back at him: "Do not pester me. You come at the beginning of the next academic year. That is all"; he so uttered and sped away from the college compound itself.

Left high and dry, both seshadri and Bhiksham returned to Prashant's room. Enroute, the two had decided not to discuss the foregone dialogues between them and the principal with Prashant. They were disheartened at nil progress for readmission. However Seshadri narrated the whole incident to his better half and advised her "Dear, you try your luck; that principal is an obstinate character. We have exhausted all our efforts, you are a teacher by profession and try your luck".

Next morning Prashant's mother, accompanied by Babu-presently working in this college as senior lecturer and long time, classmate of her son, entered the principal's room after the formal "May I come in sir" gesture

The principal did not have the courtesy to greet the lady and to say: "please come in and have your seat"; instead, he did not even look at the lady waiting anxiously to start the intended discussion.

But Prashant's mother had gone with definite purpose. She did not, therefore, mind the unpleasantries, pulled a chair herself and started. "Sir, I am the mother of Prashant .". Even before her completing the sentence, he shouted: "why are you fellows wasting my time!, I know why you have come. Yesterday, I have explained everything to your husband and your son's classmate's father Bhiksham. There is nothing more for me to add. You bring him early in the next academic year by about June/July so that he can clear the mandatory "university prescribed internal tests". He has to write 3 sets of internal tests in all subjects and for the benefit of the student best and better marks out of the 3 would be taken into account for arriving at the best average and for transmitting the same to the university".

She (Mother) intervened: "sir, you please take the internal tests right now. He has come prepared".

"You people come so late as December; you do not understand our procedures. Two sets of tests have already been conducted; only the 3rd test is remaining". So saying he continued with his office work.

She patiently explained before the principal "My son has faced an unprecedented tragedy at the hands of negligent doctors at the leading hospital at Hyderabad; he was rendered paraplegic for life and after prolonged years of hospitalization, physio-theraupic exercising, he has been restored to stable wheel chair sitting posture".

"He had always been a brilliant student. We all, including Prashant shudder to see him remaining lifelong a matriculate pass. Therefore he has firmly resolved to face all physical challenges boldly, courageously and complete his BE degree and go on further to complete <A Doctorate in Engineering>".

Nothing seemed to work with this academician-principal with his closed mind set, for he again burst out:

"Don't you understand that two sets of tests are already over. Only one set is remaining. I cannot create another set at this juncture for taking average of at least 2 sets.

She: "Sir, the internal tests are purely within the discretionary powers of the college Management. Either you please allow him to take part in the remaining 3rd set along with others and separately conduct one more test so that 2 sets of marks are available for taking the average OR you conduct only the remaining 3rd test and consider those marks as the internal session marks for award and transmission to the University. Mother's suggestion apart the principal's reaction at this juncture was beyond any sane person's expectation!

Readers! Could you kindly guess what? The principal in his usual style burst out uttering at his highest octave level:"I just cannot conduct the 2nd set of internals. I will not admit him into the final year course, if you have extra money, throw it away and go; he continued to state further: "I will allow him to take the 3rd set of internals which have been scheduled for this month and I will arrive at the AVERAGE BY TAKING 50% of the marks obtained therein. This would automatically disqualify him for writing the final university examination".

The brave knowledge seeker's mother's patience had definitely run out and obviously rightly so, for any human being on this globe. However, mincing no words, She also shot back at the principal saying: "I am also a teacher by profession. I never expected this rude behaviour from a principal who also carries the responsibility of controlling over a thousand students in the college. You must be fair to our proposal; please give me in writing your explanations for rejecting the noble cause of continuing education; of a student who was felled by an arrogant grossly negligent surgeon's scalpel for no fault of his and/ or his parents".

She went further: "Our gallant Prashant has mustered courage of conviction and convinced himself and duly motivated himself to complete his studies come what may; BUT you, as principal of a sacred educational Institute, instead of encouraging him and welcoming him with red carpet, have chosen "to shout and reject". "Please give me in writing".

The Principal however, seemed to have no regrets; had no hesitation whatever; and evidently in a fit of anger, scribbled on his letter pad the reasons for rejection.

Mother grabbed this letter much to the ignorance of the damages it could cause to him, and reminded him: "look here Mr. Principal, you must have forgotten!!! that we all human beings are puppets in the hands of the Almighty; only HE would come to our rescue and lead us through the turmoil thrown against us by an earthly mortal like you" so shouting, she walked out of the principal's room.

The situation was by all means, shocking and demanded the best of the managerial skills to find solutions calmly, coolly.

Above all, utmost care had to be taken to keep these challenging events and happenings away from our dear son for obvious reasons. We both simply drove off towards the Bay of Bengal beach and together had long and serious thinking on the benign sea beach ambience.

Finally we decided straight away to seek help from the relevant District collector / highest level District Administrator as she/he is the ex-officio <first citizen> of the concerned District constitutionally to resolve any district level issue in a natural and just way. Thus having taken the decision, we drove back home to meet with our dear son.

Needless to emphasize the importance of presenting ourselves before Prashant with smiling countenances at this crucial juncture. After exchanging pleasantries, mother strode to the kitchen to prepare some snacks for her son and the friends who had entertained Prashant throughout our absence.

Father signaled to his dear son: "sonny, let us get into the mandatory schedule- physio exercising". Ever receptive, Prashant seadily presented himself for the 2 hour rigorous schedule- 50% his own efforts and balance 50% father's, with his customary trade mark smile.

Exercising completed, the assemblage was entertained by Indira with delicious snacks.

Next morning as planned, Prashant's parents drove off to the District Collector's office after arranging friend's company. Anxiety was lit large on his parent's faces and were quite apprehensive of the events that would follow the meeting with the top District Administrator.

We approached the Collector's personal secretary and briefed him about the purpose of our seeking a dialogue with his boss. Promptly he went inside to inform his boss about the visitors. We waited outside. To our pleasant surprise she came out of her chambers after completing her regular prayers, and introducing herself to us greeted: "I do see, divine grace and aura around you. I would deem it an honour to mitigate any and all your worries which you appear to have. Be comfortable, let me share your anxiety".

This fine gesture instantly took away all our built up anxiety; mother briefed the officer about her son's predicament and the entire family's concern over the obstacles posed for rightfully resuming education of their brilliant student- son.

 While listening to the whole story, the kindly disposed lady was shocked beyond words and expressed: "How the hell, the head of an educational institute could be so unkind and cruel to kill the enthusiasm and to put out the fire in the belly, so painstakingly nurtured in the student and aspiring to complete his education confidently, and go on to acquire a Doctorate in engineering qualifications despite enforced physical challenges". She went on further: "This reminds me of an identical medical negligence case of a brilliant student, whose career had been severely jolted and virtually butchered, as narrated to me by my dear mother in law".

Quite inquisitive, she went on further: "where did this all happen to your son?; Where was he studying?; How was he compelled into wheel chair sitting position etc.- a barrage of questions to the parents!!"

Mother: "Madam, all those tragic incidences took place at Hyderabad city's leading hospital cum Institute of Medical Sciences; my son was studying in 12th standard at the higher secondary school within the township. Prashant's father was employed at a leading central public sector undertaking namely Bharat Heavy Electricals Ltd (BHEL)...."

The collector was quick to interrupt: "Indira, do I place your name correctly?; and wait a minute! Oh my god! The principal of the school where your son studied happened to be no other than my mother in law; she had most graphically described the unfortunate incident that had befallen in her pet student's life. In fact she had broken down while narrating these happenings. Now I see the pet student of my mother in law cum principal is no other than your son!. In fact she had special affection for the ever calm, non controversial, brilliant outstanding student. Oh! What a coincidence!"

Mother: "yes madam, my son's institute's principal had great admiration for him. During the time when Prashant was hospitalized in October 1990, Mrs. Padmavathi -your mother in law, happened to meet me at the hospital premises where she had come for treatment of her husband's i.e.; your father in law's ailment".

Instantly she could recognize me, as feathers of the same teaching fraternity and anxiously enquired as to why we are there in the hospital. It was noble of her to enquire about us when she herself had worries on account of her husband. She immediately chose to visit our son's ward; on seeing Prashant she could instantly recognize her pet student and collapsed on the floor. She had to be given first aid treatment".

Collector: "I get it all now. She herself went on to narrate the whole story, frequently interrupted by uncontrollable sobs.

Humanity at its best was discernible instantly. The District Collector swung into action immediately after digesting the complete unhappy episode and decided to act without any delay; she sent summons to the college principal and also to the chief of the institute's education society ordering them to present themselves before her.

Bound by the orders of and summons from their District's Top Authority, the duo- the secretary of the education society and the principal of the college, rushed to the Collector's office.

What transpired here (at the Collector's office) is beyond everybody's guess.

The principal on his way to the Collector's office room did not fail to notice the presence of his newly acquired "adversaries" – i.e.; Prashant's parents!. In particular the <heated exchange of words between him and the student's father and mother in particular, only the previous day> was reverberating persistently in his mind despite his attempts to push them out of his memory!!.

He, rightly so, did not fail to connect the Collector's summons to his outbursting incidents with the parents!; and he entered the District Administrator's room peevishly and introduced himself.

Collector seeing him: "So I see, you are the great principal of the college institution, expected to impart universal knowledge and human values to young students!!".

"Would You please answer me as to on what authority you have refused to take back Prashant for continuing his education? what you are going to blurt out. Prashant's mother has already narrated all your conversations".

"Attendance is it not? What attendance shortage in the backdrop of hospitalization continuously for nearly five years!; I can instruct the vice chancellor to waive this <so called attendance shortage>. And the vice chancellor would have no hesitation in granting permission for the otherwise bright student taking the university examinations".

The Principal in a feeble voice responded: "Madam, apart from the attendance deficit, he has to take 3 sets of internal tests; We have already completed conducting 2 sets and only 3rd set remains to be completed"

Collector: "So what?; He will write the ongoing 3rd set

with all students and later you organize one more test exclusively for him and then take the average of the two".

"What is the problem? Can you not take such decisions yourselves? Easy solutions are available; but instead, you have chosen <to add fuel to fire> by harassing the student and his parents with your third degree arrogance. You could have consulted with the education society's secretary".

She went on to give <the principal of the college and the education society's secretary> a good bit of her mind. She, the Collector, went on to chide him further: "Your actions and thoughts have brought shame and disgrace to the noble profession of teaching; have brought shame not only to this leading town of Krishna district, but to the entire state of Andhra Pradesh and the culture loving Telugu people and to our country itself."

She went on further: "I command you to treat the physically disabled boy with love and respect and do everything under your powers to help him. Firstly, welcome him into the college premises, unroll the red carpet and receive him into the assemblage of students and teachers; secondly, You create the bon- homie atmosphere and report back to me on <Action taken> within a week". So ordering the duo to start corrective action immediately, she bade them good bye".

Turning to the parents and addressing them, she had this to say: "I have given clear instructions to help you out. By the end of the week, 2 sets of tests (one common with all students and one separately for Prashant) would have been completed".

"Should you encounter any further problem, please do not hesitate to refer to me; I am here to help you. I will come and see Prashant to give him the philip and to boost further his <already acquired high morale>". The parents thankfully left for their residence to attend to their son's daily needs.

Only the pleasant aspects of Collector's advice to the college management duo were shared with Prashant as father commenced the round of mandatory physio exercising on his son. Prashant took these happenings coolly with a challenge to perform extremely well in the 2 sets of internal tests. In the meantime his father had addressed an appeal to the vice chancellor of the concerned university giving therein, brief background of how Prashant became a victim of a negligent surgeon's scalpel through unwanted and unpermitted surgery; how, as a result, his education career was severely jolted; how he fought back all odds to come to < stable in wheel chair sitting position > and therefore seeking the waiver of attendance deficits from his honoured self.

It is a heartening matter to share with readers, how the <gallant student> received a very thoughtful letter from the vice chancellor. The latter had appreciated the efforts put in by the university student facing all odds. In the letter he not only communicated the university's waival of attendance requirements but had shown his magnanimity in directing the Vijayawada engineering college authorities to conduct the Final Annual Examination at their centre, as this centre was within the university campus and had far more greater facilities to enable a physically challenged student to write the examination with greater case. All these developments, In fact, had brought only cheers and cheers in our camp and lifting Prashant's morale to sky-heights.

Suddenly Pavan arrived in our midst from his college town.

Pavan's presence gave further impetus and boosted his elder's morale further. The latter, volunteered to attend regular classes as advised by his lecturers. In the jolly company of his younger brother, he went ahead to write the 3rd set of internal tests along with other students.

Each day he was proud of his performance and waited with abated breath for the next paper!. This was the enthusiasm generated by himself duly supplemented by his younger brother!.

For Prashant, Pavan had become a friend in need, indeed. The two brothers had grown from childhood very closely affectionately. Now the duo waited and looked towards the principal for his next move i.e, his organizing the second set of internal tests exclusively for the examinee-in -waiting.

The principal, admonished as he was, by the District Collector and ordered by her to organize the second set of tests, reluctantly set papers for the test.

LO!, he was determined <to have his say> for whatever reasons best known to him and the Almighty god only. The wounded tiger as the principal had become, devised plans to carry out the District Collector's orders alright, but with an ocean of difference!; Can anyone guess how he designed, planned and implemented the Higher Authorities' orders? In revenge for the mouthful he had received from the District's Highest Authority, the principal handed over smartly, the time table for the 2nd internal tests to his student. Prashant had prepared himself for the tests according to the day to day time table; visited the principal's office room where the tests had been organized.

Promptly the test began and the examinee, handed over the question paper. It was a shock for him to see the next day's question paper having been handed over to him that day!

Prashant addressed the principal, who had himself assumed the role of supervising: "sir, there appears to be a slip through oversight; next day's subject question paper has been given to me today".

To which the principal retorted: "look, your parents proudly claim you are quite intelligent. So I have wantonly and deliberately, given the next day's paper for you to answer; you must have already prepared for all the tests in any case; is it not?". At this juncture, the young examinee expressed his resentment and shouted back at him "what have I done to you to be so harsh on me?".

On hearing the loud shouting from across the principal's room, Pavan entered the examination room in a fit of rage by pushing the door forcibly open and in a flash he was at the principal's neck and collar and questioned him: "what has my brother done to you to be given this treatment? This is simply barbaric, inhuman and cruel!.

How did you think such a brilliant, obedient and highly disciplined student deserved this inhuman treatment?".

The principal, who had apparently preplanned to take revenge also retorted: "what has happened to your elder? He has only lost walking faculties!; But he is alright with his mind and hands; Let him write".

No sane person, however cool and collected temperamentally he may be, could have kept quiet at these happenings.

Pavan shot back: "my elder, has lost all and you have the audacity to say <only walking faculty!>. Now how do you take it if I break your legs Mr. principal".

So saying he literally caught hold of his collar. This was enough to drive him jittery and he "literally" ran away from his office room and headed straight to the Education Trust chairman's chambers nearly 5 kilometres away, on his scooter. On seeing this <virtual stage encounter>, hundreds of students came out of their <internals – examination> hall, in the middle of answering the question papers!

Prashant's father, who was an onlooker so far, decided to restore calm and order immediately. He appealed to all students to go back to their examination hall as disciplined students. He promised to get back to them after their examination and keep them informed to appease their inquisitiveness. After ensuring that the students returned back to their examination hall, both Pavan and his father chased the run-away principal in their car right upto the Education Trust Chairman's chambers, which was the chosen shelter for the errant principal!; and they both did not hesitate to force themselves into the principal's hiding place!; there they encountered the terrified principal and the Education Trust Chairman doing his routine job.

Taken aback, the Chairman enquired from the enforcing visitors: "What has happened? Why both of you are here?"; and, turning to the terrified principal, enquired: "what has brought You here, away from college, in this frightened state? And that too from examination centre?".

Prashant's younger brother Pavan narrated to him the whole story behind all that he is witnessing!; The most inhuman and indecent conduct of the principal towards a student who had come to write the internal examination sitting in wheel chair is the root cause of all these happenings. At the end of it all, the Chairman saw reason and rhyme and became aware of the shabby handling of the entire <education continuation> chapter.

Taking strong objections to the principal's revengeful stance, he appealed for calm to the parents and ordered the principal: "Now you conduct the tests strictly according to the timetable given to Prashant already. You post an independent vigilance officer to supervise the writing of the test papers. I do not want you to be the vigilance officer for the test and certainly the test will not be conducted in your office room I do not want any complaint either from the student's parents or his younger brother".

With the battle finally won, Prashant coolly and calmly wrote all the test papers, bringing to happy ending this notorious chapter...

The icing on the cake turned out to be Prashant's scoring 85% aggregate, after taking average of the 2nd and 3rd test series!. Battle had been won by us and the principal remained disgraced from out of his own evil actions. **But believe me dear readers, each obstacle turned out to be a stepping stone to success in the young student's life.**

Even at this juncture there was a small melody- drama. The principal though vanquished, <wagged his ego tail>. Guess how!!!:

"Prashant now you can write the test papers as per schedule but it has to be in my room and under my supervision" so roared the wounded principal like a tiger. His father reminding the principal of yesterday's order to him from the district magistrate, warned the principal: "why do you want to give room for obstinacy? It is quite unheard of in School Management, that a principal will do vigilance duty in an examination hall!. Look here my dear principal, some independent member of teaching staff will do the vigilance duty and the examination hall will not be in the upstairs room as ordained by you; as it is very difficult to reach the wheel chaired Prashant without lift; it shall be conducted in his car with the vigilance officer sitting in driver's seat and Prashant writing the papers from the back seat. Nobody else will be present anywhere near the car, parked outside the principal's office.

Principal: "okay, okay, I have directed the physio-instructor- teacher to do the supervision. The car should be parked right in front of my office room".

Prashant's father: "Please come out of your office and satisfy for your- selves that the car with Prashant in the back seat, is already parked right in front your office".

Physio instructor promptly arrived and went round the <improvised examination center> namely, the ambassador car with a lonely "passenger" seated at the back!. As soon as he saw the student in the car he was stunned to address: "hey, Prashant! How come you are here?; I have heard all about the tragedy; but we all teaching staff admired your grit and resolve in deciding to pursue your studies from wheel chair, albeit after a break of five years. So it is you I am supposed to supervise over!".

"Oh!!, What a pleasant surprise!. We all do know the cranky decision the principal is known to take quite often. But his inhuman handling of your case has exposed his foolishness and made himself a laughing stock amongst the entire college staff.. Don't worry, you write the examination calmly and worry free in your car itself".

Prashant deeply lost in recollecting the subject matter (test paper), found time to recollect his college days where he had played tennis with the same physio master.

Prashant: "sir it is a pleasant surprise for me too. I will lighten your burden. I recollect our happy days at college and tennis field; you had been very appreciative of me all through".

"How can I be a supervisor over such an honest and intelligent personality". So saying he handed over the question paper and relaxed himself in the driver's seat!

It is all history. Prashant wrote all the eight papers for each of the 2 sets of tests continuously.

He had devoted himself fully into task of writing the examination. The lecturers, who evaluated his answer papers, were wonder struck at the remarkably intelligent way he had answered the question papers **including the totally changed syllabus in many of the subjects**. They were only too happy to allot full deserving marks for the intelligent answers.

In the result, he had scored a magnificent 85% in the aggregate- a record for the college in recent years. The principal was left speechless and shall we say, motionless also, at the foolish treatment handed out by him, to such a brilliant boy.

Dear readers, that is life!. Parents and the heroic younger brother were all overwhelmed with joy at the resounding success and achievements. Friends and even lecturers did not lag behind in showering accolades on our dear Prashant for his outstanding <achievement in the midst of adversity>.

While it was a fitting occasion to celebrate, many in

the august gathering pondered over the revengeful treatment meted out to such a brilliant, gallant student -solider. The mystery got widened as they clearly learnt that after all, Prashant was never a student of this cranky- hanky-panky principal who had assumed charge of the college administration only 2 years back in 1993 whereas Prashant would have passed out in the year1991 itself!.

Pavan and Sri Ram (the latter had been Prashant's chum in college) got curiouser and curiouser day by day at the cranky behavior of the principal academically totally unconnected with the "VIP" student.

It is not any hear say, it is no any guess work either. The truth of his cranky behavior appeared to have a link with his son- in- law being present during the historic medical misadventure on Prashant way back on 23rd October 1990 in the operation theatre as an Anaesthesist at the Hyderabad city hospital. **As a doctor (Anaesthesist) he would have definitely attributed the enforced paraplegia on Prashant, to prolonged administration of Anaesthesia as one of the likely causes and would have felt guilty!** Anyway he left the job himself voluntarily and dispatched himself to the United States of America.

Thank heavens, we have not heard of any case of overdose of anaesthisia from the USA so far!!.

Medical literature pointed out to 3 possible factors for the enforced paraplegia (our dear Prashant not excluded):-

1) Acute traction applied on the spinal cord while dissecting the unwanted benign tumour masses.

2) Interference with the supplementary Spinal vascular arrangement through ligation of intercostal arteries located along the intercostal space and entering the spinal cord through inter vertebrate foraminae.

3) **Paraplegia can also occur due to excess dosages of Anaesthesia particularly, when administered intrathecally i.e.; through the spinal cord. (It is a well recorded fact that Prashant remained under the influence of General Anaesthesia several hours long after the butchery surgical procedure was completed and shifted out of the Operation Theatre to ICU for intensive care).**

Sudden exit of his son-in-law from India to the USA, and the same principal (and father in law of the anaesthesist), making detailed enquiries about Prashant and his family in far off Hyderabad city- could they be pointers to the guilty conscience and cranky behaviour of the principal!

COLLEGE LIFE AT MACHILIPATNAM

With all hurdles crossed with grit and determination and leaving behind all unpleasant history to posterity, the young challenger marched forward with head held high. Regular college going restarted; now it was not the library but he entered the class room where he was welcomed with cheers by his new class mates and lecturers alike.

Pavan addressing his father: "Daddy, now everything is streamlined. You both parents are absent from your work places for too long ; I will take care of my elder brother with support and help voluntarily pouring in from his class mates; you both can freely resume your duties at Hyderabad".

His mother: "Dear, it is nice of you to suggest our getting back to our respective work places. The care- taking load is quite heavy on your young shoulders. My leaving leaves a big gap in kitchen duties".

Pavan: "Mohan Ram is standing by us like the great rock of Gibraltar. Moreover he has already planned with his wife Krishna, to replace you in the kitchen. You therefore can leave for Hyderabad peacefully".

Pavan had kept Mohan Ram fully informed. The next day we were all pleasantly surprised to find Mr & Mrs Mohan Ram in our midst with their bag and baggage!.

This magnanimous arrangement paved the way for the overstressed parents to leave for Hyderabad the next day for a short stint back at their works.

Mr. & Mrs. Mohan Ram lost no time in greeting Prashant: "Dear, hearty congratulations to you on your HE R C U L E A N efforts and achievements. You have brought glory to your family, to our township and to the society at large. Keep it up!; We are here to replace your parents at least for a short spell".

Prashant: "Dears uncle and aunty, I just do not have words to express my gratitude for the love and affection being continuously showered on me".

With the exchanging of pleasantries continuing, Mrs. Krishna Mohan Ram had quietly slipped into the kitchen and returned to his room with steaming hot tea pot and biscuits.

Pavan in total wonder: "Aunty! What a surprise! You have already taken over the kitchen!?; from now on, we will have delicious Andhra dishes!".

Mrs. Krishna, hugging Pavan affectionately: "It is my pleasure; you both brothers are free to demand your choice of the palate"; sipping hot tea Prashant profusely thanked aunty and turning to his younger:

"From tomorrow onwards, you will have to get up at least 4 hours before, to prepare me for journey to college. I am keen to see how you can manage to wake up from deep slumber to which you are habituated since you were a child!!".

Pavan:"Uncle Mohan Ram would sound <the air base camp> alarm to wake me up. Don't worry!".

Prashant: "Do remember, it is just not, your morning preparations alone!; You have to attend to my morning duty; you have to exercise my lower limbs as part of mandatory physio therapy. This would require yet another hour. So be prepared to get up at least 2 hours before sunrise!".

There was perfect harmony sliced with cracking of Jokes between the two brothers since their childhood. This childhood upbringing clicked at the nick of these trying times.

Pavan, a live wire, as always, did not give room for any laxity but instead, joyfully took on the duties as the clock ticked away from 4AM to 5AM and speeding away to 8AM even. He would lift him from bed and transfer him to wheel chair ready for breakfast at the stroke of 8 in the morning.

Transferring him from wheel chair to car; and Mohan Ram driving away Prashant to college; transferring him from car to wheel chair and wheeling him to class room- all became a regular routine- as regular as the Sun rise daily.

Pavan, after settling his elder in the class room, would return home around 9AM to complete all his morning schedules and would drive back to college to be in "attendance" for any movement from class room to class room; or class room to library. This close association with the college atmosphere and his joyful disposition, brought Pavan affectionately close to all of his elder brother's friends. Prashant drew inspiration and self boosted his morale to astonishing high levels in this benignly pleasant atmosphere.

Such was the bon homie created, that nobody noticed the passage of time –a staggering 2 months period!!

By this time Prashant's parents returned from Hyderabad after a short stint with their respective professional duties.

It was a pleasant ceremony for handing over charge from the highly affectionate Mohan Rams back to parents.

Mohan Ram: "I would be very much missing the jokes being shared between the duo brothers".

"We have no words to express our gratitude for the care and service to Prashant during our absence; we are very fortunate to have friends like you": thankfully reciprocated the parents.

Mohan Ram: "Please mention not; I am part of your family; I thoroughly enjoyed the company of the two brothers joining them as a third brother. The atmosphere, even while doing rigorous exercises, was so charged with life- full of laughter and mirth. As an airman, I had lessons to learn from these duo; how to face a difficult enemy!".

"I am deeply moved by the dedication of the younger brother to his elder. It was a treat to watch Pavan performing duties to perfection; showering love and affection all through smilingly; despite the strains and stresses of duty".

Parents: "We too are deeply touched by the warmth of affection shown by you and your lady". Profusely showering accolades on Pavan, Mohan Ram had this to say: "It is difficult to assess who underwent greater hardships- whether it was Lord Sri Rama or His dear younger brother Lakshmana of the Ramayana epic".

Mother: "Is it not undoubtedly, Lakshmana?; At least Sri Rama had the company of His consort Sita by His side".

Mohan Ram: "surely it was Lakshmana, who accompanied his elder brother voluntarily to serve Him in the forest at the cost of his newly married wife Urvashi's company.

Prashant is very fortunate to have a "Lakshmana", in his younger brother, constantly putting efforts to keep boosting the morale of his elder to greater heights day in and day out. These fine gestures, plus, his sacrificing one year of his academic course in engineering, both aspects, perhaps deserve a mention in the <Guinness Book of world Records>; my contribution pales into insignificance in comparison!. Of course the two brothers had built up this attachment from childhood.

****

CHPTER- XII

THREE CHALLENGES

Family sat together to chalk out the future plans to face the three challenges: 1) Education; 2) Mandatory Medical attention; 3) Litigation in Courts of Law

Father to son: "Dear, you are such a progressive oriented person; you concentrate only on studies, yes studies of not only completing the BE Degree but pursuing it further and acquiring <Post Graduate and Doctorate in Engineering>."

"You had always been a great achiever; you have the vision to see the road ahead even beyond dead ends and, create new paths to march forward uninterrupted. Where majority would have fretted and fumed at such tragic crossings in life, you our dear, remained cool and collected, never losing your goals set for yourself".

"Do not bother about our inconveniences and your mandatory schedules. Life should go on and blossom" so declaring profusely patted his back.

Prashant: "Daddy, I am game for the future plans. But what worries me is, how we can simultaneously tackle the other two tasks namely: 1) continuous medical

Attention and 2) start of the litigation proceedings against the negligent doctors and the hospital institution as well, in Courts of Law".

Father: "For medical attention we will arrange for a professional nursing help and a qualified and certified physiotherapist for exercising all joints, at home itself. As for the task of preparation for litigation, first and fore-mostly, we should be in the know of what went wrong; how it all went wrong; and how it resulted in physical handicap life-long; how it could have been avoided or could not have been avoided at all; were there any compulsions for the hasty decisions to conduct <Surgery as the only remedy>..."

"Scores of such issues have to be thoroughly addressed; studied & investigated".

Pavan suggested: "Father can totally free himself from medical attention necessities and totally concentrate on litigation.

Mother: "Pavan and myself will take care of daily necessities. Sharada and Ananad from Mohan Ram's family; Ashok and Anupama from neighboring Bhat's family; Asha, Shubha and Raghu from Murthy's family are ever ready to hop- in with helping hands; **you concentrate on your office work (for sustaining family income) and preparation for litigation.**

Each one started in right earnest with his/her designated tasks -With Prashant seriously studying; His father serious both at work and totally involved in preparation for litigation.

PREPARATIONS: FOR LITIGATION in Courts of Law/FOR WRITING EXAMs for Final year Degree Qualification

Prashant and party returned to Hyderabad residence, during the preparatory holidays for final examination.

As already planned father dived into huge volumes of medical literature, publications to get at the truth of the tragedy. This writer and his family including Prashant are indeed grateful and lifelong indebted to knowledge sharing by eminent professors in medicine and medical practices. They have been gratefully listed as materials referred to, in the Bibliography chapter at the end of the book.

Further we are indebted and grateful to scores of authors whose publications are condensed and made available through <Medline Data Base (National Library of medicine, USA) and PUB MED (National Library of Medicine USA>

We are also indebted and grateful to libraries - in charge/ officers at various medical colleges cum hospitals including the AIIMS New Delhi; NIMS Hyderabad; St John's medical college hospital Bangalore; Escorts medical college library at New-Delhi, Bangalore medical College, Saint Mary's hospital Hyderabad, KIMS Bangalore. Yes all these Institutions' library officers <bent over their backs> to enable this writer (father of Prashant) to acquire sound, authentic medical knowledge to expertly analyse the tragic, unwanted surgery strike on our dear Prashant's physique and to come to dispassionate, unbiased and Jurisprudential Conclusions

Knowledge acquiring mission completed (spread over a period of six months); Prashant's father joined hands with a senior Advocate, one Mr. S. Rao (he practiced as senior Advocate at the Apex court of the country, namely, the Hon'ble Supreme Court of India)

The drafts of the petition were written and rewritten, after detailed discussions on legal and medical aspects between father and the legal counsel duo

Finally on the 9th day of April 1993 the <Original Complaint Petition was filed before> the Hon'ble National Consumers Disputes Redressal Commission (abbreviated NCDRC), New Delhi.

On the other side, Prashant dived fully into the Engineering subjects including those where the syllabus/syllabi had under gone drastic changes.

At long last, there came an intimation, from our appointed legal counsel informing: "Be ready for 1st hearing in May 1993 at Delhi".

Prashant's father: "what is your advice Rao?; Should we go over to New Delhi for the first hearing along with Prashant?"

S. Rao: "It is, indeed, advisable to take Prashant along, to be present before the Hon'ble NCDRC".

Pavan: "Let my brother and the legal counsel reach Delhi by Air".

His father: "Pavan dear, you also accompany your elder brother and the legal counsel in flight; parents and your uncle Krishna however, will come by train, for obvious reasons of economy, and reach Delhi at the same time. My ex–employer, head –quartered at New-Delhi has kindly arranged guest house accommodation along with a chauffeur driven car for our movements from Guest house to the NCDRC court and back until the end of First hearing".

As planned, the two batches reached Delhi guest house. **Next day morning parents got up by 4 AM to attend to morning duties to Prashant, including mandatory physio- exercising**; and after breakfast we all journeyed to the court and arrived promptly by 11AM. But surprises galore greeted us!.

Pavan: "Daddy, the first level for the lift is virtually on a mountain top!; We have to climb 20 steps!; OMG!!".

Father: "It is all in the game mates!; one, two, three here we go", so saying Krishna, Pavan joined father; the three together lifted the wheel chair - seated litigant. Hardly had we climbed 5 steps, a fourth helping hand appeared from nowhere and started to lift Prashant along with the threesome.

Father: "It is very kind and noble of you sir, to offer help in negotiating the cumbersome manual- lift starting Level".

"Please mention not" came the reply.

We all reached the court hall and settled down for our case to be taken up. As the Hearing Bench settled down at the Altar of Justice, Prashant keenly having a look at the August Bench, whispered into his daddy's ears: "Look daddy, do you recognize the Hon'ble Presiding Judge!!"

Pavan: "Oh! Yes, he is the same noble personality who only a few minutes ago, had offered his helping hand to all of us as we were lifting Prashant manually up to the start level of electric lift".

"What a pleasant surprise!; What a magnanimous and noble personality the Hon'ble Judge is" :so exclaimed all in the Petitioner's camp in one voice.

Krishna Mama: "Nobility displayed is Justice delivered!: We are sure the proceedings will be absolutely smooth and balanced in the hands of these Noble Judges".

This chance incident had its own effect; the Presiding Judge addressing the parents had this to say to begin with: "Why did you trouble the Petitioner in bringing him all the way from Hyderabad to Delhi until absolutely required ; this could be at the final arguments stage which will be definitely several hearings / sittings away".

While this was the disposition on the part of the complainant/petitioner, the legal counsel for the Opposite Parties had apparently hatched entirely different plans to thwart all our initiations!!; Guess how?!. Raising from his seat the legal counsel (for the OPs), pleaded: "Your Honour!, One of my kith has suffered an accident; I therefore seek the Leave of the Hon'ble bench, on humanitarian grounds, to defer the hearing to a later fortnight". The Hon'ble Bench somewhat embarrassingly, granted the appeal and posted the case for a future date although they were aware of the ensuing hardships for the handicapped complainant.

Left with no alternative, the entire company of the Petitioner had to return to Hyderabad till the next hearing a month away. But here again, Prashant was in the limelight demonstrating his <Pacific- Ocean- magnitude> composure, despite the compulsions of his having to take the Delhi trip again within the next month. While he and his mother returned to Hyderabad by air, the legal counsel and his deputy returned to Bangalore by air. Prashant's father and Younger brother however returned by train.

Father to his son: "Dear Prashant!, Your friends at Hyderabad will receive you at the airport and drive you home; they will take care of all your daily needs till we three arrive by train 2 days later and take over our duties. Are you game for this dear?!".

Back at home the rigorous- duties- schedule had to be kept going. However all these difficulties were taken in good stride- ranging from studies, medical treatment of bedsore wounds, physiotheraupic exercising.

He, matter- of- factly announced: "Dear, your college- mate Satish has planned to visit you this afternoon".

Prashant: "Oh! You mean that break- dancer Satish!. He would not break his dance once he starts; we friends only have to apply brakes on him"; laughter all around.

Pavan: "Dear, Your casio- master Ashok, Your tabla

-master Srinivas also are visiting you and I have planned to join them all with my guitar .How do you like it?"

Prashant: "Oh!, that will be simply great fun!; We will have a music concert but without a conductor?! Otherwise we will have neither western music nor jazz!; So I will have to conduct the show myself?". Laughter again!.

At the appointed time all friends arrived and the "music concert" began in right earnest and went on endlessly till late evening hours. Although he also enjoyed the music concert, but burdened with enforcing schedules, PRASHANT's father reminded all concerned: "Boys, now it is time to begin physio therapy exercises, please".

Pavan beckoned to Sharada to take over the exercising assistant's duty: "you hold the left leg firmly when I start with the right and vice -versa"; "One, two , three ..", Pavan started pulling the right leg and Sharada **firmly straightened** the raising left knee!.Do **you guess how? Pavan** noticing something strange urged: **"Sharada, how is it that Prashant's left knee, which you are holding in check, has turned deep blue!?"**

Sharada: "I just did my duty in arresting any movement of the left leg as you started exercising the right leg ".

Prashant in lighter vein: "Goodness gracious! You have transmitted your whole weight on my leg! My dear sister, at this rate you will make my life very happy as you would have left no life in the leg to suffer any more!".

The whole gathering went hysterical with laughter and "begged" Sharada to leave Prashant alone!!

The ambience around Prashant was thus always kept lively by his friends and well wishers. That was the secret of eternal smile on his face; the secret of incessant overflowing enthusiasm and high morale. He could therefore, concentrate on his preparations for examination with all seriousness and concentration.

The time arrived for taking Prashant to write his final Degree examination at Vijayawada city which offered better facilities for the physically challenged.

Readers may recall that the Vice Chancellor of his University had graciously waived off attendance shortage and also permitted the young student to write the final examination at the much nearer and more convenient and wheel- chair friendly center. **Prashant began his final assault to conquer name and fame**.

Waking up at 4AM early morning, father approached his son: "Dear, now you have to be awake as I start with your morning ablutions, to be followed later by physio exercising; we should be there , at the college premises at least a half hour before 8AM ,the scheduled start of examinations.

Prashant: "I am already awake daddy. Please get me today's examination subject book. At least for half an hour I can glance through and refresh my memory". Father patiently conducted him all through the drill and readied him for the next mandatory schedule; Pavan the designated physio master arrived: "daddy, you please relax a bit as I start the 60-minutes exercising schedule", so uttering he started off promptly. By 7AM,

Prashant was transferred into the wheel chair ready for breakfast and take off to college.

While the whole world slept, our dear Prashant, his younger brother and father had to be active for the mandatory schedules. It had become a daily routine leaving no room for any leniency. Quite often parents themselves were unable to hold back their tears at these compulsions enforced on their very dear son life-long from this early age. What a twist of fate for the helpless but brilliant- best student since his childhood! All living beings have 24 hours in a day but dear Prashant had to manage all within 18 hours after allowing a minimum of 6 hours for his enforced compulsory activities not at all required by common healthy people; situation tough and difficult though, was boldly and smilingly faced by Prashant and his affectionate team of attendants.

Each day he would perform very well in the examination and return to hotel like a gallant soldier having vanquished the enemy, the eternal beaming smile never to disappear from his face!.

Even a strong atheist would not hesitate to see the hand of god in going through such ordeals by us mortals. The schedule gone through meticulously for a full fortnight, all students, juniors although, and staff gathered to bid him farewell. Each one present on the farewell occasion saluted the bravery, steadfastness, grit and determination of the VIP-knowledge seeker-Prashant that was!. The young student had established eternal bond of relationship with them all. He thanked them all profusely, attributing his successful completion of the education-mission, to their unstinted help and cooperation.

Next day morning Pavan assisted his daddy in packing up for journey back to Hyderabad. The journey by car was different this time. All felt completely relieved of anxiety that had been built up for writing the examination.

Prashant: "Oh! What a relief ! As of now; however, there is no time to relax. Every day of the 5-years period lost, has to be recovered".

Pavan: "Dear, you can seriously think of taking up a mechanical engineer's designer job or a stint with software development in Information Technology field; both offer great prosperity and of course they are disabled- friendly".

Prashant: "We can contact our age- group people who are learning software development skills offered in our BHEL Township itself ".

Pavan: "Yes, you are right; Ashok, the ever enterprising friend of yours, has started IT software development programme for novices at his residence itself located within our residential township".

The journey of 500km was not at all felt in the midst of Discussions, jokes. Prashant was only too happy to be back home after the great achievement.

All friends, neighbours welcomed the adventurous company with cheers, appreciations, admirations for the gallant soldier; immediately on return home, Pavan went ahead to contact his elder's friend Ashok for the IT software learning programme.

Ashok overwhelmed with joy: "It will be my honour and privilege to enroll your brother and my chum for the IT software programme. From the beginning I knew your brother as an intelligent and determined personality. 5 years break!; Wheel chair bound for life; medical attention daily without any let-up for hours on end!. Despite all these obstacles, my chum has achieved the nearly impossible!!. Kudos to him; please bring him along. By tomorrow I will be ready with a wooden ramp at the threshold entrance to my humble residence- cum-institute, to welcome Prashant".

Pavan did not fail to notice tears rolling down Ashok's cheeks! He and his father would drive Prashant to the IT center every day. A full 3 months course gave our dear, all elementary start up knowledge to operate computer and to write software programmes in basic languages; his teacher as also others in the family and circle of friends were thrilled at the speed of his acquisition of knowledge and skills in the entirely new IT field.

The great day dawned on the family. Anxiously awaited result from the university did arrive. He had passed out of the final BE degree examination with flying colours; professors and lecturers from his Machilipatnam college were overwhelmed with joy and were quick to transmit the exciting news: "Prashant, great indeed; we all, are so proud to announce that you have passed out with distinction and honours ; your final battle gloriously won, you have brought name and fame to our institution. We all, including the Top Management , have inscribed your name in the < scroll..> of Honour> Three cheers !, hip- ip, hip- ip hurray !"

Prashant responding in sheer delight: "I have no words to thank you all for this thrilling news. It is a great moment in my life. This achievement would not have been possible but for your stinted cooperation and herculean efforts; your contribution to my success is unfathomable and worthy of being etched in letters of gold. I shall remain grateful in all my life, to all your morale boosting efforts during my traumatic period".

All our family members and well wishers congregated at our residence to shower: "Prashant, heartiest congratulations! on your great achievement. It was a great moment to celebrate. None in the family and none of his friends had even dreamt that such a joyful day would arrive for a physically challenged person whose condition was in no way better than an young baby requiring round the clock attention; unable to turn in bed by himself; unable to remain in sitting position even for a fraction of an hour, not to speak of walking deficit enforced.

Prashant had risen like a colossus; had risen like a meteor through sheer determination and tireless efforts from himself and with his full family support. This could not have been achieved by even the bravest of brave humans without continuous propping up by HIM- the creator; the Lord Almighty. Prashant too, had realized and acknowledged the hand of god in his astounding achievement this.

Notwithstanding these electrifying moments, the family had to continue the journey, the journey of life paved with some excitements here and there but obstacles unabated for the major part. Prashant's father retired from his service to the BHEL organization on attaining the age of superannuation with effect from June 1994. Although his company offered him a Senior -consultant's contract for one more year consequently to continue to live in the company's residential quarters and avail medical services for Prashant (purely on grounds of his physical challenged condition), We had to weigh in the alternative of his starting off with earnings more conducive at the IT capital city of Bangalore than the hitherto Hyderabad on one side, and the offer from Prashant's mother's school on the other side.

Like a silver lining to the dark clouds of financial strangulations, the principal of Indira's erstwhile school suddenly appeared in our midst. Pleasantly surprised, Indira greeted her and profusely thanking her for her concern for our family's welfare exclaimed: "I just cannot believe my eyes; my beloved principal is with me in my humble home".

The two embraced each other and tears rolled down their cheeks profusely. She (the principal) made detailed enquiries: "How is your dear gallant soldier-son Prashant? ; is there any improvement in his health condition?".

Indira: "you would be glad to see that he can now sit in the wheel chair for hours on end; rigorous physio-exercising, both in the morning and evening, has helped him with improved general health: he has gained in confidence to face obstacles for his future life".

Principal: "I see what all you said about him. It must be HIS Divine Grace. The credit for all these progress and achievements goes in no small measure, to his younger brother's, his parents' and his friends' devoted service". Turning towards Prashant, she smilingly blesses him:

"Dear, I have heard a good lot about your efforts to complete the interrupted education despite great odds; you have lighted a beacon to show the path of progress to the whole world. Oh my god! , what a determination!; what a grit beyond compare ! My heartiest congratulations to you on these Herculean efforts".

Prashant thanking her: " My mother has high reverence for you and your predecessor for the benevolent approach to all teachers. For my mother the school was a continuation of home".

Principal: "It is nice of you to hold the school Management in such a high esteem; your mother worked with extreme devotion to her teaching job. She went on to earn the distinction of being one of the pillars of our Institute".

"As a token of our love and appreciation, we are requesting her to come back to school now that your health has vastly improved and stabilized ; moreover, your family needs financial support at this juncture when your father has retired from service", the principal added

Indira: "I am thankful for your kind gesture in taking me back after nearly 4 years of break".

Principal: "Do not worry; we have not treated your long absence as any break in service but only considered it as <Leave of absence without pay>".

Indira voiceless, speechless with these gestures coming from her School Management , silently nodded her head in approval and embraced her.

Principal: "I can easily visualize that you cannot devote all the standard twenty six classes per week; you cannot, I am also aware, take home any unfinished school work either".

"The school management had already debated these salient situations and had come up with decision to allot you only 12 classes per week; you will be enabled to spend the remaining years of your service peacefully. Further I am happy to announce that you will be entitled to retirement benefits if you make up the shortage of six months in your continuous service spread over 15 years".

This kindly disposed principal had developed great affinity for the highly devoted teacher in Indira. When the latter was in hospital serving her son for months on end, the principal would make it a point to visit her and her son for enquiring about the health and improvement. Keeping in mind the continuity of her service without break, the principal herself would have prepared a long leave application only to take Indira's signature !, and she would immediately record her < leave granted without pay> orders on that leave application!; **such was the divinity and bon -homie displayed by the principal towards her <better than best> teacher!.**

And the < Indira teacher> as she was respectfully known to the entire school, followed suit. Once again she had become a regular teacher; on her first **reappearance day**, she was accorded a rousing welcome and reception by all her erstwhile colleagues, non teaching staff not excluded.

She dutifully completed the six month regime. Notwithstanding the pain in her heart, she thoroughly enjoyed her revisit to school entirely due to the love and affection showered on her by the kindly principal and staff and colleagues. At the end of it all, she had to call it <permanent leave–taking>. The School Management most reluctantly accepted her resignation; and she was given a tearful and touching farewell.

With 8 years of service still left for normal retirement, all retirement benefits including gratuity were promptly handed over to her with best wishes for bringing her dear son Prashant back to normal with her filial love and divine care as soon as possible.

****

CHAPTER- XIII

BEGINS LIFE AFRESH AT THE HOME TOWN OF THE FAMILY- BANGALORE CITY

Like the <Last supper>, the family members had their last serious meeting at Hyderabad.

Mother suggested to her dear son: "Dear sonny, we have crossed many a hurdle and achieved many laurels and accolades. It was possible only through your sheer grit and determination and above all, with your most positive attitude to life ahead.

Not to undermine the noble help and encouragement received by us from the large conglomeration of our friends, Kith and kin, well wishers both at Machilipatanam and Hyderabad towns, You have converged on your choice of profession between teaching and or software development. In either case Bangalore will be the most suitable place for us to settle down" .

Pavan suggested "It is not only our home town but also called the silicon city for IT hub ; there are a number of eminently popular training centers, easily reachable by you. So I hereby put my stamp of approval on our dear mummy's proposal!; do you get me steeve!"

His father and Krishna mama in one voice: "There cannot

be   a better choice as we have long standing connect with our home town people. Our home/ house will give further boost to our efforts to settle down".

Resolutions thus passed by the < family court>, the entire setup moved once for all and forever to Bangalore.

Pavan went around Bangalore without any further loss of time and selected <Aptech center> located about 12km away from our residence, as the best Soft-ware recruitment Centre

Addressing his elder, Pavan announced: " Dear, you have already acquired the basics of the computer soft-ware. Now it will be easy for you to acquire higher professional grade knowledge and skills in different languages such as C, C+,VC,VC+" .

Prashant : "Your suggestion and choice of IT training center is quite OK for me . I am game for the decision". But, "listen dear Pavan, now you have to go back to college to continue your studies".

"But dear me, don't forget father will be alone; economic strangulation will not permit engaging a chauffeur": so chipped in Pavan with his thoughts .

His father instantly intervened: "do not write off your dear daddy simply because he has retired from service!; recollect! Who does the physio exercising regularly vigorously for hours on end!- your daddy and mummy is it not ?; then where is the problem !"

Pavan: "I see the self confidence of our daddy ; after all it comes from his own mouth quite assuredly and confidently". Decision taken, promptly Pavan and his father left for the former's college town to ensure that he is resettled comfortably.

His father returned the next day to Bangalore. We had to reach Aptech training center sharp at 10am . This time schedule dictated our preparation to start at least 4hrs before. Prashant's father ably assisted by Indira had no difficulty in getting him readied without skipping the mandatory schedules. He drove Prashant to training center. The newly acquired Maruthi van came in handy for the journey. The van had been suitably modified to make it highly physically-challenged friendly. Father would drive off with his VIP passenger- son to the training center12km away. On reaching the destination he would enlist the help of security guard on duty to transfer him from car to wheel chair. The next move, many a time was not without hurdles!; guess why and what for?; the electric power supply would <go witch hunting> for quite a few hours daily because of transmission overloads and consequent load sheddings . To reach Prashant to the 3rd floor where the training facility was located, father had to device a number of novelties!!.

The security guard would guide the wheel chair up to lift entrance alright. But father would climb the entire flight of stairs to reach the lift control room on the top most floor (5th floor) ; enter the engine room and slowly, carefully release the brake step by step, to enable the powerless lift inch downwards manually. The lift would thus be brought to the zero level. Gopinath, the security guard, would wait patiently for Prashant's father to come down the flight of stairs to assist him to wheel Prashant in to the lift. closing the collapsible type lift door entrance himself, as a safety precautionary measure, father and Gopinath would, like true sports, climb all the flight of stairs to the highest roof top from zero level, enter the lift head room and would, this time operate the handle of the geared motor axle and gradually <lift the lift> in notches slowly and steadily from zero level to third floor.

We both would dart down to third floor and take the waiting VIP passenger out of the lift and perambulate him into the class room! This exercise of manual lifting had been a regular feature. In a span of six months this extra ordinary feat had to be performed at least a dozen times for taking up Prashant to 3rd floor and as many number of times to bring him down to zero level after the end of training for the day.

While Prashant was busy receiving training, father would spend his 4 hour- waiting period in the car itself parked a furlong away.

Around 2:30 PM the reverse routine would start! Father meticulously, would drive his son back home

His mother-Indira would be waiting at the residence gate to receive her dear valiant- soldier- son smilingly. The entire process of transferring Prashant to wheel chair was combined handled by the parents smilingly with even broader smile from the <Never say die> , <Dear man divine!, stop not till you reach the goal> Prashant. Such commandments to enrich humanity practiced and preached by great thinkers and saints like the swami Vivekananda, like the Commandments enshrined in the sacred Bhagavad- Gita guided his life. Nothing is impossible for a determined brave heart; <come what may!, Succeed, I must> was the adrenalin, freely flowing in his well built otherwise healthy body and mind . Prashant sailed on and on undaunted.

****

PRASHANT'S-An Incredible Life Journey!!!

1998 Prashant's first job (in wheel chair) at Covansys MNS

At Covansys chennai year 2002
(22 years old)

CHAPTER- XIV

BEGINNING OF PROFESSIONAL CAREER AT BANGALORE 1996

Six months of disciplined learning had added to Prashant's necessary vigour to step into the chosen profession. Along with the software languages learnt at AP Tech Institute, he added a few more to his knowledge kitty. He expressed his desire to earn by starting computer classes for beginners at home. Mother offered to finance computers and required furniture as her gift with blessings;

Prashant:" Our neighbours Raja, Sheela , Shubhash are quite eager to learn basics of soft ware applications. So let us start off with these three pioneer customers".

Pavan jumped at this initiative and enthusiasm; strongly hugging him said: "I am proud of my senior brother: Best of luck; nothing can stop you".

Prashant: "How can I stop anywhere midway ! . You have transferred to me Alpine mountains' proportion momentum through your loving care and attention and devotion".

"You will be required to partner me in future for higher and higher assignments. It is therefore time for you to go back to your university and come back with your Bachelor in Engineering Degree duly acquired".

Pavan:"I just need only 2 years; will keep visiting you in the intervening holidays. After all my university town-Shimoga is just a few < cricket balls throw > away distance".

The trio of Raja , Sheela and Subhash had promptly reported as obedient students; mother lighted the lamp as symbol of knowledge and progress and blessed both her sons profusely. It was a great moment in the family.

The<Sree Ganesh > inauguration had been successfully completed. Pavan left for his university town with all vigour and enthusiasm to return back with added strength.

In less than a month's time, Prashant's training center had gained reputation. His bright student Subhash had this to say: "sir, are you ready to take on 3 more students (they are all my class mates)?"

Prashant: "The training center can run in batches of 2 hours duration each. So I am game for more inflow of students; and turning to father he suggested: "let us add 3 more computers. After all , my dear father is there to finance from his retirement benefits!"

Through word of mouth, the students' strength rose sharply to fifteen . The young software engineer managed all of them in three batches expertly with time to spare.

One fine morning Prashant receives a call: "Hello Prashant, I met your father recently and discussed about your plans.   I am only too happy to request for your professional help in preparing working drawings for the manufacture of electrical starters in our factory".

"I am very much eager to meet you; I have heard a good lot about your achievements even from wheel chair"so aired Mr.Vasudevan desiring to help the physically challenged but gallant soldier

Prashant:" uncle, you are welcome any time; I will be only very happy to assist you in your requirements".

Promptly arrived the industrialist and introduced himself as the Managing Director to Prashant: "I am Vasudevan. I am sure you will be interested in helping me by way of preparing engineering drawings using computer aided design software (CAD)."

Prashant: "Surely uncle, I am interested in taking up this professional task";

 It was a cake walk for Prashant's entry into professional field.

Besides discharging the training responsibilities, he produced the first set of working drawings and was curious to present them at the factory himself to his newly acquired client. His father only drove him to the client's place. Vasudevan took pains to explain his product namely electric motor starters.

Prashant: "should you need, I am prepared to discuss with shop production engineers on the drawings prepared".

Vasudevan: "I have gone through the detailed working drawings. They are perfectly okay"; so saying he profusely complimented him.

With this start, CAD assignment became a regular business; in fact, the MD Vasudevan promised to add further orders from the small- scale industrialists located around his establishment. With income raising slowly month- on- month, Prashant's confidence also went on reaching greater and greater heights.

Encouraged by these developments, he decided to spend some devoted time exclusively to qualify himself with a few more computer languages in order to make himself more easily eligible for higher professional career jobs.

Parents and Prashant could not afford to go soft on the other mandatory schedules- especially physio- exercising and medical attention for the bedsores which had been thrust on him He took the challenges smilingly and started to manage both the mandates equally effortlessly.

This was not all. A balanced mind and body were a prerequisite for sound progress in profession. Yogic exercising was also started. A yoga master agreed to visit him at his residence itself in view of Prashant's heavy schedules; controlled breathing exercises called <pranayama>, universally practiced for astounding benefits of health of both mind and body, were promptly started. This went on to benefit his general health. Visiting his family on his first vacation, Pavan noticed a sea of change in his elder's busy schedules; but did not fail to notice the huge burden of expenses certainly not at all commensurate with the moderate earnings.

Pavan to his dear parents: "How are we going to meet the growing expenses? After all we have to spend a fortune even for preventive check up of Prashant's health parameters; not to speak of hospitalizations now and then, due to urinary tract infections (UTI); due to bedsore infections and not to speak of visits to experts for periodic consultations about the status/ progress/ correctness of schedule for continued physio- exercising, preventive and curative medicines not excluded.

Father: "Per force we have to find solutions to make both ends meet. Pavan's getting into earning position will take at least 2 years from now; and even then we cannot expect to tide over the financial strangulations fully".

Mother: "why do we have to keep taxing our minds? After all, things must brighten in future; our two children will definitely go from strength to strength in their professions.

Let us utilize the big financial source available handy!"

Pavan:" "Dear mom, you have already sacrificed a lot by selling off your lovingly acquired ornaments; you have reduced to zero, your retirement monetary benefits ; you are not behind father in spending at least 10-12 hours a day to look after my dear brother. How much more you want to sacrifice?".

Father: **"That is the humanely human-mother, ever ready to sacrifice all for bringing up her off-springs which trait places all mothers all over the globe, on a high pedestal so revered and held sacred. That is why many cultures across the globe covering all humans look to mothers < as divine as God>; <Matru devo Bhava> is practiced from decades.**

All in family: "Let us either mortgage or out rightly dispose off our housing property. After all, property, since ages, has been considered< a stand –by security in distress>. Seven long years have passed since the tragic medical negligence "gift" to our family. Let us generate a < Corpus Fund > to see us through the present enforced monetary strangulation ."

By now, Pavan had completed his Engineering Degree with distinction and was looking to walk into professional field.

Prashant: "Kudos to your achievements in completing education! ; I suggest that you acquire additional qualification ; through post graduation you can go for Masters in Engineering or…."

Pavan: "wait a minute, wait a minute folks; the need of the hour is to meet both ends meet. Let me start off with earnings and later on do my PG course"

Prashant: "That sounds Fine; if you take up the IT field, it would compliment my efforts also".

Pavan decided to go all out to acquire software development skills from within the city limits itself.

Thus the family moved to a new rented house; new set up-a full 15km distance away from the old just recently sold off residence!. New friends had to be made. With the positive attitude displayed incessantly by Prashant, it was no any uphill task at all; no any miracle. Soon he was surrounded by new acquaintances ever ready to contribute their bit to his life for making it better and better

Every evening family would discuss over dinner, the future plans. Prashant expressed during one of those dinner gatherings: "teaching is imparting new knowledge to youngsters. I do make a few bucks from the same alright. But I am keen to acquire higher and higher skills to be a top class IT professional; meeting people in that profession would hasten my learning".

Pavan: "wait a minute dear, I have heard of a genius in this line of service having overcome similar odds like you".

Prashant: "Hey! That is it. Try locating him immediately and let us invite him to our place"

Pavan returned home from his office fully excited: "Hey look dear, I have fixed up an appointment with one Mr.Niranjan who works as manager in Philips (India) Software Ltd".

The next day, we both met the Public Relations manager of the Software Coy.

PR executive: "you please wait here as I request Niranjan to come downstairs to meet you"; we eagerly waited for the VIP to arrive downstairs. Lo! He arrived in a flash in his motorized wheel chair bringing it to a full stop right at our toe tip! and straight away introduced himself to both of us.

So quick and alert was Niranjan; both of us were instantly taken aback by his dynamism. And our first thoughts on meeting him were: "How at last we have found a match for our dynamic Prashant. Soon we can see him also coming out of his closeted enclave, join a large band of companions and grow fast.

We invited Niranjan to join us for lunch the coming Sunday itself. Prashant was too anxious to meet this new acquaintance. At the appointed hour Niranjan arrived promptly with his wife in his self driven car!

Prashant was the first to greet the guests on their arrival, he was quick to point out "hey Niranjan how come you are at the driver's seat?

Niranjan smiled: "I could not continue to depend on the way- ward chauffeur. He was quite irregular in driving duty. **So I went ahead boldly to get my car retro-fitted for self-driving !.** Despite physical challenges, I could drive the car all by myself with all controls –clutch, brake, accelerator controlled by hand only!. I have the permission from the State transport Authorities as well".

Prashant: "Niranjan that is simply fantastic .I am also tempted to ask my daddy to retro-fit our car; I appreciate your bold initiative".

Niranjan introduced his better half to the family: "She is quite a morale booster for me. She keeps on giving ideas continuously to make me more and more independent in life"

Indira welcomed the new guests "we all in the family stand enchanted at the breath taking maneuvers including modifying the car itself to be <wheel chaired person friendly>; please let us know where you got it all done. Behind the success of every man there must be a lady".

"I would be glad to meet that great lady today": Prashant's mother added on.

Niranjan entering the house was quick to notice his newly acquired friend Prashant's escapades in his house.

"Hey Prashant, how come you have a gymnasium in your house!. Ah I see, you have also opened training school at home itself; very encouraging indeed".

The two friends seemed to have become pals forever- a case of < true love at first sight>; long after having had lunch, the two pals were found enthusiastically continuing their conversation; perhaps sharing their life experiences abundantly mixed with jokes and laughter.

Parents and Pavan in particular were all delighted at this new friendship.

Niranjan to Indira: "Please permit me to address you as mummy and your husband as my daddy. At the first sight itself I have found my parents in you. I had been missing my life givers since their deaths two decades ago. I value my acquaintance with your enlightened family".

Parents: "Niranjan, you are welcome .It is our pleasure also".

Prashant: "Look Niranjan, I have been thinking of joining a software company where I can learn, contribute and of course, earn decently".

Niranjan: "Dear Prashant, I am quite impressed with your inroads into the IT field; you come out, join any company; there are empteen number of them for your asking. I am confident of your instant success with your self- acquired skills".

Prashant and family saw the guests off after late lunch. But the bon homie and the astounding success story of Niranjan thrilled the family resulting in long discussions, even after his exit, for the whole week.

Result of the first meeting was there for all to see. The next week itself Prashant had transmitted his bio data and CV to at least a dozen software enterprises. Such was the level of encouragement Prashant had received from Niranjan as further supplement to his already built up high morale. He continued to draw and store therein tremendous inspiration from many a great artists scientists, men of letters, freedom fighters and physically challenged personalities reaching Alpine heights in their chosen profession.

Who has not heard of :

1) the great Christopher Reeves –an American citizen nay, a citizen of the globe, who acted as <Superman> in comic series and who became a famed Hollywood star despite being confined to wheel chair due to a mishap

2) Stephen Hawking a British physicist of world fame despite his quadriplegic challenged condition

3) Commander Kohli of the Indian army who became wheel chair bound for life in military operations but who did not allow his enthusiasm and bravery to be effected a wee-bit and went on to climb, wheel chaired, the great Himalayas and reached fame of Himalayan heights.

4) The famous Indian Musician (vocalist) Madurai Mani Iyer who rose to become a house hold name across the sub-continent despite being completely vision handicapped; and the list of such eminent men and personalities who led their lives transforming all the way their physical handicap into assets to achieve glory and prosperity, name and fame remained endless in Prashant's dictionary.

With this fine self-discipline and encouraged to the hilt by his dear parents; very affectionate and highly attached dear younger brother Pavan, host of his relatives, well-wishers and friends; Prashant started applying his mind and soul into every task he assigned unto himself. So much adranalin flowed in his body, so much self-boosted his morale; so much fire he generated in his belly that there was no stopping him from venturing into any field. He read and re read books on great leaders including the father of our nation, including chacha Nehru, Sardar Vallabh Bhai Patel who earned the nick name of <Iron man of India> by his sheer devotion, love to his motherland; Babu Rajendra Prasad, Subhash Chandra Bose, martyrs Bhagat Singh, Chandra shekar Azad and Rajguru and scores of great sons and daughters who shaped destiny of our motherland.

He was intensely interested in sports, debating skills. He always looked all round for opportunities to be grabbed .**Luck would never desert the bold and the courageous**

PRASHANT LEADING HIMSELF ALL THE WAY

****

CHAPTER- XV

FRONT FOOT FORWARD ON PROGRESS PATH

Prashant was busy as usual with computer classes for business and his project work. The door bell rang. His mother Indira opened the door to Shivesh- Pavan's friend.

"Come in Shivesh what a surprise visit".

Shivesh: "Aunty I have come in a hurry to collect the book on VC++ which , I had lent to Pavan sometime back".

"You will get your book alright. By the time Pavan comes down with the book, hot steaming coffee will be ready please wait a bit": so said Indira

While waiting for the coffee, Shivesh saw a wheel chair roll out of a room. He was surprised to see Prashant on a wheelchair. Shivesh asked the obvious question to Prashant and got a very brief response from him. Shivesh was very disturbed that Pavan had not mentioned anything about his brother to him.

After a few moments, Pavan arrived and both set out to office, As they left the compound, shivesh could not control his emotions. He was touched seeing Prashant in great spirits inspite of his situation. At that very moment he promised Pavan that he will do whatever it takes to help Prashant.

In the coming weeks, Shivesh managed to get the whole story out of Pavan. He was soo impressed with Prashant's attitude and achievements that he took it as his responsibility to help Prashant t achieve his dreams of getting into the Software Industry.

Less than a month after Shivesh had met Prashant, he had managed to convince his close friend Sunil, a budding enterpreneur, to meet Prashant.

When Sunil came home to meet Prashant; very much to his surprise he encountered a beaming bright face sitting in wheel chair!. "Hi Pavan, who is this Sunlight in your house?" anxiously enquired Sunil.

Pavan; "I am happy to introduce my elder brother Prashant to You; please meet him".

Prashant welcomed the visitors.

Sunil: "Nice meeting you Prashant; I see you are surrounded with table top computers and computer books ; I take it that you are also a computer expert".

Pavan explained the entire background of his elder entering into the IT field.

"It is interesting indeed; I am pretty sure you must have mastered several computer languages" .

Prashant : "Teaching and learning are part and parcel of my life. Whereas I do teach freshers, I have learnt C,C+,VC languages at the APtech institute ;. A few more languages like JAVA, enterprise JAVA, I have learnt on my own" .

Sunil set aside his hurry for the moment and got into deep discussions with Prashant on various computer languages and the skills acquired by him thereof.

Finally Sunil expressed: "It is simply astounding that you have mastered several languages in such a short time; I think I found an electric live wire business partner in you, for my Coy. I am planning to conduct a seminar on< a new language > recently introduced by one American IT specialist-Mr. MOUBREY.

"As a matter of fact, the author of this new language Dr. Thomas J MOWBRAY is also expected to join the seminar. All big bosses of IT industry in the country have already planned for active participation. I offer you to speak as a free lance speaker (a wild- card entrant) in the seminar".

Prashant: "Dear Sunil, many thanks for your accolades; but I am quite apprehensive to straight away jump into the speaker's fray; I do not mind a listener job for me!"

Sunil reacting instantly, had this to say: "Oh my dear Prashant . I have gathered in this very first meeting of we two, that knowledge wise you are second to none; you have already graduated , as far as my assessment goes, from speaker- designate to speaker- professiona!. I have noticed that you are already close to the language <Corba>; it is a higher level application of JAVA and enterprise JAVA which are already in your acquired knowledge kitty. By tomorrow itself, the necessary reading material will be at your doors. I am quite upbeat about your preparations for the seminar within the next week itself": so complementing Sunil and Shivesh took leave.

Pavan "cajoled" his elder brother into accepting the wind fall offer to participate in the seminar.

Prashant: "Sunil appeared to have stormed into my life!. It was very nice of him to offer me straightaway, speakership role at a National level seminar being attended by experts and Chief Executives of many top IT companies. I am too raw even as a student to participate in such an important and high level seminar".

Mother Indira quipped encouragingly: "Dear, we all know, through your grit and determination that you are <second to none>; we are certainly proud of that status of yours; you are not participating in the seminar as any competitor; look at the same from other angle; it is an excellent opportunity for you to interact with luminaries in the field and in the process you will be richly benefited both in knowledge and skills. I bless you and pray to god to shower you with great success; do go ahead;. Do not lose this wind-fall opportunity".

Mom's encouraging words did seem to have profoundly influenced the young Prashant . Sunil promptly sent the necessary reading material and he started to prepare in right earnest even by burning < midnight oil> .

Came the auspicious day of 23 Jan 1998 (nearly 9years into traumatized life for the family). Prashant was wheeled into the conference hall at< hotel Capitol> Bangalore just adjacent to VIDHANA SOUDHA the seat of the Government of the state of Karnataka. Many luminaries in the IT field made their presentations before the August gathering. They were all well received; then came our dear Prashant's turn. At this juncture mother's anxiety knew no bounds; as a natural corollary she sent out her prayers to Almighty to bestow success on her son.

Sunil the organizer of the seminar introduced Prashant to the audience thus:

"Ladies and Gentlemen, you will now listen to a talk on<Corba language development for software solutions>. Mr. Prashant was a brilliant student of mechanical engineering; his career at the final engineering stage, was severely jolted by a medical grossly negligent non-consented major surgery that resulted in his confinement to wheel- chair lifelong. He had to spend five crucial years in hospital and in rehabilitation; notwithstanding this severe setback, he fought like a valiant solider and not only completed his engineering course with honors and distinction but also acquired professional computer programming skills through computer training lectures and also self-study. He is a freelancer. Now over to Prashant".

Once he entered the dais there was no stopping him.

He spoke, demonstrated his theme fluently through projecting charts on to the screen. Audience heard him with rapt attention .It was a highly knowledgeable dignitary audience from all companies in the IT Field. At the end of his hour long presentation, the enlightened audience gave the speaker a standing ovation for the highly practical rendering of a relatively new chapter in Information Technology.

Sunil proposing vote of thanks , had this to say: "Dear Prashant, you have held the huge audience of highly knowledgeable professionals in the IT industry spell bound by your skillful and absorbing talk ; it is all the more a greater achievement coming as it is from a freelancer. I am sure one and all present here share my thoughts".

"Yes" reciprocated in chorus the entire audience. Prashant's parents and his dear younger Pavan were all moved to tears at this great moment.;

He undoubtedly felt profoundly encouraged and thanked Sunil for having given him this wonderful encouragement and opportunity.

Sunil in reply "You have enhanced the prestige of the seminar organizers . It is we who have to thank you".

All returned home after dining out. Next morning, Prashant was in for even greater surprises!

Mother reading the morning newspaper rushed to her son: "You have done it. You have done it; front page has captured your fine moments of yesterday's seminar. The newspaper did not mince words in praising you and carried the headlines < Stephen Hawking of India> Prashant, wins the < Corba Professional Award of the year 1998/99> . The article paid rich tributes to you for the enlightened talk".

"The credit of my success goes mainly to Pavan and parental encouragement that always kept on boosting my morale and held me high on the pedestal" : thus he shared his joy with family members.

Hardly a week had elapsed there was a telephone call from Sunil.

"Hi, this is Sunil. The Award- < Corba Professional of the year > will be presented to you by the National IT Industry Chairman who has kindly accepted our invitation for the presentation ceremony. You have done us proud. We welcome you and your family for this great moment to receive this Award before an August gathering of giants in the IT field at the same venue as the seminar, exactly a week from now".

The newspaper coverage had drawn attention of many a chief executives in IT industry. Mr. Subramanyam CEO of < Covansys Bangalore > lost no time in registering himself for the glittering presentation ceremony .

Came 30th January 1999. Prashant with his family was present in time for the occasion. Many dignitaries had graced the occasion. Covansys Coy boss Mr. K.Subrahmanyam was promptly present. The All India IT industry Chief Executive inaugurated the ceremony with his eloquent tribute to the Awardee. While expressing his admiration he embraced Prashant and offered him an invite to join his team at Delhi in shaping and directing the future of software industry in the country.

Prashant in reply: "I am thankful to you Mr. President Sir, for the glittering offer. I seek your continued blessings. At the present juncture I am unable to leave my home town because the local doctors have drawn strict schedules of physio exercising; regular monitoring to prevent muscle wastages that invariably haunt all paraplegics.

Mr.K. Subramanyam who had turned a great fan of Prashant went on to heap eloquent tributes on him; offered him opportunity to join his team at Bangalore.

Thus opportunities knocked at the valiant professional's doors. It was a proud moment, moment of honour and recognition more glittering than gold; many such offers came knocking at his doors.

The next week itself Prashant received a call from CEO of MNC- Covansys: "Hi, Prashant, this is your well wisher KS (that is how I want you, Prashant, to address me); why don't you join me at our Airport road office for job placement discussions. Let my office know how you are arriving and at what time so that I can make arrangements to receive you into our office without any difficulty.

Prashant: "Sir, I am delighted at your call; surely my father will drive me to your establishment in our car. I will be carrying my wheel chair also; 2pm tomorrow suits me."

KS: "That would be fine; you are welcome".

Prashant had chosen to opt for this computer coy despite interview calls from Wipro and two other IT companies in Bangalore. The personal interest and affection shown by KS enabled Prashant to opt for this MNC.

Next day promptly we reached the gate of Covansys ltd on old Airport road. To our surprise the CEO himself was present at the gate to welcome us. "Welcome, welcome, Prashant; your father need not worry how to get you into the office".

So saying he embraced him and started moving the wheel chair himself right up to the lift door entrance. Such fine gestures from the top boss himself gave Prashant great encouragement.

KS introduced his Coy's Technical team to Prashant saying: "these 3 guys, our Coy's Technical Directors, will search your soul and brain deep alright. But I am pretty sure you will land up the other way around! ; Wish you all the best"; with these words he departed from the interview room and chose to give company to Seshadri.

KS went into deep conversation with the interview candidate's father: "Now you tell me how it all happened; how you parents and his younger brother have all managed to keep his morale so high? I am quite eager and anxious to know all about this gallant Prashant".

Seshadri explained the entire background right from his childhood till this traumatic stage due to botched up surgery; how he fought against all odds to complete his engineering degree at far off Machilipatnam; how he aligned himself to the IT software axis; how he started training novices in software programming skills and who alongside enhanced his own skills for taking up higher assignments.

Totally engrossed in these detailed narrations, KS came out with these remarks: "It is really a highly absorbing battle to come up trumps in life despite enforced physical challenges; your detailed narrations have captured my mind and soul; you have succeeded in giving interview before me on behalf of Prashant!".

"Prashant's composure and beaming smile and the glow in his eyes have impressed me about his in- built Capabilities at the first sight itself. Let us have some coffee before one of the 3 Technical Directors, reports to me on the outcome of his discussion with the young aspirant".

As the two of us started sipping coffee, Technical Director (TD) Mr Srinivasan came out of the interview room beaming with smile. Holding my hand he said "Mr seshadri, I am proud of your brilliant son; he has impressed me quite a lot".

An hour later yet another TD arrived in our midst and appraised his company's Chief Executive KS, about what went on inside during interview discussions with Prashant.

"Sir", he reported to his Coy's CEO - KS: "Prashant is Simply wonderful ; he will bring name to our institution".

Yet another hour passed; the last of the three Technical Directors arrived in our midst along with Prashant and reported to his Chief about the outcome of the interview.

Looking at the smiling faces of Srinivasan, Mathews and Venkatesh, KS summed up: "Your smiling faces are enough indicators about your impressions on Prashant and about my choice of the candidate for interview! Is it not? I am sure I have you threesome's sanction to announce to anxiously waiting father of Prashant, the result of your interviewing!!"

All three spoke very high of the candidate ; KS turning to Seshadri: " You have a diamond in your family; please part with that diamond for our company. Please wait a wee bit before we hand over the precious Appointment Order".

<Prashant came and conquered Covansys> all within a span of a few hours; had cornered the glorious appointment order the same night! This was his first job that opened the doors for earning handsome income.

Back home, Indira and Pavan had spent highly anxious moments all this while. On seeing the beaming faces of father and son, they were able to make out the results of the interview.

Mother to Prashant: "Congrats for your success".

Prashant: "Mummy , I have not even announced the result; how come you have guessed right!".

"My confidence in your capabilities apart, your beaming smile has given you out": patted mother smilingly

Prashant's father: "Yes, you have rightly forecast. Now prepare his avowed weakness for < cocoanut burfi >; let us celebrate his success with it".

The Chief Executive (Mr KS) had left no stone unturned to make his new entrant's work place totally wheel- chair friendly; overnight ramps were built alongside steps and raised floor levels; approaches from one office room to others to conference halls, library, canteen, play area for recreations were all suitably modified.

And when Prashant did arrive for his first working day, he had no difficulty in reaching his work place at the number –seven floor from lift. This gesture itself had boosted his morale; Giving him a rousing welcome, KS introduced Prashant to all fellow employees, peers and senior executives. The benign working atmosphere was totally in contrast with the enforced hospital atmosphere and style, he was forced into, all these years. This was instrumental in bringing back the childhood dynamism and enthusiasm.

Prashant was blessed with a decent job alright. But it was no easy cake walk to the parents in readying him to leave for the office! after attending to all the mandatory requirements .

It was a rigorous preparatory duty for his mother in the kitchen as well; being wheel- chaired Prashant's restricted movements demanded care and caution even in his diet food intake, meticulously balancing intake of proteins, carbohydrates, fats in order to avoid increase in weight; to maintain hemoglobin levels, blood sugar levels in short to keep him fit like a fiddle, as an equally mandatory necessity.

The morning had just not started as yet but so much activities around him mandated!.All these had to be gone through smilingly and dutifully.

Pavan would start playing on the flute in different ragas set to mis- matching "taals" to wake up his elder!.

Prashant: "Dear me, I am already awake ; You are trying to send me to sleep again with your <marvelous> rendering on the flute!". The entire morning environment was thus kept vibrant and jolly

Prashant was game for all these. We all foursome in the family could maintain this happy disposition Continuously for days, weeks, months and years on end.. Music in the background always set the tone for all activities till he was transferred to waiting car.

The car had been suitably modified, altered to enable his easy entry into and exit from the automobile which he had expertly mastered all by himself with small assistance from outside. All these stresses and strains of shifting and travelling also became a routine; he would gladly attend to his work.

The first to greet him, daily, was no other than KS himself. "Good morning Prashant! Are you comfortable? How is the project progressing?".

Prashant would explain the previous day's work done

and the day's planned tasks. KS would thus enquire, encourage his beloved employee and leave for his work after patting him on his back.

Once he sat in front of the computer, there was no disturbing him; he would be lost in work unmindful of environs around.

With his positive approach to work, he would start with his team mates on the tasks set for the day; and then briefly discuss the plans to take the project further and subsequently concentrate on his own assignment. This routine was followed religiously regularly.

This method of working endeared him to one and all, enthusing them to give out their best.

This did not go unnoticed by his seniors either.. His slogan < Work smilingly; See the results for yourselves > caught the imagination of all his team mates and created a very positive working environment. And when it came to lunch break, there was no discussion on work but only relaxing, sharing jokes; thus making the break hour lively and worry free.

The stress of working continuously had to be taken off with periodic breaks for sipping coffee. And the 10- minutes' period immediately before lunch break, was utilized by one and all for performing light exercises which helped everybody to relax. This also did not go unnoticed as one of the measures for increasing productivity at work. Working became a pleasure to one and all.

****

CHAPTER-XVI

ON DEPUTATION TO SINGAPORE

One fine day KS approached Prashant's table; and wished him "Good morning, good news".

Prashant: "With your encouragement, mornings will always be good sir. But curious as I am, what is the good news?"

KS: "Your predecessor had tried his best to crack at the most demanding customer from Singapore, namely, Citi- bank. I thought you would fit into his shoes and do your utmost to please that VIP customer for us. How about that change?"

Prashant: "I am always ready to face challenges sir. Doctors from IMS Hyderabad have already challenged my very posture!; I shall give it a fair trial" .

KS: "That is the spirit; I have already talked to our officer at Singapore to ascertain if the entire premises are suitable for you. I am happy to share with you the glad message from him that the entire Singapore city is physically challenged friendly; roads, rail, buses, taxis, residential places public parks included.

Prashant: "The assignment proposed for me at Singapore is simply exhilarating, but, sir, what about meeting my requirements of medical services; medical attention which are mandatory (enforced)?".

KS: "Oh! You need not worry about all these pre- office and post- office activities; we are fully aware of the tremendous care and attention being given to you by your devoted parents day in and day out. As they happen to be the fittest and most appropriate 'attendants' to be standing by you, Your employer Company will take care of their journey and stay at Singapore".

Prashant: "I am overwhelmed with the company's attention to minutest details of my requirements; I shall deem it an honour to take up this assignment as our company's prestige".

KS: "I knew you would respond positively for this new assignment. Citi- Bank Singapore is a highly respected customer of ours but equally tough demanding quality results without even a day's deviation from contracted time frame. I am confident you would do well to share this onerous responsibility".

Accordingly visa permits for Prashant as well as for his parents, travel arrangement with insurance coverage and stay were all meticulously arranged through the Coy's liaison officer stationed at Singapore. He was one of few employees who had been honoured with higher assignments and responsibilities in such a short time.

Prashant returned home with so much good news tucked under his seat. Giving his customary trade mark smile to mother: "mummy there is good news for all in the family!".

Anxious mother: "Your face is trying to give out something!! What is it? Come on; don't keep me in suspense?"

Prashant holding his mummy's left palm in his hand went on: "Oh mom!. This life line in your palm indicates change of residence for you very soon. You see I have become a palmist/ astrologer".

Indira: "What change of residence? Dear ; we have built this house and occupied it only a fortnight back. Your astrology is at least a fortnight behind!!".

Prashant: "I am reading your palm into future and not the past. Do you get me mom?".

"Then come out! Don't keep me in suspense any further!!" said mom.

Prashant at long last, broke the glad tidings. Pavan returned home late in the evening . While sipping coffee, he (Pavan) came to know of the Singapore trip. He was also equally overjoyed and raised the question of occupancy of the newly built house during our trip abroad.

Prashant: "Don't worry folks. My close friend, recently married, is searching for renting an accommodation. He will take good care of our residence. So let us offer him our residence till we return back.

The grand day arrived. It was a very happy moment for Prashant at his Bangalore city office when he was given a highly affectionate sendoff headed by no less a dignitary than the CEO himself. His immediate seniors and peers were present to see him off at the airport.

Air India, the winged carrier, had taken notice of their special passenger and made all arrangements to ensure that he was boarded into the aircraft comfortably with seat selected carefully at the door entrance. An aisle seat had been chosen to enable the passenger to be transferred comfortably and conveniently from corridor- friendly wheel chair.

In less than 4 hours we had landed smoothly at Singapore International Airport. It was a pleasant treat for Prashant's eyes which, had, unfortunately got used to hospital beds and environs. The liaison officer stationed at Singapore was there to welcome us all. Soon we were on our way to hotel where accommodation had been arranged. It was a delightful drive from airport to hotel in a highly equipped taxi.

This taxi, pseudo named 'luxury London Taxi', had special features as different from normal cabs. High roof passengers' cabin area designed perhaps, for the very proud, conservative and immaculately dressed English man and his counterpart- the English Lady to enter the cab without taking off their customary head gear!.

(After all who does not know the conservative English who traditionally refuse to take off hats(lady or gent irrespective of) in public but who deem it, a sign of honour, a sign of admiration for the opposite sex to take it out and put it back at the <appointed place in the human frame> namely on the head!!

Further, and most importantly from our dear Prashant's special requirements point of view, this luxury taxi had a telescopic sliding foot rest that could be slided on to the road pavement from car floor to enable the passenger to be wheeled in/ wheeled out and retracted into the car floor during journeying.

On arrival at the hotel we were ushered in with all hospitality and soon found ourselves relaxing inside the spacious room.

Prashant started his work from the next day itself. The same <luxury London taxi> was booked for enabling him to reach office a full 10km away from the hotel.

When the taxi reported at the hotel, we were pleasantly surprised to see the same Mr Yoe at the wheels who had brought us from the airport the previous day.

Yeo: "Oh! La la! You are the same yesterday's passengers!".

Prashant: "Yes, Mr. Yeo, I could recollect you and your jokes during yesterday's drive. Can you please take me (accompanied by my parents) to the central business district area's most popular < millennium towers > where my client- Citi bank's office is accommodated".

Yeo: "It would be my pleasure La (by now we had got used to the suffix "La" by most Chinese citizens during their conversation!!); don't worry La ; I will reach you safely with you securely seated in your wheel chair itself inside the cab!!. Duly assisted by Yeo, Seshadri ushered in Prashant seated in wheel chair, into the cab. The retractable telescopically sliding foot rest came in very handy for easy entry in to and later, out of the cab.

Yeo: "Oh la! Your destination has come la". So uttering he immediately came round to the back door; slided the foot rest onto the <millennium plaza> pavement and gently brought his VIP passenger down.

Thanking Mr. Yeo, Prashant told he would call him in the evening for returning to hotel after work .

Yeo assured he will promptly report within half hour on receiving phone call.

Prashant: "I would be very happy to take your help daily for both ways journeying".

Yeo: "you just have to call me 20-30 minutes before you wish to start back. This would be the permanent arrangement from your hotel/ residence to office and back".

Prashant: "Daddy, did you notice foot path very wheel chair friendly. I think I should be able to manage all by myself". So saying he wheeled himself right up to the millennium towers and as the glass doors opened by themselves (optically controlled) he could reach the lift entrance straight away. It was a pleasing experience from there on because he could also enter the lift and reach his designated office on the 21st floor all unaided.

From cab to the work place he managed all by himself unaided; totally exhilarating experience indeed.

Promptly arrived the CEO of Citi- bank and greeted Prashant in customary Chinese style and introducing him to his colleagues: "Here is your new colleague from the Indian sub continent. Let us all give him a warm welcome".

Prashant cheerfully acknowledged the warm welcome from his colleagues: "teaming with my already present colleagues Raghu Ram and Dileep, we will all strive to make the project a resounding success".

And here at the work spot he would open out his heart and mind on a scale befitting the efforts put into him, It did not require even a week's time for him to adjust quickly to the new environment and he started off meticulously displaying his total dedication to work at City bank. Colleagues all- including Indians, Chinese, Malays, and Americans created lively productive ambience through their love, affection and respect for the brave soldier. This boosted his morale sky high; created a positive atmosphere to bring out the best in him.

It was time to move away from hotel to a cosy home atmosphere.

Deepu (Prashant's colleague): "Prashant , we will hire a 3 bed room apartment so that your family and my family can stay together sharing all house hold duties. Further I could be of some help to assist your father in carrying out your daily mandatory tasks".

Prashant: "Dear Deepu, it is a welcome suggestion. Let us go ahead".

A spacious 3 bed room accommodation was fixed on the prominent Rangoon Road with the help of local estate agent.

The lady owner- a Chinese citizen, welcomed us all to her apartment but expressed a small concern.

Indira to the flat owner: "you are free to express your Concern".

Owner: "How many times a week you use the kitchen?".

Shell shocked Indira replied: "Why this concern! We are used to cooking each of the 3 meals whether breakfast, lunch or dinner, daily".

Owner: "Oh my god! I just cannot believe. Do you mean to say you spend nearly six hours a day in the kitchen !".

Indira: "If guests like you arrive in our midst, six hours are just not sufficient! Kitchen activity may go on even upto 10 hours at a stretch per day!".

"We Chinese in general, hardly put the kitchen to use once or at best twice a week!"

"This is the "newest" news to me. How do you manage then the minimum three meals daily?"

Owner: "Oh! Our husbands enjoy food outside and we do not like to be left behind in the kitchen. Scattered around each locality there are restaurants by the dozens. They offer clean food you see!"

Indira: "I see your point; but do not worry about the up keep in the kitchen; we are used to maintaining it spic and span and no less cleanly than the drawing room or the guest room".

Owner: "Oh! You have answered my worry; wish you good luck and happy stay in my house. I hope you do not mind my periodic inspection visits!!"

Indira: "You are most welcome as my guest".

A new environment at Singapore? Anew set up? Anew set of readjustment in life style? Certainly not for Prashant or for his parents. What adaptations had taken place since his taking up the jobs in India came good here also. There was no difficulty to continue life in this metro city. After all, parents who stood by him 24hours a day, were always by his side and the new home had all the arrangements in continuation as at Bangalore back in India.

Prashant in a chat with mother: "I have noticed during my daily drive to office and back that the local government has taken care to ensure that even private and public buildings are physically- challenged friendly; not to speak of roads, foot paths. So it is quite easy for me to go places effortlessly through lifts/ ramps.

Mother: "We both spend our leisure hours, as you are away on work duty, walking around our locality, travelling around in local transport; we have also noticed the special concern shown by the local government in making the whole city wheel- chair friendly".

"When you come back home, you can relax in the nearby parks or spend hours in the super market, shopping at all floor levels which you always loved to do!"

Singapore, to our dear Prashant was a second home away from home. He got used to travelling to office and back home all by himself without father's escorting him. Either Yeo or Rita would take care of him excellently. Thus encouraged to the hilt, Prashant would put in 10-12 hours of work a day and return home smilingly looking always relaxed.

"Hai Prashant, how come you return home after 12 hours work beaming with smile and looking fresh as if you are ready to go to office again!. I return home damn tired to the bone !" so shared Dileep his daily routine.

Prashant : "Daddy shall We start with physio- exercising ?; after all I have been sitting all through the day at office".

Dileep overhearing this conversation exclaimed: "Oh my god, where from you get this extra shot of energy and that too at the end of a tiresome day! ?"

Prashant's father answering Dileep's anxiety: "your surprise is but natural. But the mandatory medical attention requirements pre, peri and post working hours have trained and trimmed Prashant to be ever active"!

While father was busy exercising; mother and Pooja (Deepu's better half) would be engaged in the kitchen for preparing delicious north Indian and south Indian dishes for dinner. Then we would all assemble for dinner. Lo! Jokes galore! Sharing of new experiences galore!

Prashant: "Hai Deepu, did you notice small heaps of oranges there all along our drive to the office? I was tempted to stop the car and collect them for morning breakfast!"

Dileep laughed loudly: "When I had arrived at Singapore earlier than you , I was also tempted and did not hesitate to pick up at least 3 heaps by the road side; no body prevented me either".

Prashant: "You stopped on the roadside!. But here I am, getting tempted with oranges each day offered by the office boy as I enter my office for work!".

Dileep: "And what did you do with those oranges?"

Prashant: "why this question?. They were given to me and I gladly relished eating them".

Dileep laughing aloud: "My goodness gracious! You know why the orange was given to you? It was given to you to offer it to ghosts at every nook and corner of our office. This month is called the < month of ghosts >. It is a Chinese practice to appease ghosts with such offers and beget their blessings in return".

"If you have eaten that orange then please bless me as ghost!". All of us had a hearty laugh at the dining table; life was tuned for ever with laughter. After all "laughter is the best medicine".

Prashant did not let go his spare time to be wasted. He planned sightseeing in and around Singapore.

Prashant: "Hai Deepu, next time when we return from office let us visit the < Intourist> office to ascertain the places of tourists' attraction. We can plan to visit them one by one during each week end".

Dileep: "I have collected already brochures of all tourist spots; shall we plan to visit <the indoor culture beehive named Duran>; the <indoor stadium>; the famous Japanese gardens; the equally famous <bird park>

Prashant: I have heard of a famous Indian by name Mustafa who has pioneered and painstakingly built a big market enclave starting from selling goods on roadside. Today it is a land mark of Singapore; that great bazaar popularly known as < the Mustafa> offers ease of access at all floors to my wheel- chair, offering all articles of use from electronic goods to provisions to dress material to gymnastic paraphernalia.

In less than six weeks he had carved out a covenanted place for himself. On a fine day the CEO sprang a surprise by visiting Prashant at his work table. "Hi Prashant we are very much pleased with your total dedication. The project has gained tremendous momentum with your efforts; keep it up; I want you to guide yet another project simultaneously with another team. I know that additional responsibility is no any burden for you".

Prashant: "I am honored with your offer. I would put in my best sir".

CEO: "you will be given an international mix of team mates for the additional project; you can start off from the next week itself".

Prashant handled both the projects deftly; simultaneously much to the admiration of the City Bank Management.

It was indeed a tough job to please a demanding customer like City Bank .

<City Bank never sleeps > so went the proud slogan. But < City Bank never allows its employees to sleep be either > < would the complete working scenario> so claimed the employees!.

Success flowed into Prashant's path .

The CEO was all praise for his work; He sprang a surprise:"Dear Prashant, we want you to join us permanently on our rolls .you can guide a number of ambitious projects"

Prashant " Sir ,I feel highly honored with the offer . I have to return to my employer at Bangalore, India to take up equally important projects for which the Local Management has already drafted me in advance. Moreover I have to pursue the already established rehabilitation activities that had to be given a break in view of this present assignment here".

Where majority would have, in all probability, grabbed the attractive offer, Prashant had deep rooted responsibilities of his professional ethics in not deserting the parent company. Seven months of stay at Singapore had enriched him in all fronts including his professional skills. In the midst of busy work schedule he had carved out time to visit all important places in Singapore.

All had left lasting impressions on him. On the day of returning to his mother land, Yeo was there at the wheels to take him to the airport. Prashant was used to interesting discussions with both Yeo and Rita while driving to office and back. They both were highly informed personalities, widely travelled allrounders.

Rita the stop gap driving help, in particular had so much in common with Prashant. She had been a software engineer prior to taking up this < road adventurous profession > of driving her own taxi!

She would profusely share her past experiences. Suddenly these happy driving moments came to a halt. Both were very depressed and morose at Prashant's departure from Singapore. Quite an interesting and nonstop speaker as Yeo was, today he was quiet, simply driving without a word coming out of his mouth.

Prashant: "Yeo, I am missing your jokes very much. This "white elephant", as you had nick named me, is saddened with your silence. Why la!?"

Yeo, pointing to the speaking parrot gifted to him by Prashant said: "today you are going away la?; so I am speechless but the parrot will speak la". We all easily gauged the depth of his emotions. He was not only speechless but tears had been rolling down his cheeks.

Prashant ever readily carved out deep impressions on each and every person he came across; Yeo and Rita were no exceptions.

****

CHAPTER- XVII

BACK HOME IN INDIA

Prashant had gained good lot of experience of the Outside world. Living in most friendly Singapore city, he had let go his mind to enter and acquire various cultural and extra-curricular hobbies and went on to add photography, bird watching to his already existing list. Back home he started looking to pursue his acquired hobbies. But alas!, conditions around in cities and towns left much to be desired. Having travelled with all wheel chair disabled friendly facilities in Singapore he had difficulties back home. However his parents, dear younger brother and the family chauffeur were there available handy to take him places all around

He decided to take up the <cause of the differently abled > having facilities for visiting public places, parks as noticed and enjoyed by him at Singapore.

One day he straight away drove to the city administration office and sought appointment with the Chairman of the City Borough.

Chairman: "come on in Mr. Prashant. What can I do?"

Prashant: "I have come to live permanently in Bangalore. But I find differently- ableds like me encounter good lot of difficulties to criss -cross city public places, parks and other facilities without an attendant's help. Although I am fortunate to have people around me to help me out, what about scores of other similarly challenged persons? I thought if necessary you would visit Singapore our neighboring country.

Everything is friendly there, whether it is entering a public transport vehicle such as buses, trains, even taxis or visiting public places shops, hospitals, play areas, cinema halls, market places.

It certainly does not cost any big fortune to provide these small little facilities nor do they require any Einstein brain (to design and produce such facilities).

Chairman of City Borough: "I appreciate your initiative and thoughts. We had been thinking on similar lines for quite some time now".

Prashant: " Building a ramp alongside flight of stairs in bus stations, railway stations and all such public places, dedicated lifts for reaching different floor levels all by themselves, sliding platforms from bus entrance to road level to help wheel chaired to reach the inside of the bus from street pavements vice versa are only a few examples of numerous facilities provided as a matter of factly in the great city of Singapore. I had the pleasure of visiting Germany, France, Italy, and Switzerland where all public facilities are most friendly to all differently abled persons. What we require is the will to create such tailored facilities; what is called for is EMPATHY and certainly NOT SYMPATHY"

Chairman of City Borough: "Your suggestions are highly motivating; we will carry forward your thoughts and start translating them into action sooner than later".

"We would be delighted to have you in our midst at the same office next month enjoying the ramp along office entrances, optical delay operated door entrances etc. Keep in touch as our city's proud citizen".

Prashant: "Please make my Country proud by providing such facilities. After all our motherland is second to none in industrial progress and economic growth".

Chairman: "You are most welcome any time; we are indeed proud of you".

Prashant conveniently included such social services in his daily/ weekly agenda. The Singapore visit had been a shot in his arm and he was always upbeat whether at office or off duty hours. Back at Covansys in India, he was all exuberance personified. The Top Management was game for all his brilliant suggestions whether on work procedures or involvement of personnel for company's faster growth or the enhanced friendly working environment and culture, and received them well and acted upon willingly at god speed.

Fire in the belly, his suggestion on < deliniation of responsibilities> for completion of the projects and assignments in time was yet another well received and implemented suggestion, duly demonstrated in his work also.(After all, software industry's watch word is<timely complete the project or else cough up heavy penalties >).

He looked 360 degrees around always and did not necessarily direct his thoughts only on work and work. He introduced light, short exercising schedules during appointed periods immediately preceding lunch break and evening tea break. Lo!,these thoughts duly implemented, with the Management's approvals had salutary effect on high productivity. An employee undoubtedly brings out the best in him when the Management provides him a relaxed environment for dedicated work.

By such suggestions Prashant created a win- win situation both for the Management and for himself and employees. His alert CEO boss did not fail to notice his escapades into higher productivity at work. On a fine day he walked to his work table to announce:"Dear Prashant, here is good news for you. You are going to Madras where our head office is located".

"Sir may I know the tasks for me at our head office!!": exclaimed Prashant.

The CEO: "You have done our company proud; you will go over to H.O to receive the coveted < Best employee of the Decade> Award".

Prashant: "Sir, award for the best employee in a decade!!; But I have just completed only five years of service in Covansys".

CEO: "We are aware of that; you are most deserving of it even then".

Prashant: "I am honoured sir, I need permissions for my younger brother to accompany me".

CEO: " Undoubtedly travel arrangements are already made for both of you for next week itself."

Prashant shared these glad tidings with his colleagues who were all thrilled at the honour being bestowed on him much earlier than the scheduled decade.

All colleagues in chorus: "Dear Prashant you richly deserved the honour".

Prashant: "I must acknowledge it was not possible without your cooperation. After all it is only team work".

 Back home after day's work, he thought it fit to share first with his parents and his affectionate younger brother.

As Pavan received him at the main gate, Prashant had this to say: "Hai look, I have some good news for the family; you have to accompany me to Chennai this coming Monday!".

Pavan expressing his surprise enquired: "Hai, what is this good news!"

Prashant: "CEO of my Coy called on me at my work table and announced the happy recognition of my work declaring that I have been conferred < the Best Employee of the Decade> honour , although I have completed 5 years i,e,; half a decade only".

Pavan: "That is greats!. This recognition has come to you through your hard devoted and intelligent work. Right now I am starting my preparations for the journey".

"Look mom, look dad, Prashant has brought one of the 'pleasantest' news for our family".

Prashant's mother: "From the kitchen itself I have overheard you two brothers conversing; hearty congrats to you dears both , for the well deserved gift".

Seshadri chipped in: "There cannot be any gladder news. We both parents knew confidently that hard efforts put in do not go in vain and will always, as rule, stand rewarded. We are all proud of your achievements".

As scheduled the two brothers reached Madras by air and a little later reached the Head office of the company.

There were surprises in store for him! CEO the affectionate Mr. KS, had readied himself to receive Prashant and greeting him affectionately had this to say: "I am proud to welcome you for the Award ceremony; come on in, you can refresh yourselves at the guest room a bit and proceed straight to the main hall".

The two brothers quickly refreshed themselves and soon presented before the August gathering. The kindly Mr. KS was there to welcome Prashant on to the dais and introducing him:"Ladies and gentlemen, I am happy to introduce to you; our company's chief architect who has brought glory and laurels in such a short time. What it required a full ten years, Prashant has achieved the name and fame in less than half that time. He has demonstrated to one and all what highly productive devoted work can achieve".

"In his short stint with our very demanding and highly prestigious customer namely Citi Bank Singapore, Prashant has come up trumps. It is no secret that Citi Bank straight away had offered him their Management

Cadre job during his stay at Singapore Chairman of the company, visiting Directors from the Corporate Office (head quartered at New York City), all took turns to greet and honour their VIP guest for the day. It was a great day in PRASHANT's life but more memorable in the back ground of the obstacles, hardships he smilingly overcame. How did he do it?

Prashant's life had always been aligned with surprises and happy events despite his physically challenged condition. One of the many happy incidents in his life was an announcement by Pavan, his younger brother, about his having befriended a smart beautiful girl named Swetha during his sojourn abroad.

Lo , Prashant was quick to pull his legs : "You fellow,you were reluctant to go abroad on deputation because you did not want to leave me alone .Now you are giving us the gladdest on earth news about how you are 'hooked' by a beauty. Well, well, first of all accept our heartiest congratulations".

Swetha took the first opportunity to visit the family at Singapore where Prashant had gone on deputation from his Coy.

The first to welcome Swetha into the family was dear Prashant himself : "I was feeling our family is incomplete without a girl Now I feel god has favoured me with a beautiful sister."

Swetha responded : " I am only too happy to join your family ; I have heard all about your steadfastness, determination and achievements even from wheel chair from Pavan. I look upon you as my guide and inspiring brother"

Prashant's similar escapades into life with absolutely open mind and happy disposition are countless indeed.

The other day ,when the young   Pavan & Swetha couple were blessed with a new addition ,it was again Prashant who took the lead in expressing the family's joy and went on to christen the baby girl <Tejal Nidhi> (meaning 'Beam of light'of the family & 'Treasure' of the family)

And when the second child was born to Pavan-Swetha couple , he, the same ever smiling Prashant was the first to greet his nephiew-a baby boy, and christen him

< Roshan Dhruv > meaning 'Brilliance' and ' Pole Star'

Prashant , by virtue of his broad outlook, went ON and ON in LIFE unstoppable

****

CHAPTER- XVIII

OBSTACLES TURNING STEPPING STONES FOR SUCCEEDING IN LIFE

Behind these great moments of glory; behind the smiling face, Prashant went on to write history, history of rock solid determination to overcome obstacles, impediments in the path of his progress.

As if not to be out done, there have been empteen number of instances and incidences which could have proved nightmarish to one and all, except Prashant of course.

One of those pre-employment days, Prashant and family were on a trip to Chennai for medical consultations with a well-established center for neurosciences. As we settled in our berths in the reserved compartment of the Hyderabad Chennai super-fast express train, there came dashing a fellow passenger of our train at the last moment. Entered, he, hot headedly, summoned the ticket examiner on duty from the adjacent bogie and seriously questioned the railways official "How do you expect me to travel with this handicapped passenger with his paraphernalia of wheelchair, back rest etc.;".

The ticket examiner coolly replied: "he also has a berth

in the same coach reserved weeks earlier. What is your worry? What is your problem?"

Not the one to give up easily, the hot headed passenger retorted: "how do you officials mix up normal and handicapped passengers in the same coach and went on further to add "you better shift him to other coach". Prashant listened to all these orations alright, but gave one smile at the agitated fellow traveler and went into silent mode. Parents of Prashant , the ticket examining railway official all remained cool and chose to answer the agitated passenger's queries.

Abruptly came yet another shot from the agitated mouth!. This time it was more funny: "Mr. Railway official, would you shift the wheel chair passenger to other coach or shall I pull the chain to prevent the train from steaming off!!"

The Railway official lost his cool and in no time ordered him to leave the train forthwith. Otherwise we will throw your luggage out of the coach and hand you over to the railway protection force on charges of disruption of peace, obstruction of movement of train. You will not be accommodated in any reserved coach either.

Prashant's father coolly addressing the agitated passenger advised him: "you are fluttering your feathers for no fault of any one in the coach except perhaps yourself at the wrong end; take it calmly and have a pleasant journey yourselves allowing others also to enjoy the journey".

Heated outbursts apart, a dignified strong willed gentleman citizen like Prashant, did not deserve to be in the company of such lunatics. Admiring was the way he faced off this incident and many more beyond count!.

Yet another incident that < cockled the brains > of even steadfast, strong willed personalities cannot go unwritten!

But again, It was however, no cake walk into the professional field for dear Prashant. Quite often in the day he would express: "I am proposing to work outside instead of sitting and doing projects at home".

Seshadri: "your ideas are simply marvelous; you have the knowledge and wherewithal to take up challenging assignments .I will speak to a few of our family friends for your entry into professional field. Pavan and his father lost no time in locating a private entrepreneur having his set up within 5km radius from our home. Promptly Prashant was invited for discussions on placement within his organization; the very next day he wheeled himself inside the interview room for discussions, as parents sat outside anxiously waiting for outcome.

Sreenivas , the CEO of the IT company came out: " your son has done extremely well in placement discussions. He is highly knowledgeable. I would like to consult with my business partner to decide on the project. I will get back to you within a day or two" ; promptly our Srinivas came back on phone and addressing Prashant's father: "Mr.Seshadri you see, my working business partner was also pleased with your son's performance during discussions. But…."

Seshadri: "why this <but> is coming in your way".

Srinivas: " Mr. Seshadri, you see my partner feels that Prashant's working from wheel chair would be a distraction and disturbance to all in the company. .Ours is a small company that would be easily tempted to enter into protracted dialogues /discussions every now and then with Prashant as to how it all happened to him".

Seshadri: "Good reasoning to reject a talent! Well, that is your decision to let Prashant into your company or not. But Mr. Srinivas! Don't you realize you have done a great disservice to yourselves by allowing your mind and thoughts to differentiate a person from his/her physically challenged condition even without verifying <how tall Prashant is in his profession!>".

"Well, certainly do not bother to rethink. We ourselves would not like to serve in such an environment headed by misconstrued thoughts; thank you for all the troubles taken in assessing the candidate" so uttering father wheeled out his dear son Prashant to his car parked outside.

Dear readers! Could you guess what was the reaction from Prashant? He simply said: "you have replied the company boss most fittingly. Let us not be here even for an extra moment! Daddy"!

Disappointments had no place in Prashant's personal diary!. Hell bent to overcome obstacles, he moved on, utilizing each obstacle as stepping stone to success.

On yet another sunny day, father sounded his dear son Whether he would like to work on a specific IT application field called <SAP> in a reputed IT firm. Always game for new attempts, he readily agreed to go over for discussions with the international IT company located within 10km radius from his residence.

Seshadri decided however to deal the job - search exercise differently. He straight away drove all alone to Roberts IT systems located 10km away from our residence.

Meeting the Human Resources development boss of that coy in her cabin (she happened to be a lady;): "Madam Sujatha Rao ,I am glad to introduce myself as father of one dear Prashant who has qualified himself in the IT field. He is well informed in VC, VC++, Java applications. Here are his CV/ bio-data . He is a keen learner and has fire in the belly to achieve milestones in his career. He is quite agile in his motorized wheel chair and has travelled extensively in the country. He does not allow the wheel chair confined position to interfere with his ambitions to be a top professional in the IT field. He can travel widely without any hindrance being assisted by his car driver whenever needed".

"Please do go through his CV/ bio data and feel free to invite him for discussions on placement in your company at your earliest convenience": So saying Seshadri gave all the contact details including e-mail Id and took leave of Madame Rao for the day.

The family promptly received the much expected phone call the very next day from Sujatha Rao of <Roberts IT systems>

Sujatha Rao: "Mr.Seshadri you see, our working team of experts has perused the bio data of your son -Mr. Prashant; they are very pleased to get into discussions with him. But we in the HRD have some queries about his wheelchair sitting postures".

Seshadri on the other side of line;. "Your query is a bit surprising to us all ; seated in wheel chair he can access every nook and corner of any premises provided of course, these premises are physically differently abled friendly; requires nothing more to deliver results as he has learnt to lead on his own prowess.

Best way is to have discussions with him in his computer management skills and have your own assessment of his personality.

Sujatha Rao: "But Mr. Seshadri, you see, we may find it difficult to provide access to wheel chair at all locations including library, conference hall. Moreover he may be required to put in 10-12 hours of efforts every day; also go over to our customers' premises for discussions on the projects."

Seshadri: "Madame Sujatha Rao, I think you have started interviewing the wrong candidate! . As I told you, your interview team should have the first hand assessment of the candidate. But you seem to be putting your wrong foot forward more particularly so coming from a human resources development officer!. I wonder whether your enlightened company's Top Management shared your views; so let us call it 'quits' at this stage itself. We are not interested in joining such a team with such closeted minds; perhaps you may repent for your mis-thoughts some time later in your life .So saying, he took leave of the HRD self styled genius. Although Prashant was not told of all these negative thoughts of HRD officer, he managed to read his daddy's mind!!.And the ever alert highly balanced personality, took it all in his stride without a single comment!.

That was the stuff he was made of; he had made himself of; < **come what may! Stop not! Reach your goal utilizing the divine traits gifted by HIM, the Almighty God to every being humans included!** >. These principles always guided him even from his childhood.

His family apart, doctors and other medical personnel who were in constant touch with Prashant also did not fail to notice the enthusiasm in him, the fire in his belly to move forward despite obstacles on the way. In fact, quite often the doctors would invite him to their wards for counselling the depressed patients because of their physically challenged conditions. Such gestures had high impact on them; boosted their morale resulting in achieving their goals

****

CHAPTER- XIX

CLIMBING THE LADDER

He was always on the lookout for assignments even more challenging and even more rewarding. It was his ambition to reach for greater name and fame in the software industry although a designer's job also fitted into his profile all right

He had heard a good lot about another multinational company namely "Infosys Technologies" doing excellent business in the IT industry, besides offering challenging opportunities of growth. When he e-mailed his CV and bio data to <Infosys Technologies> for possible openings into that company, he was immediately contacted and invited for a detailed technical discussion < at **his** earliest convenience>.

With the traditional smile duly displayed, he approached his mother to break the good news. "Mom, by next weekend, I should be proudly entering into an MNC company with vast avenues for faster development. I am seeking a change for higher responsibilities and attendant higher emoluments, and keen to make up the times and remunerations I have inevitably lost hitherto".

"Dear, I am confident of your success in life and even more confident of your making- up the decades of professional growth you have been compelled to lose due to enforced physical challenges and enforced year on year hospitalization. Bless you, go and attend the interview and come out with flying colors": mom managed a broad smile despite tears rolling down her cheeks.

"With Pavan and you parents always around, I can sky-rocket to success"; so uttering, he wheeled closer to his mom and instantly wiped off her tears and gave her a big smile.

The very next morning he received an invite for technical discussions with the MNC's Top Technical team. Pavan the younger, drove his brother to the MNC and promptly ushered him into the conference room.

"Best of luck dear": so, he wished him with anxiety writ large on his (Pavan's) face [as also his father's]. At the end of nearly 2 hours Prashant came out of the conference room promptly wheeled out by the Technical Team Member himself. Father and younger son were quick to receive their VIP family member and lost no time in profusely thanking the Member for his fine gesture in wheeling out Prashant. "Oh!, Don't mention any thanks": smilingly replied the Coy Executive. "It is our privilege to <have caught the rarest of rare fish in the IT profession>. He is welcome to join our Management team from today itself ".

"He will be looked after and cared for with all attention to all his elementary needs and compulsions".

Prashant returned home after the technical interview and straight away wheeled himself into the kitchen knowing full well, mummy must be busy preparing delicacies for him.

"Mummy, I have a big surprise for you: close your eyes"

Mom, promptly obeying her dear son's commands opened her eyes only an instant later, Lo! What did she see in her palm?: her dear son's appointment letter and box of sweets!!!.

"Astounding dear sonny, the appointment letter that is!. In one go you have made good all losses in salary of the previous five years"!: so exclaiming she bit off 2 pieces of sweets in one go.

For a full half hour he went on to graphically narrate his heroic technical discussions that went on for more than two hours in one go!:

"Mummy, the Technical Committee made me highly comfortable throughout the discussions. It did start off on a highly inquisitive note", "how the hell the doctors at the IMS blundered to send you into < a   wheelchair bound position> life long? Have you not dragged them to Courts Of Law in your country?; it was only later the committee returned to the subject matter of technical discussions!.

MOM: "I was always confident of your outstanding performance in the interview. I recall how in the previous company; you were compared to a < diamond > after technical discussions; what title you have managed this time to make us prouder?!".

Prashant smilingly narrated: "you have guessed it alright mom, I told the committee after the interview that < it will be my privilege to contribute to the growth of the company>"

Smart came the reply from the Committee Chairman: "Dear Prashant, where were you hiding all these years? We are lucky to have caught the < rarest of rare fish >. You are welcome to join our Team of Management from this very hour".

Mother instantly went into her seclusion into the pooja room to profusely thank the Almighty God for HIS continued blessings on us and our prodigy son.

Her thanks to HIM at HIS LOTUS FEET got multiplied several times as HIS Blessings came to us at our hour of pain and suffering and very timely indeed.

By the following month, Prashant had become a proud < Infosysian>;. He found, the very first day, his new Company is highly employee -friendly and employee-oriented. The Chief Executive always treated himself as < only first amongst all equals >. The very first day he was surrounded by one and all of employee- force to welcome him into their fold.

"Dear friends" addressing the gathering the Chief Executive said: "Let us all welcome this bold and brave Prashant into our fold. He needs no special introduction for; most of you must have come to know of his credentials through the internet already. Let us be < careful with him> in all aspects of office décor!;

guess why?; we may all find ourselves in court room answering his charges .He has the distinction of pulling up errant doctors in the Apex Court of our land!" ; bursts of laughter greeted the newcomer. "Prashant will lead the < Finacle project group >. All you youngsters please join hands with him and continuously strive to make the Project an outstanding success".

He was overwhelmed with joy at the warm welcome into his new office. He returned home after first day at work with his trade mark smile beaming .

Mom the first to greet him home queried: "Dear, how was your first day at the new office?".

Prashant: "Simply exhilarating mom! The atmosphere is simply marvelous; the office looks located in the middle of a botanical park!. Just in front, I can see through the window and enjoy water fountains. In the background of the fountains are green foliage that are a treat to appease the appetite of a botany research candidate!. With my motorised wheel chair, I can move around from one office building to other; to canteen building located on a hillock top, to library, to conference hall in a dedicated building, all by myself unaided!. It is a huge campus and calls for movements nearly 3-4 kms a day; **the beauty of it all, these wheel- chair friendly facilities have been created on war footing exclusively to take care of the Company's first differently abled employee, that is me!**

Even the ATM level has been lowered to suit my sitting posture for ATM card insertion.

It was my dream to work in such an atmosphere. I am excited to share with you that this dream has been fulfilled".

Mom: "**For you, an enlightened, determined gallant soldier nothing is impossible**; the Almighty will always be standing by your side. The society will follow suit. Don't have any apprehensions in life dear. Success will never ever desert you. In fact it follows you like your shadow wherever you traverse day in and day out.

Prashant always stood, moved around with confidence, with high morale continuously ensured from his near and dear ones.

He was fortunate to have enjoyed outstanding differently abled facilities at all places whichever he visited; even his sojourn to foreign countries either for work (Singapore) or pleasure trips (to Europe); whether it was to get lifted up to second level of Eiffel Tower in Paris to have a panoramic view of that beautiful vast city or to enter the Gondola boat and ride through the famous Venice city's criss-cross canals or enjoying panoramic view of Kaula Lumpur from atop the Twin towers of Malaysia or the automobile museum at Stuttgart (in Germany)

He needed only a few weeks to get into the feel of work and march to high performance and achievement levels. He was instantly rewarded with higher and higher responsibilities. Soon he was elevated to be team leader to control a larger group of software professionals located at different away- centers geographically; as wide and as far as Chennai, Hyderabad, Pune and Mangalore.

Through tele- conferencing he could unite all the teams for achieving the set targets in time, comfortably, easily, and appreciatively. He never looked back at the tragic past that had forced him into wheel chair. On the other hand he would innovate at work, constantly carrying the team with him. Alongside the development of this team, he developed his personality also getting strength of steel to tread new paths. He had practiced many difficult maneuvers in handling as independently as possible his wheel chair transfers.

He had developed confidence therefore to move away from home town/work headquarters to away–centers just with the help of his chauffeur. He supervised and guided his away-center colleagues and he had no hesitation or difficulty in meeting these duty requirements hassle free with only the ever-ready driver by side. Wherever he went, he spread cheer and brought smiles on his colleagues' faces by quoting smilingly his own challenging physical conditions. That would be the end of their worries for the duration of the day at least and his benign treatment would have already spurred them into efficiency and productivity at work. Knowing him very well, the <yesterday's off mood employees> would dare not appear in front of him the next day with any semblance of worry either on their faces or in their minds, because they would have turned around to face obstacle, irritations, smilingly from the previous day itself. Prashant would feel proud of his contribution to peace in the otherwise restless family without even visiting them at their residences but controlling only remotely!.

****

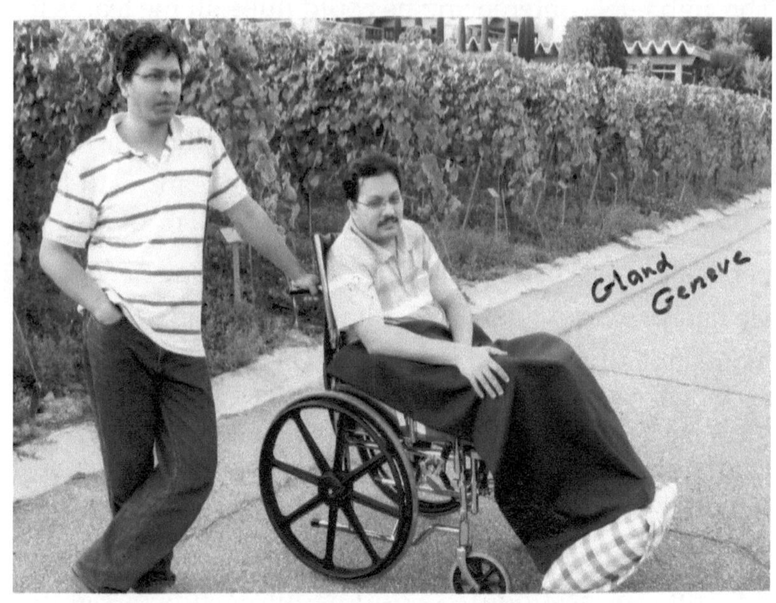

(35 years old) Holidaying at Geneva Swizerland with
younger brother - Pavan

35 years old ; Reaching Height! on to of Alps-Shilthorn 2970 mts
height with"eskimoed" father

on way to Louvre Museum Paris with parents and
sister (-in-law) (35 years old)

CHAPTER- XX

HERCULIAN PREPARATIONS FOR THE GREAT LEGAL BATTLE

It was well neigh impossible to get on in life with enforced expenses mounting by leaps and bounds. Physio-therapic exercising by the day, by the noon and in the evening; total attention to morning ablutions, to bath, to aseptic dressing of bedsores wounds; helping Prashant for wheel-chair transfers had all to be meticulously performed. They all needed energy, time and money not excluded!

There was no chance of meeting these huge expenses as also on medicines by any individual's earnings (father and mother had retired from service, younger brother having not completed his education). **Recourse to litigation in the Courts of law for directing the negligent hospital and negligent doctors to cough up the huge monetary compensation was the one and only solution**. Prashant's father took up the medical knowledge gathering duties.

Prashant's maternal uncle- Ananda Murthy took upon the responsibilities of locating an upright legal counsel for fighting our case in the Courts of Law. Mr. Seshagiri

Rao a senior advocate practicing in the Hon'ble Supreme Court of India, readily offered his services after getting first hand information of the case as also the necessity of litigation.

The two got down to their allotted businesses quite seriously. The legal counsel went into all aspects of medical negligence; Studying in the process, the Consumers Protection Act passed by the India Parliament in 1986; diving into scores of medico-legal cases. Prashant's father understood clearly that the onus of proving the medical negligence squarely rested on his shoulders. His project took off into a fine start when he started consulting medical text books at the various medical college libraries at Delhi, Hyderabad and Bangalore cities which he had to frequently visit.

Glued to the computer he could cull out vast medical data from various web sites like <Medline Data site>, <Pub Med site>. Through discussions with professor of Anatomy at the Bangalore city medical college, he could grasp a clear picture of the tragedy that had befallen his dear son; fusing together the medico technical and jurisprudential knowledge collected by the Duo painstakingly, a draft of final version of our complaint in the form of Civil Appeal was initiated by Seshagiri Rao the legal counsel: "Let us both be very clear in our minds, that we have to clinchingly convince the sitting Judges about what all happened, how it all happened, how it could have been avoided; How there were no any urgencies for the surgeon to even by pass biopsy procedure i.e. <putting surgery before the full diagnosis>"

Legal counsel: "Yes I think we are on the right track for information gathering ; needless to emphasize that the information so collected must be duly supported and evidenced; must be free of all rancor and devoid of any bitterness towards the medical experts although they only perpetrated this calamity.

Prashant's father: "Everyone in the family, everyone in the vast circle of our friends and well wishers do hold the doctors' profession in high esteem". He went on to add further: "After all that noble profession had come into existence with the sole objective of mitigating sufferings of humanity through diagnosis, through complete diagnosis before starting the treatment for cure".

 Each of the Duo started off with open minds, in their respective projects with plans drawn to meet bi- weekly for exchange of information hitherto collected.

Came the first knowledge exchange meeting; the legal counsel suggested: "give me a brief on the anatomy of the body parts involved in the tragedy"

Prashant's father: "Basically, Mr Seshagiri Rao, we are ready to fire the first salvo against the Duo doctors for not even completing the diagnosis first.

"Factually ours is a case of caused paraplegia i.e.; caused non- functioning of the spinal cord in the thoracic region".

"The spinal cord is a very predominant part of the human body's both CENTRAL and PERIPHERAL nervous system. Any physical disturbance to this system will surely and certainly cause very serious damage to bodily functions. They are termed -"quadriplegia and or paraplegia".

Legal counsel: "But you told me that Prashant has suffered paraplegia? Is it different from quadriplegia?".

Prashant's father: "Certainly the two are different. If a surgeon wrongly damages one or many of the 12 segments in the thoracic region, the result is paraplegia where the affected patient loses control (both sensory and motor) of all parts below that level. And in the instant case he has lost control from 4th level of thoracic spine resulting in paralysis of both the legs from thighs to feet; resulting in loss of urine voiding control, and stools evacuation control; all these damages are permanent and lifelong!

Legal counsel: "So then, this action of surgery has taken away his walking faculties?"

Father: "Not only walking faculties dear Rao, he cannot sit without all-round support; he cannot stand; he cannot walk; he cannot turn from one supine position to others; he cannot get up even in bed to sitting position. In short he has been reduced to the state of a <living vegetable> - quite helpless and dependent like a baby child.

All these and scores of attendant problems have been enforced on our dear Prashant **not for a few days or months but life long** . The damages are clearly substantiated in medical text books in the event of botched up surgeries.

Legal counsel: "Dear Seshadri, I am recollecting my middle school knowledge of Hygiene including elementary anatomy of the human body. But you have gone very deep into the subject".

Seshadri: "we have to clearly bring out the seriousness of the damage caused before the Honourable Judges and Members of the Jury in a language easily comprehensible to non-medical people .Being non-medical men we have made a good start in comprehending the seriousness and the whys & hows of the damage.

Legal counsel: "Certainly we are on the right track. Let us bring into discussions whether the surgical procedure decided by Dr. Vaidya and blindly implemented by Dr. Adimanov was the only and only procedure under the circumstances".

Seshadri: "Oh no! Dear Rao, the procedure was definitely faulty without a shadow of doubt and crystal clearly. **The investigating medical men were duty bound to have completed diagnosis first; consulted with their professional colleagues next; carried out further diagnosis/ diagnoses as per mutual consultations; inferred from such detailed investigations, whether there was any urgency/ emergency and such other thoughts before announcing to the patient under investigation (certainly not on the Operating Table) and also to his family members and attendants, the need for the next procedure; the likely consequences of the intended procedure; the risk benefit ratio of implementing the prescribed procedure or postponing the procedure etc.**

Legal counsel: "you have aroused enough fire in my

belly to acquire more and more medical knowledge of the functioning of the human body!"

Seshadri: " <Necessity is the mother of invention>; we are in dire straits economically to meet the exponentially mounting medical expenses. We will fight tooth and nail for Justice for being awarded with adequate monetary compensation to enable our dear son to lead a decent life with dignity albeit in wheel chair sitting condition; albeit having to undergo mandatory physiotherapic discipline; albeit having to periodically undergo medical checkups as preventive and such other enforced mandates attributable solely to the butchery acts of the medical self- claiming experts".

Legal counsel: "I have dived into several medico-legal cases that have already been disposed off. In quite a few cases, the Courts of Law have sought an independent medical witness to establish negligence or otherwise".

Seshadri: "Prescribed medical text books, publications from enlightened medical luminaries have discussed in details the various Dos and Don'ts in surgical procedures and for that matter even in treatment with medicines".

"Extensive scrutiny of these publications revealed clearly **the importance of total knowledge of the complete diagnosis prior to any curative prescription; mandatory consultations amongst medical experts as second and even third opinions, before even penning down the prescription alternatives".**

"Dear Rao I will be strongly supporting your judicial

prudence with clinching evidences from the enlightened publications by enlightened medical experts".

Legal counsel: "The battle is half won even before the start of the litigations, when we are on the right path of evidence with no acrimony or bitterness towards the Opposite Parties. We will sit down right away and start the final draft of our Appeal/ Petition". So deciding Seshadri and the legal counsel started off in right earnest. We had to discuss, rediscuss each and every argument before finally inking them. The legal counsel had firsthand knowledge of the scores of hardships the family and dear Prashant had to undergo mandatorily when he chose to stay with us for a full week and partake of the ups and downs, jokes and gimmicks that helped to keep the morale upbeat.

Draft of Appeal finalized, printed and sufficient copies taken, the Appeal was filed before the Hon'ble National Consumers Disputes Redressal Commission (abbreviated NCDRC) at the country's capital - New Delhi on 9th April 1993, The Hon'ble Court acknowledged receipt of the complaint/ Appeal and posted for hearing in May 1993.

Readers may recall from the previous pages how Prashant and party encountered a noble person who readily offered his helping hand to lift the wheel chaired from court entrance level to lift starting level -a full 20 steps above!; And that noble personality was no other than the President of the NCDRC court! He had directed us not to trouble Prashant in coming to court at the initial stages of litigation.

The next stage of proceedings i.e.; first hearing in May 1993 was therefore attended by the legal counsel and seshadri 'sans' the Petitioner/Appellant. The Hon'ble Bench had gone through the Appeal running into seven hundred and fifty pages and appeared to have gathered the central focal point whether negligence has been brought out clearly or not. The legal counsel, appearing for the Appellant petitioner, began the hearing proceeding by making a powerful statement. "Your Lordships!, **I am going to unfold the tragedy that has been brought on an young, enterprising, healthy, sport loving boy and class topper in studies also, at the prime of his youth for no fault of his and for no any seriousness in health;** some unwanted masses had grown in the thoracic region that required firstly and fore- mostly, a biopsy procedure to ascertain whether the masses were < benign or malignant> in nature and **only after knowing the results of biopsy further procedures had to be deeply thought of**; discussed with panel of doctors and other expert before even pronouncing the curative procedure let alone implementing the prescription. The only symptom they had was occurrence of light transient fever that lasted for a few hours and disappeared with one tablet of 500mg paracetamol. This condition prior to start of any investigation , has been clearly noted by the examining doctors and recorded also in history sheets (which are filed as evidences); it has also been recorded in medical case history sheets by the attending doctors that Prashant was hale, hearty, he was well built well nourished, not anaemic or cyanosed or jaundiced, no clubbing of pedal edema present; BP:120/80mm Hg; CVS: NAD(Nothing Abnormal

Detected); chest, lungs: clear; haemoglobin, BUN, creatinine, FBS urine examination: All normal; as part of investigations X-ray had been taken which revealed presence of tumour masses in the posterior mediastinal region with erosion of 2nd,3rdand 4th ribs on the left side : CT scanning also taken which substantiated the X-ray findings".

Your Lordship: "it is exactly at this juncture that total diagnosis including ascertaining the nature of tumour masses through fine needle aspiratory biopsy, had to be resorted to as the first step".

"MRI scanning at this juncture would have given further details about the extent of masses extending into adjacent organs within the thoracic region".

"My lord, it is understood by even a common man that a MRI scan would reveal all. But unfortunately the self-proclaiming experts in medicine have not utilized this diagnostic tool even though this hi-tech facility was available in ready- for- use- condition in the same Hospital and Institution of Higher Learning. This, Your Lordships, constituted the first instance of negligence".

Legal counsel for the Petitioner continued to aver:

"The investigation process started correctly alright with fine needle biopsy under ultrasound guidance. This procedure did not involve any surgery at all and much less did not require even local anesthesia for pricking a fine needle into the backside of our dear Prashant".

"LO! What was the result of biopsy?   No conclusive evidence!",was the recording of Dr Vaidya. It is baffling how highly qualified and mature doctors could conclude < no evidence > when huge monstrous tumours have been confirmed as existing by prior CT scans and X ray!!; **Ordering a repeat of FNAC biopsy by itself constituted a serious negligence Act, when MRI -a non invasive, non anaesthetic diagnostic tool was not thought of.** Strangely however, Dr. Vaidya thought it "fit and proper" to continue with FNAC biopsy procedure for second, third and fourth attempts again without any conclusive evidence and finally ordering< excision biopsy through thorocotomy> **without, even at this late stage, resorting to MRI scanning, constituted the highest degree of negligence!**

"Your Lordship, even a common non-medical man would have suggested obtaining a second opinion, a third opinion from medical experts available by the dozens in the same Institute of Medical Sciences!. Alas !, this also not done; **and taking out a micro grain sized sample by a minor surgical procedure involving a minor incision in the thoracic region also could have delivered the desired result.** Leaving all these simple non invasive procedures, the operating CT surgeon went ahead with opening out the entire left hemi thorax after giving general anaesthesia and 'scourged' out the whole of the masses from the thoracic region (as against the requirement of a tiny, micro sample) for conducting laboratory investigation to determine the pathological nature of the tumour i,e; whether benign or malignant. **Ah!, what a whimsical and damaging procedure !: <operating first and biopsying next>. This is akin to putting the proverbial < cart before the horse >**

It is obvious even to a common man that any further procedure had to be, threadbare discussed with a panel of specialists pinpointing the pros cons of removal of the entire masses; pin pointing the risk benefit ratio of the intended procedure carried out then or postponed to a later date/ or attempted to be cured with oral medicines etc.

Any such decision should have been discussed with the grown up patient himself besides explaining in clear language, understandable to parents, attendants present there; the pros a cons of the intended procedure.

Alas!, no such steps were taken by the negligent doctors.

The Hon'ble Presiding Judge at this stage intervened and asked: "What has the advocate for the Respondent doctors to say on the hitherto presentation by the legal counsel for the petitioner?". "I seek the Leave": the Counsel for the Opposite Parties interacting: " of the Hon'b le Court to **aver that my clients have done their best and it was only the rarest of rare cases that paraplegia had set in despite following the procedures followed the entire world over".**

"Objection my lord, objection my lord; I seek Leave of the Hon'ble Court"; so spontaneously reacted Prashant's father from the gallery.

"Special Leave granted to reply": announced the Hon'ble Presiding Judge.

Petitioner's father: "My objection to the averment by the legal counsel for the OPs is that paraplegia has been caused by the scalpel of the operating surgeon thoughtlessly without even establishing the pathological nature of and extent of involvement of these extra grown masses with the adjacent organs in the posterior thoracic region".

"Half baked knowledge applied on the Petitioner by madly driving the scalpel through mass of inter costal arteries and exiting nerves from the spinal cord has resulted in paraplegia. It just cannot be attempted to be explained away light heartedly without proof. I have painstakingly collected clinching evidences to prove my point from various publications and medical journals. Here are ready copies of these evidences (already annexed to the main petition vide page nos….)".

Hon'ble Presiding Judge: "I understand your anxiety and pain as father of the affected boy. We shall revert back to you at the arguments stage; till then let your legal counsel continue with the presentation on the legal aspects".

"I am very much obliged Your Honour" so stating, the Petitioner's father took his seat in the gallery bubbling with anxiety to explain the whole gamut of mis-actions, non-actions and mal-actions by the notorious duo of Physician and CT surgeon namely Dr. Vaidya and Dr. Adimanov.

With the arguments by OPs completed, the Hon'ble President directed the Petitioner's father to resume his arguments.

As the aggrieved father of the gallant soldier Prashant went on unfolding medical facts after facts the Presiding

Judge intervened: "I have gone through the petition papers. But I do not find many of the references being quoted now."

"Your Lordship!, we are only quoting from the medical records handed over to us by the Hospital Authorities at the time of discharge": So replied the legal counsel for the Petitioner

"There appears to be deliberate wanton conspiracy to withhold vital treatment details by the OPs from the preview of the Hon'ble court to save their skins":the Petitioner's father submitted before the Hon'ble bench; he went on further, to state: "The Hon'ble Court may be pleased to order the OPs to explain to the entire humanity, all the details of development that were caused by them in their Hospital Institution which virtually kept our dear Prashant imprisoned for seven long months continuously as against a maximum of <half a day required for biopsying >.

"Then there is something greatly amiss between the papers submitted to this Court and those being referred to by the Appellant". Sensing mischief from the Hospital Authorities, the Hon'ble Court ordered the OPs: "We now direct you to submit forthwith <every bit and piece of paper and documents > which would detail out the treatments during the seven months'long stay in the OP1 institution".

The Court simultaneously directed the Complainant: "It is desirable that you supplement your evidences that seem to be, appreciatively, derived from authentic

Medical literature, medical publications , by producing a medical expert as witness on negligence. The Court would find it easier to adjudicate in the matter".

It was a Herculean task to locate a medical expert, who would readily come forward and express his opinion, apparently, against his own professional community!!. We had to run from pillar to post exhausting the lot of all our family doctors, our acquaintance doctors, family friends' acquaintance doctors, our own relatives practicing medicine. It was only a gentle "sorry, I cannot go against my professional colleagues", **although I feel the damage was definitely avoidable"**. These sympathetic words would at best, serve the purpose of the proverbial <crocodile shedding its tears>.

At this juncture the legal counsel suggested a way out of the predicament.

"Seshadri, fortunately for us, there is one upright personality who practises medicine as a renowned neurosurgeon; he works at the leading multispecialty hospital at Bangalore. Let us try": so stating he straight away made a call to this specialist and briefed him about the requirement of medical witness for his close family friend in distress and he handed over the phone to the Petitioner's father to continue.

"Hello doctor, it is my privilege to get acquainted with you through our legal counsel"; he continued further: "my son, a brilliant engineering student **has been felled by the scalpel of a CT surgeon who operated on his dorsal region** with sole intention to take out a tiny sample for biopsying for finding out the nature of the tumour masses whether benign or malignant; but landed in rendering him paraplegic from T4 level and below!. I would need your help as a medical witness, to express your considered opinion on this tragedy **only on its merits**; we are stuck at the medical witness level".

 From the other end, the specialist doctor advised: "you can bring all the medical records in original along with pre-surgical diagnostic reports and preoperative X ray/ CT scans; and if not the pre, at least the post operative MRI scan, discharge summary to enable me to go through and study the case **and offer my comments dispassionately". He also promised: "my opinion will do full justice to the required line of treatment, without being influenced either by the patient's pathetic condition of health or by the length of acquired degree qualifications of the operating surgeon".**

These words were indeed soothing very much like finding < an oasis in a desert>. Prashant's father decided to take the trip to Bangalore to consult with the angelic doctor. Before leaving Delhi, the immediate necessity of a wheel chair for Prashant had to be met; wheel chair buying at Delhi was not without emotions and tears flowing from Seshadri's and senior counsel's eyes; if the tragedy had not taken place, it was the most befitting time in Prashant's life to present him with a <Honda City model> car. Painfully but meticulously we finalized on a good wheel chair and readied it for parcelling to Bangalore.

With all medical papers and documents Seshadri headed to Bangalore city by train. The 36 hours journey from

Delhi to Bangalore was more trying for the body and mind than even trekking along the Himalayan slopes to attempt to reach Mount Everest peak for obvious reasons of anxiety about the possible outcome of meeting with the neuro expert at Bangalore and even greater anxiety about the unfathomable degree of success or failure of evidences to support our complaint against the negligent doctors.

As planned we met at the super specialty Manipal hospital in Bangalore where the upright surgeon was the Head of the neuro surgery department. The chance meeting was an instant morale booster for Prashant's father; exchanging greetings he promptly explained briefly the tragic happenings and handed over all original medical records.

Dr. Hegde meeting with Prashant's father a while later, after going through all medical records, expressed his shock and dismay at the happenings to an young upcoming boy:

"You see Seshadri; I notice from X ray that he had extensive growth of tumour masses in the posterior dorsal region and those masses appeared to have caused erosion of ribs. CT scans also confirmed these findings. **Are there any MRI scans done before surgery?"**.

Replied Seshadri: "Unfortunately doctor, MRI scanning was done only post operatively"

Expert: "Oh my god!. Things would have been altogether different if only the Magnetic Resonance

Imaging had been carried out as part of preoperative diagnosing process". Appearing quite disturbed, he went on to state: "MRI scanning would have revealed involvement of bone and soft tissues of the body besides indicating clearly the extension of these extra grown masses into the spinal cord area. I see the report of the ghastly damage caused. It is very sad indeed. I am ready to come and record my opinion and statement before the local court of law in Bangalore".

This heartening consent was immediately communicated to the Hon'ble NCDRC Delhi who promptly organized with the Bangalore Urban Consumers Disputes Redressal Commission for recording the statement <Chief-examination> and cross examination by the OPs **at Bangalore itself with a view to not disturbing a busy medical expert.**

Finally Dr. Hedge's statement was recorded in the presence of the President of the Commission and, as per the due process of Law, the OPs' legal adviser was allowed to cross examine the Prosecuting Medical Witness. The entire recordings were later transmitted to the Higher Court at Delhi for further consideration.

A careful reading of his statements, brought cheers to the complaining party as it was loaded with helpful **witnesses for** smoothly and firmly **<prosecuting the guilty!!>.**

The OPs also, on reprimand from the Hon'ble Court for withholding and suppressing vital treatment records, submitted a 120 pages treatise on the entire treatment

from day of admission to day of discharge with a copy to us.

The stage was set for final battle in the Hon'ble Consumer Court. As expected both the parties were summoned to Delhi for arguing out their respective contentions on negligence or non negligence spanning April 1993 to 1998.

The intervening period from date of complaint in April 1993 till the arguments stage in 1998 was quite anxiety-causing for Prashant as also to his parents and younger brother.

Learned counsel for the Opposite Responding Parties took the witness box and taking oath started his arguments: "I will speak only the truth and nothing but the truth"; he went on: "Your Honour, in their distress of paraplegic condition of their son, the Petitioners have overstepped their ethics in blaming the doctors belonging to the world recognized noble profession, for having caused unjustified damage. A true and devoted help to the patient has been construed as a barbaric act. My clients' intentions were only noble, meant to help the patient; unfortunately < the rarest of rare > unpleasant development has taken place. **It was only after opening out the thoracic cavity the surgeon noticed huge lobulated masses.** He could well imagine the extent of damage these masses would inflict on the patient if left alone; went ahead and took decision to remove all of them   once for all to make the patient free from any serious ailments in future. **During this process of**

excision unfortunately, the< rarest of rare paraplegia> occurred < in spite of good intentions >".

He continued: "instead of accepting the situation, the Appellants have gone on to tarnish the name and fame of the experts".

"Dr. Vaidya is a highly qualified and experienced internal medicine expert with credit of having published over 100 articles on various aspects of internal medicine".

"Dr. Adimanov is a highly skilled cardio thoracic surgeon having vast experience of performing several hundreds of surgeries in the thoracic region ; **such eminent experts are dragged into litigation in the Courts of law by the 'acknowledgedly' aggrieved Petitioners** causing unfathomable pain in their hearts and serious dent on their name and fame in their professions".

"The two doctors, from diagnostic stage to surgery completion stage, have only followed procedures and practices of the entire medical world. My clients (doctors) want that this case should be withdrawn forthwith unconditionally, otherwise they reserve their rights to file a counter complaint for putting to disrepute all their achievements in the medical profession".

The Presiding Judge directed the Petitioner's legal counsel to reply to these averments.

In reply the Petitioner's legal counsel submitted before the Hon'ble Court: "Your Honour, I will be pleased to argue on all judicial aspects of the case. But I appeal to the Hon'ble court to grant Leave to the victim's father to argue on all medical aspects of the case. The victim's father- Seshadri has put in extra- ordinary efforts in discussing with doctor anatomy professors; consulting with dozens of enlightened publications stored in various web sites like <pub-MED> and <MED LINE DATA BASE>; also he has visited various medical college libraries at Delhi, Hyderabad (the OPI Institute's library also!), and Bangalore and studied in depth and stamped his acquired knowledge with discussions amongst well known doctors. At any point of time his intentions were clear: how it all happened to an upright brilliant, highly active boy who was not only outstanding at studies in the academic field but also in over a dozen sports .He also evinced keen interest in music and had acquired debating skills; was this tragedy not avoidable?; why it could not have been avoided?; where was the urgency when there were no symptoms / no   visible manifestations either physiological or neurological?

****

CHAPTER- XXI

HEARING OF THE PETITIONER'S TIRADE AGAINST THE OPS AT THE NCDRC COURT

He Seshadri, has the inputs for all the above detailed queries and hence our Appeal before the Hon'ble Court to permit him to answer or raise all medico legal issues throughout the stages of hearing, submissions or arguments in person".

Presiding Judge: "The court has no objection to the above proposal. However care should be taken to ensure only one speaks at a time".

Petitioner's legal counsel: "We are very much obliged Your Honour. We will ensure strict order in presentation of our case at all times".

Seshadri: "Your Honour, I am the father of dear Prashant - a victim of thoughtless, brainless actions and half baked procedures enforced on my son by the OP doctors. I am grateful for the permission granted to me to highlight the gross, criminal negligence acts of OP doctors. I swear before the Hon'ble Court that there is not even an iota of acrimony or vengeance in all the medical knowledge which   I am going to present before the Hon'ble Court. The knowledge of the damages caused has been dispassionately culled out from intensive study of medical text books, periodicals journals etc as already averred by our legal counsel".

"First of all it is to be made abundantly clear that Prashant was admitted for< a biopsy procedure only> albeit through a mini surgery; that procedure had been given the title <excision biopsy by thorocotomy>. By whatever name it is called; whatever be the title it is given, it was explained to us (the patient under investigation and his dear younger brother and his parents very much before the start of the procedure), that a small incision will be made into the thorax,< a tiny sample of the tumour masses would be taken out> and sent to the institute's laboratory for histopathological examination to rule in/ out malignancy or benigness of the tumour: **it was also clarified by the medical doctors that any further action would be decided only after the result of the biopsy"** **(OP4 's recorded evidence available as his Cross examination by the Petitioner); assurances given, the designated** patient was wheeled into the Operation Theatre on the 23rd day of October (1990 year) at 9AM promptly.

The attendants were hoping everything would go well as it was only a minor surgical procedure and they also entertained hopes of seeing their dear one in less than an hour.

It was well past 10AM, the anxious younger brother enquired from every medical staff exiting the OT; but no news of his elder brother from them!. **Also no news**

on the outcome of biopsy. Time ticked heavily for us; anxiety grew to Himalayan proportions; it was well past 12noon, **a full 3 hours since entering the OT**, but no news!

As tempers were raising high within the attendants' camp, **they noticed Prashant being wheeled out on a stretcher straight towards intensive care unit!**

There was no trace of the operating surgeon; no trace of any medical doctor either, the nursing sister pushing the trolley paused for a moment and announced to the anxious attendants "the patient is still under the influence of General Anaesthesia. It is an emergency case and hence being admitted into the ICU. You can speak to your dear much later" so stating she continued her paces towards the ICU!

Presiding Judge: "Do you mean to say that no doctor came out of the OT to briefly appraise you attendants, of these happenings inside the OT?".

Seshadri: "Precisely Your Honour, this was the major lapse. The world over, the operating surgeons do come out of the OT to brief the anxiously waiting attendants; but alas!, not followed in our case. This, Your Honour, coupled with more than 3 hours of surgical procedure caused immense worry, anxiety beyond words for description".

"However the OT nurse came out to brief us after admission into the ICU and held a large sized tray in front of us. On seeing kilograms of excised out tumour masses in the tray, Your Lordship, all of us wanted to know whether the patient underwent a biopsy procedure or a major surgery inside the OT".

"Your Lordship, it is a tall story which I would like to unfold before the Hon'ble Court".

"The 3 ½ hours procedure from 9AM to 12:30 noon inside the OT clearly indicated that the operating surgeon has gone ahead with surgery not only for biopsy but also for <curing> (as evidenced by OP4 before the court) at the same time through whole scale, total excision of the invading masses, and the result is there for the entire humanity to note!- Patient paralysed LIFE LONG from T4 level of thoracic region and below with **<loss of sensation and modalities of power> in the entire lower body with no hope of recovery. On enquiring with medical literature, this happening is clearly attributable to 1) either wrongly applying traction to these masses (confirmed to be neurological in nature) 2) and/ or interference with blood supply to the spinal cord".**

"The two major reasons for causing paraplegia to the patient have been graphically explained by Dr. Thomas Gray a renowned neuro- specialist in his treatise entitled "Anatomy". Dr. Gray is popular in medical world as Father of Anatomy; therefore the point arises as to how the CT surgeon Dr. Adimanov, did not involve a team of specialists including a neuro surgeon; a neuropathologist and a neurologist".

"It has been recorded clearly in the pre –diagnostic instant case documents including X-Ray and CT scans and Operation Notes, that three consecutive ribs had been eroded. **From this point of view alone the investigating team was duty bound to have included an orthopaedic surgeon as well".**

"Before applying his scalpel as CT surgeon, had he involved/ consulted with the neuro experts and ortho experts he would have got sufficient warning of the dangerous consequences of injury to spinal cord, as these tumour masses had grown, as distinctly indicated in CT scans, over the boni- structures and including the multi - million dollar spinal cord through IVF-openings (the Inter Vertebrate Foraminal- openings)".

"And as a part of the team, the neuro surgeon would have firstly warned the operating team about the easily possible damage to spinal cord".

"My lord, the negligence act has started from here; without ascertaining the histopathological nature I,e; whether malignant or benign, how could he have gone ahead with total removal through total surgery? **Then what for they made big announcement that our dear Prashant is to undergo a mini surgery for biopsy sake".**

"The CT surgeon, **days and weeks before excision,** had the knowledge that the tumour masses have grown extensively covering large vulnerable parts of the < under investigation> patient's thoracic region".

"How has he failed to analyze ,when he was seeing through his naked eyes ,that these tumour masses have, by applying constant pressure, eroded 3 consecutive ribs i.e.; 2nd, 3rd and 4th? Does it require a PhD in

medicine to interpolate, on the spot in the OT, that these masses could have, easily and surely, entered the spinal cord area through the inter vertebrate foramen (ivf) between 2nd and 3rd ribs as also between 3rd and 4th ribs? AFTER ALL a first year student of medicine being taught Anatomy in the first class knew that.

The multi- million dollar and multi functioning spinal cord is housed inside the vertebral column, **god** WHO has created this universe including humans, the flora and fauna, **has intelligently created gaps between two adjacent vertebral bodies for the spinal cord to receive arterial blood supply; to exit venous blood supply; to exit central nerve roots to various organs for sensory and motor control of all human activities"**.

"Any thoughtless incision in this highly sensitive and vulnerable area, can and will definitely cause serious damages; and that, My Lord is exactly what has happened. Simple pre- surgery knowledge of the tumour masses extending vastly and that too in the posterior region with erosion of three consecutive ribs was sufficient to have taken series of measures as enumerated below:-

First and foremostly, why MRI scanning was not resorted to even at this belated peri- surgery (during surgery) stage?** My discussions with empteen number of doctors including anatomy specialists revealed undoubtedly, the most likely involvement of the spinal cord with these extra grown masses.

Secondly, even after making a tiny incision as part of mini surgical biopsy, the CT **surgeon was duty bound,**

forgetting all other thoughts, **to primarily know the nature of tumour masses and therefore to have sent, on top most priorty that fine sample to laboratory to ascertain the nature of the tumour.**

If the tumour was non malignant where was the hurry to proceed without consulting with other specialists and also the patient after allowing him to come out of GA;

If the tumour was malignant, where was the competence of this CT surgeon to deal with such huge masses extending everywhere including inter costal space; And why has he not referred this case to cancer care unit if at all it existed in the same hospital, otherwise, to cancer specialty hospital outside?

And because of erosion of 2nd, 3rd and 4th ribs (as admitted by OPs) why did not this arrogant CT surgeon consult with an oncologist and an ortho surgeon?

"My lord, all these highly sensitive, highly vulnerable issues, sure & certain medical deficit causing possibilities have been thrown to winds **and this callous, arrogant, unconcerned CT surgeon Dr. Adimanov, has simply gone ahead with total removal".**

"Further Your Honour, the CT surgeon has blundered in apparently not waiting for the biopsy results although it would have taken (and in fact factually taken), not more than 20 minutes and the result was not only <non malignant> but these masses were neurological in nature and the lab technician in consultation with

other experts has correctly identified these masses as <plexi form neurofibromatosis >. With this knowledge of neurological nature of the tumour, only a senseless, brainless surgeon would not have involved a team of neurologists including neurosurgeon and neuro pathologist and ortho surgeon in the surgical team; And this team by dint of their collective knowledge and discussions would have conducted several other diagnostic tests; non invasive MRI; mapping of blood supply in this heavy traffic thoracic region, to rule out possible damages to adjacent structures".

"The neuro surgeon would have had the expertise in handling neurogenic tumours in close proximity to spinal cord; would have intelligently, skillfully separated these masses from central nerve roots in the inter vertebrate foraminal region; none the less importantly, blood supply arrangement to these tumours should have been< mapped> as part of diagnosis before applying the scalpel.

Dr. Judo Folkman an eminent cancer specialist...has brought out clearly in his publications that no tumour mass can grow in the body without blood supply specially nut sized or larger sized; and the Hon'ble Bench also can visualize that the huge masses in the instant case of Prashant could not have grown without enough blood supply".

"SADLY, Your Lordships, this confirmation of the butchery act, has come from the CT surgeon himself who has admitted in his Operation Notes (AND

these have been filed as evidences as annexures to the Original Petition), that <Two inter costal arteries were ligated as they were found feeding the extra grown tumours >".

"Consequently, the SUPPLEMENTARY blood supply arrangement to the spinal cord through the intercostal arteries had been severely interfered with and resulted in paraplegia. This fact is also borne from the statement of a neuro specialist friend of family who was discussing the damages caused in the instant case. He went on to suggest that the **interrupted blood supply to spinal cord could have been restored, if the operating surgeon had immediately, reconnected the ligated arteries**; as if to add insult to injury, the butcher Dr. Adimanov had <applied traction>. (this is only parliamentary medical language; otherwise in lay man's words- he has pushed, pulled, dragged the spinal nerve roots from their mother spinal cord during large scale removal of masses very much like a lion tearing its prey). Alas! what a skill displayed by a highly qualified and self boasting experienced surgeon!!??".

"My lord, I have briefly brought before the Hon'ble Court the senseless, ghastly murderous acts of the Opposite Party no 2, the CT surgeon, in handling the most vulnerable part of the human body next only to the brain, most barbariously, comparable only to a carnivorous animal tearing its vanquished prey; and not caring to preserve the blood supply to the spinal cord".

"What a display of knowledge from < a Medicinae

Bachelor & Bachelor Surgery (MBBS) qualified doctor!; nay, even further <Doctorate in medicine (MD); not to stop here even further < M.ch> -Post Doctorate qualified doctor !!".

"Such a highly <London to Delhi> long qualified doctor does not think before cutting off, not bothering if the same arteries in the intercostal space also supply blood to the spinal cord. This barbaric act of unwanted, thoughtless surgery has caused in medical parlance "Ischemia of the dorsal spine" (caused no supply or even reduced supply to dorsal spine in common man's language) resulting in paraplegia on the Operating Table itself in the Operation Theatre.

"And this Dr.ADIMANOV, **has the arrogance to state that he has followed the procedure practiced across the globe and further goes on to justify "I tried to help the patient".** But the actual damage is borne out not only in medical literature but also substantiated practically, beyond shadow of any doubt, by the MRI scanning; unfortunately this clinching conclusion has come only after the damage i,e; post operatively when the same MRI scan would have crystal clearly, most authoritatively clarified during pre operative diagnosis itself."

"This constituted, Your Honour, the highest degree of deficiency of service and Himalayan proportions of negligence".

"**As if this damage is not sufficient, post operative care of the lowest degree has resulted in various other deficit/ complications in the hapless patient!;** such as pressure sores that continued to haunt him and torment him for years on end (15 long years!!). Besides, these pressure sores have caused yet other complications that forced him to stay in the same hospital continuously for seven months at a stretch!. Although discharged after seven torturous months, Prashant remained a patient only and compelled to be hospitalized elsewhere totaling nearly 900 days".

Pre-operative Total Diagnosis, Peri- operative Care and Caution   and Post- operative Intensive Monitoring of the Recovery, are the basis and hall-mark of any medical surgical procedure. These have been thrown to the winds at all the 3 stages as enumerated above.

"This, Your Lordship is only a brief description of the damages caused; it is only < a tip of the iceberg of damages inflicted >; misery pain and suffering imposed not only on the hapless Prashant but on the entire family and close associates whose help was necessary, mandatory during the entire period of rehabilitation".

"And this magnanimous help was rendered most selflessly although beset with many a disturbances in their normal life activities. And all this through out life!!"

"Your Honour, we are aware, damages inflicted cannot be reversed for quite a few decades to follow. **As per present day developments in medicine, cure may not at all be possible for the gallant Prashant's life tenure! .On the other hand medical care and attention are mandatory for the rest of his life. No miracle can make him walk; no miracle can reverse the incontinence of the urinary** bladder; no miracle can restore the natural evacuation of stools; nothing short of physio-therapic exercising by the sun rise, during the mid day and after sunset only will prevent wastages of muscles; no miracle can avoid deployment of nurse by the day and by the evening; no other way to transport him from home to office and back except motorized wheel chair, hand pushed wheel chair, chauffer driven car; regular visit to hospitals for periodic check up as preventive measures mandated; enforced ailments needing hospital admissions and treatment therein; and this list is endless!. Where from money will flow to meet all these enforced expenses? Certainly not from the father who is going to attain the age of super annuation in June 1994 ; certainly not from mother who has already bid good bye to her teaching job for obviously reasons".

"Your Honour! We have therefore approached this Hon'ble Court of law for awarding sufficient monetary compensation to lead life of semblance of dignity although with imposed handicaps".

"And the gallant Prashant is game, sportive to get on in life decently despite odds. He displays exemplary courage; and his morale is ever high and determined to break many a barrier and raise meteorically in his chosen profession of Information Technology. He has all the traits in him to be a highly successful professional engineer PROVIDED of course , he is supported strongly monetarily and continuously cared for and attended to.That is all YOUR LORDSHIPS .I am very much obliged for the Leave granted to me for describing the damage

Caused ,torture imposed on the entire family including our very dear son, the gallant Prashant".

Apellants' arguments completed, the Hon'ble Court directed the OPs to take the floor and to present their points of view.

The Counsel for the OPs did rise in response and started off: "Your Honour!, OPs have considerable sympathy for the complainant and his father. But all the Ops- 1 to 4 seek the Leave of the Hon'ble Court to state that they have made every attempt to safeguard the interests of the complainant to save from the ailment he suffered!"

And went on to add further: "a surgeon or a medical practitioner cannot be considered as an insurer against the accidental slip but he is expected to exercise such care as a normal skillful member of the profession is expected".

"Your Honour , I would like to add further that most of the annexures filed by the complainant for arriving at the quantum of compensation are self- serving documents and claim is totally exaggerated and ill founded; however the IMS (the OPs' Institute of Medical Sciences) is very much willing to get the matters adjudicated and requests for appointment of necessary Commission to enquire into the matter by visiting the Institution itself (as it might be difficult for it to establish its version correctly at Delhi, a different place far away from the hospital city of Hyderabad)".

The counsel for the OPs went on and on further and in his anxiety to defend his clients, made several Clinching averments that served the Appellant's cause of compliant more favourable!. Inadvertence!! Or should we call it road end!; called by any expression or phrase , it was sheer non knowledge, non comprehension of the damages the extra grown masses had caused by way of eroding 2nd, 3rd and 4th consecutive ribs (consecutivity indicated seriousness and vastness of damage). To add to their misery of disjointed arguments, the OPs have gone on and on and stated: **"since rapidly growing benign lesions also erode ribs, a biopsy of the mass to confirm the diagnosis is a must to plan the future course of action"**.

"And before surgery, the parents were explained about the plan of management viz thoracotomy will be done **and a piece** from the mass will be sent for **histopathological examination and further management will be based on the report and the local pathology". The pathology dictates the operative procedure"**.

OPs have gone on to state further: "A thorocotomy was done and part of the tumour was sent for frozen section biopsy which revealed benign nature of the tumour. The lesion on the operating table looked more than benign in terms of vascularity and multiple lobulated masses spreading into various muscle planes of the chest at several places including the inter costal space and along the course of the ribs starting from the vertebral body to the anterior part of the ribs".

"The help of neuro surgeons would have been taken by CT surgeons, if the tumour has got any intra spinal extension. If intra spinal extension is known pre-operatively, CT surgeons and neuro surgeons would join together to plan the operation".

"After excision of the tumour, the complainant-patient developed paraplegia; spinal complications of neuro- fibroma like paraplegia are known to occur but extremely rare. As and when it was realized that the patient had paraplegia, further investigations were done on emergency basis like MRI and necessary steps were immediately taken in consultation with the neurologist Prof. JMK Murthy to contain it. With all the experience and in the necessary circumstances as warranted by the exigencies, OP 2 acted with utmost care to safeguard the interests of the patient at the time of performing the operation and also during the post-operative management. OP2 is well experienced and well aware of the anatomical structures and the safety of dividing the inter costal arteries, **the ligation was made beyond the spinal arteries were given off!!"**.

The complainant in keeping with decorum and dignity of the August Court, displayed the expected silence till the averments of OPs' legal counsel were completed!.

"My lord, I seek the Leave of the Hon'ble Court to expose the hollowness of the OPs' justifications and explanations":so pleaded the PETITIONER'S FATHER .

LEAVE SOUGHT WAS READILY GRANTED by the Hon'ble Court

"It (The micro-surgery) was, as already discussed earlier,

primarily meant to ascertain the nature of the tumours before the next course of action. **Who had given him permission for the uninformed major surgery against the planned mini surgical biopsy?**

How could he, the butcher-surgeon, even after knowing the pathological nature of the masses as benign and < plexiform neurofibromatosis >, go ahead with total removal? without:-

a) Informing the patient and his attendants of the risks benefits

b) Co-opting a neurologist and neuro surgeon even at this belated stage, for carrying out additional diagnosis/ diagnoses to rule in/ rule out intra spinal extension with a view to avoiding easily possible damage to spinal cord

c) And further diagnosis to ascertain the vasculature to establish where the hell from, these unwanted masses got blood supply to grow so fat and extensive, when it is clearly known to even first year student of medicine, that large masses cannot simply grow like that without blood supply!! (Ref. Dr. Judo Folkman in his publications on vasculature of tumours.)

d) And further diagnosis through MRI scanning of the spinal zone; MRI scanning is known, the world over Your Honour, as the finest pin- pointing and effective diagnostic tool to ascertain the extent of these tumour masses spread; involvement with one/

many/ none of adjacent structures in the posterior mediastinum including the spinal cord.

And the OPs simply wanted to escape by stating <any further investigation such as MRI was found not necessary as CT scans had given sufficient information about the extent of tumour; MRI cannot reveal any pathological nature of the tumour (this averment of the duo, on MRI – scope, is quite out of the human world!; for, no sane person expected < a photograph to reveal goodness or bad traits or sweetness of the photographed >)

What a 'Nobel Prize' winning study by professors of Internal Medicine and CT surgery?!. Ah!, Kudos to their Mch Qualifications!; Kudos to their decades of experience!! (both these 'medical legends' had crossed 40 years age mark confirming thereby they had at least 12-14 years of experience). Even a man on the street has the knowledge that CT/MRI/X-ray or a photogragh for that matter, can only take picture/ scans of the targeted organs/ structures, but certainly not the chemistry of tumour.

And we non medical men can, after browsing through medical literature on the internet state emphatically as to "how qualified   men of medicine ignored erosion of three consecutive ribs which clearly evidenced definitely possible involvement of spinal cord through the 2 or 4 anatomical holes: between 1st to 2nd rib; between 2nd to 3rd rib; between 3rd to 4th rib; and 4th to 5th rib".

"Your Honour it is not all. Even the medical men have recorded in their own generated clinical summary records, nearly 4 weeks prior to surgery that:-

"< Evaluation showed a mass lesion in the left upper chest with erosion of ribs and vertebrae > as per the OPs' own created record i.e.; the discharge record;, even the Hon'ble Members of the Commission have keenly read and noticed that "the size of the tumour mass was 4cmx4cm and much more ; so huge as to occupy entire upper left hemi thorax and this was extending extra-pleurally and posteriorly into inter vertebrate foramen; and there was 1cm size opening in the vertebral body exposing spinal cord at T4 level". All such details could have come out pre operatively, only if these and self proclaiming Professors of Internal Medicine & CT surgery, had ordered MRI scanning and Myelography.

Simply delivering lectures/ issuing statements like: <MRI scanning was not necessary>; <MRI cannot reveal pathological nature of tumour>; <There was no indication for myelography or angiogram>; etc, **serve them best as only <WHITE LIES>.**

As if, the 1cm size opening in the vertebral body has been carved out not pre-operatively but only peri operatively!!

As if the masses have extended extra-pleurally and posteriorly into intervertebrate foramen not pre-operatively but only peri- operatively!!

Were these duo self proclaiming Professors in Internal Medicine and CT surgery, ignorant of the dangers to

Spinal cord with such a vast spread of tumour masses in the posterior region of thorax?

Were the duo also ignorant of the immense possibilities of these extra grown tumors drawing blood from intercostal spaced arteries which anatomically also supply blood to spinal cord?

Why pre operative MRI scanning was not done to precisely fix the extent of spread of these tumours into various adjacent organs such as 2nd, 3rd and 4th ribs and also into spinal cord area through inter vertebrate foramina?

Why arterial blood supply mapping was not done to ascertain where from these masses got their blood as food to grow so sumptuously and extensively?

 And for an averagely informed doctor but fully devoted to his profession, these are not hypothetical, but only mandatory to even take a decision on paper, let alone implementing such a decision; these are mandatory to make sure that while dissecting an unwanted tumour, you the surgeon with scalpel, should be 100% sure that you are not disturbing any other healthy parts, organs and structures in the vicinity of these unwanted/ unwelcome extra grown masses.

What if, a thoughtless surgeon, while performing a pre-operative permitted Caesarean section, noticed a cyst in the uterus of an young/ middle aged woman and decided to remove the uterus altogether!. Take a guess; what would have been the outcome of such a decision?!. Such a case has practically happened in Canada; and the victim has challenged the erring doctor in the Supreme Court of British Columbia ,Canada; and the Hon'ble Apex Court has awarded huge monetary compensation: REF : Murray vs Mc Murchy (1949) DLR 442 (1941) I WWR 989!

The mandate of taking decisions only after collective thinking, collective consultations has been brought out clearly by <**The Royal College Surgeons**>, who have come out with a highly practical publication "on total knowledge not that which is contained in the brain of the designated surgeon only; but total knowledge gained and pooled together from other colleagues, specialists and their brains".

It certainly is not , a case of <too many cooks spoiling the broth>; but a glaring case of good number of opinions saving life / lifelong damages through collective knowledge, pooled knowledge , seeing the problems/ ailment/ disease from all-round angle.

Looking at the disease as to how it has manifested

1) As an intruder into the body from outside?

2) As case of malfunctioning of the organ/ adjacent structure of the human torso?

3) Due entirely to non -functioning?

4) Due to mis- functioning of the affected organ or structure of the human torso?

Scores of such thoughts should and must have been placed on the table, discussed and rediscussed; findings/ conclusions authenticated by additional diagnosis/

diagnoses and only then arrived at a practical prescription/ treatment whether surgical or otherwise

Who has not heard of the adage <measure ten times and cut the cloth once>

A few souls on earth may argue otherwise but what stands out predominant, is that the sacred < Balance of Law > always remained unruffled by arguments and counter arguments, by evidences and counter evidences; by chief examinations and cross examinations ; except to tilt in favour of Absolute Justice, Absolute Truth. The globe is maintaining its dynamic equilibrium only because of Absolute Justice being practiced by the Upright Independent Judiciary across the globe, my beloved motherland included.

As ordained, Prashant got justice from the NCDRC when the Hon'ble court pronounced its Judgment Order dated 16th Feb 1999 thus: <We have carefully examined all records and relevant medical literature and make the following observations:.

<Records and averments show, that while handling the case OP2 and OP4 focused more on whether the mass was benign or malignant; rather than ,on its location and extent of its spread. They failed to take due cognizance of the fact of erosion of T4 vertebral body already recorded in the CT scan findings as also in the evaluation notes (on 29.9.1990) of OPD; this information on erosion of vertebrae was with the OPs on 29/9/1990 itself> i,e; more than 3 weeks before that black day of 23rdOctober1990.

< But OP4 and OP2 did not put together the   aforesaid information and did not feel it necessary to carry out further pre operative tests (facilities for which were available in OP1 Institution itself) which would have thrown light pre operatively, on the precise location and extent of the tumour>

The Hon'ble Court also relied on the Absolute Truth stated by the medical expert witness (Prosecuting Witness): <diagnostic procedures are used to precisely locate the tumour, its extent > and further goes on to rely on: "Available medical literature has also noted the usefulness of advanced investigative techniques in the pre operative assessment of mediastinal tumours".

"According to King, Smith (supra), contemporary imaging techniques (including Computerised Tomography –CT, and nuclear Magnetic Resonance Imaging - MRI) have increased the clinician's ability to identify anatomic relationships and their clinical significance; they have dramatically altered the pre operative assessment of both pulmonary and mediastinal tumour (page 632); In a discussion on mediastinal tumours, they have observed that diagnosis evaluation begins with chest radiography in several views; followed by CT and MRI - a non invasive diagnosis modality thought to have great potential for imaging the mediastinum, especially for vascular lesions".

"Myelography has been considered an essential part of the evaluation of the posterior mediastinal tumour lying very close to the vertebral foramina but this invasive procedure has also been replaced in many cases by CT of the spine!!".

The Hon'ble Court thus , have left no stone unturned in accessing the whole truth and have, in the process, acquired substantial authoritative knowledge of medicine and human physiology. Alas these Protectors of Human Life through selected medical practices have failed in this duty which only is most elementary and mandatory before applying the scalpel on the Almighty created Prashant's torso!!

And the Hon'ble Court went on further < the plea taken by OPs that it was most uncommon of complications, fails in so far as the minimum of pre operative and operative care was not taken by them. There was injury to spinal cord **and it was damaged consequent to the operation and there was reduction/Non supply of blood to the spinal cord. OPs have not been able to explain why removal of a benign tumour in chest wall resulted in spinal cord injury and paraplegia.**

"There was lack of proper appreciation" (the aggrieved father of dear Prashant had stated in his deposition before this Hon'ble Forum, that it was sheer arrogance on the part of OP2 and OP4 to project themselves as possessing all the knowledge in the medical world and **that it was only their half baked knowledge that is the root cause of this ghastly tragedy**) "and assessment of the neurological implications of the pathology and spread of the tumour due to which the surgery was performed without the complete involvement of the neuro surgeon;

this was a serious lapse on the part of OP2 and amounted to negligence and lack of care and therefore deficiency in services in the operation per se".

The Judgment Order went on further to pin point the deficiency in services of OP3 who was then the Director of the Institute besides being a neuro surgeon himself, had also been negligent in

1) Not having a discussion meeting of the clinical physician and the surgeons in the relevant lines(including himself)

2) Not planning the surgery on right lines

3) Not performing the surgery along with CT surgeon as a team.

Although the Judgment Order goes on further suffice to draw to a close as reproduced here: "From the aforesaid discussion we are clear in our minds that there was negligence and deficiency of service on the part of the OPs in the different stages of the case.

****

CHAPTER- XXII

WAITING FOR THE NCDRC COURT'S JUDGEMENT ORDERS

The family started to look for the land mark Judgment Order to reach their hands. After all, several weeks had elapsed since the great pronouncement by the Hon'ble court. All leading newspapers carried in bold print the extracts of the land mark Judgment.

But the court certified copy of the Judgment order continued to be evasive to the rightful Appellants / Petitioner.

Prashant's father to legal counsel: "Mr. Rao, how is it we have not received the certified copy of the Hon'ble Commission's Judgment Order?

The legal adviser: "It is strange that even I have not received the Order at my address as well , although it stood duly registered with, and taken on records of, the court; I will find out what was the delay for, when I visit Delhi next month".

Prashant's father: "Let us shoot a letter to the registrar of the Hon'ble NCDRC at New- Delhi"now itself.

Legal Adviser: "Yes I shall send the letter today itself".

The letter was promptly dispatched by the legal advisor on behalf of the Complainants.

Smart came the reply: "we have already dispatched the certified copy of the Judgment Order to you- the complainant's legal advisor and to the petitioner, by post in Feb 1999 itself".

Legal counsel addressing a reply: "I am surprised, Dear Registrar sir, neither of us have received any communication from your side till date, that is a full 2 months from the date of Judgment Order. I will be thankful for your kindly faxing me the scanned copy of the acknowledgement from our side if at all you think the post has been really dispatched from your end and "acknowledged as received" from our end". I smell some foul play by the Opposite Parties in collusion with antisocials."

We decided to wait patiently for a few more weeks.

Again came the reply from the registrar of the NCDRC in the month of June (a full 4 months after the pronouncement of the land mark Judgment Order) insisting on the <Already dispatched> status. Quite anxious to get at the truth of the matter and quite disturbed at the inexplicable inordinate delay, the agitated father of ever calm Prashant called Delhi on Phone:"Dear Registrar Sir, please do not mind our persistent enquiry on <alleged> dispatch of the Judgment Order certified copy ; be surely convinced, about our not having received any communication from your office and about our not having signed any acknowledgement slip either.. .The matter is grave, serious. We do not hesitate to file a conspiracy complaint against the OPs before the Hyderabad City Police Commissioner for most apparently, fraudulently forging our signatures of acknowledgement, if and if you restate that your office has definitely dispatched and if you show us proof of acknowledgement".

We waited with abated breath for all our queries and for that "Historic "alleged acknowledgement slip (if at all, any!).

There came a local Bangalore city phone call, from a totally unknown person: "This is Sudhakar, a coffee shop owner seeking to speak to father of Prashant. Am I speaking to the desired person? Are you the bother-in-law of my close friend HP Ananda Murthy from whom I have heard about the tragic medical misadventure in your family?"

Prashant's father: "Yes Mr. Sudhakar, you got it all right; how can I help you?".

Sudhakar: "Sir, please accept my share of concern for the tragedy imposed on your family .Just recently in the month of August 1999, I lost my 13yrs old daughter to a medical mal- operation at Bangalore city's leading hospital. I have consulted with my neighbour and close friend who happens to belong to that noble profession of doctors."

Prashant's father: "It all sounds very strange and coinciding too!. Please accept my heartfelt condolences on the tragedy at your door step also".

Sudhakar: "Before I proceed further , please let me tell you that we have found out from the Government of India Gazette publications about your son's case being disposed off after total hearing of witnesses and counter witnesses. I have collected a copy of the Judgment Order also. By all means, this sacred order is a great land mark; the Hon'ble Bench of the NCDRC New-Delhi have clearly ruled the gross negligence of the doctors and the medical hospital institution and also awarded Rs15.5 lakhs as monetary compensation".

Prashant's father: "Mr. Sudhakar! Your phone call is simply sacred to us. We have been waiting since Feb 1999 for the certified copy of the Judgment Order. Now, your news comes to us like < The Savannah from the Heavens above>. Sudhakar, I want to personally meet you immediately".

"I am myself very keen to meet with you all; shall definitely see you today itself with a copy of the landmark Judgment Order": so saying he rang off the phone.

There was tremendous anxiety to possess that < sacred Order> at the earliest and rightly so, father wanted to dash off to the caller's residence himself .Suddenly the door bell rang and lo!, A tall figure standing at our doors announced: "Hello Prashant, I am Sudhakar who spoke to your father only an hour earlier; I am pleased to handover this Judgment Order copy in your Appeal Petition before the NCDRC, New Delhi",

Elated with joy, Prashant lost no time in being the first to read the relevant Order. His mother, his dear younger brother, his father all jumped into the reading fray and were all thrilled beyond words at the most favourable Judgement (Order).

"We all thank you, dear Sudhakar" interrupted Seshadri: "what you have handed over to us, is more precious than its weight in gold!. We have been waiting for this prized possession for over 6 months as of now", Thank you, Thanks a million".

Immediately our legal counsel Mr. Rao was informed of the good news and was invited to rush to our home. Equally anxious all these months, Mr. Rao the legal counsel, darted to our residence and was there within the next hour!

"Please let me read the Judgment Order": so saying he took the Order in his hands and after carefully going through, he spoke at last "It is simply wonderful".

"It is a land mark Judgment as far as pinning down the doctors for their gross criminal negligence, in causing the life shattering damage to our sweet Prashant. Let me read through the pages and lines on the compensation aspects as well", so uttering, he quickly waded through the thick of papers; but suddenly we all noticed his face turning grimmer and grimmer!.

Father: "Mr. Rao, all of a sudden the glow has disappeared from your face giving way to frowning why? What is the matter?"

Rao: "Oh ! , What a disappointment on the compensation aspect? We had clearly shown detailed just and realistic calculations to the Hon'ble Court during the arguments' stages; we had put up bold front in explaining the enforced expenses thrust on us before them; But awarding a meager "Two Pence equivalent of Rs.15.5 lakhs" against our justful calculations amounting to over Rs.580 lakhs is simply alarming": so saying he decided to straightaway start preparing for Appeal before the Higher Court for enhancement of compensation.

While this was the mixed reaction in the Appellant's camp, the criminally negligent doctors were perhaps celebrating gleefully, the occasion!!. Guess why? What for? They knew very clearly that Prashant and company cannot even Appeal before the Higher Hon'ble Supreme Court of India due to time delay factor. Provisions do exist in law to appeal before the Higher Court for any redressal but only within a time frame of not more than one month from the date of Judgment Order. Here it was!, the Opposite Parties were gleeing on the prospect of the complainants' Appeal for higher compensations being rejected outright on this <time barred >score!. Doctors, the Hospital Institution's Management, were all tuned to parting with the trivial compensation of Rs.15.5 lakhs as directed in the NCDRC Order. There was no end to partying on the prospect of having to pay only a smaller amount as compared to Rs.580 lakhs claimed.

Prashant the gallant fighter as he was already, did react at the mean compensation, grossly insufficient to meet even the enforced car driver's salaries for 10 years let alone till his old age and what to speak of tens of other expenses all enforced!.

"Mr. Rao, who will meet, this singled out expenditure (on driver alone) beyond 10 years?" angrily, for the first time, retorted Prashant.

"Where from we can meet scores of other enforced expenses as earlier discussed ?".

"Let us meet immediately and draft our Appeal to the Higher Court".

Rao (the legal advisor): "There is a big hurdle, a negative blockade for our next step!.The Higher Court may outrightly reject our Appeal on grounds < time barred beyond allowed time of one month>; we have crossed all grace period limits allowable .

Prashant: "Do not worry Mr. Rao: My dad is there to prepare **a powerful Appeal for condonation of delay, nearly 7 months delay, occurring for no fault of ours".**

Father: "Mr. Rao, you know that we are all waiting with abated breath to receive the Judgment Order copy from the registrar of the Hon'ble NCDRC at your address duly registered with them ; as also at the complainant's (address) ; We have made several attempts at the National Commission also".

Rao: "you have given me the leads correctly".

Seshadri: "I am pretty sure the Opposite Parties in connivance with courier/postal authorities would have "managed" either 1) < to stall movement of the registered letter of NCDRC from Delhi city itself >; or 2) must have managed with the courier/postal authorities at the receiving end to delay <delivery indefinitely> or 3) to declare <the post lost in transit>".

Rao: "I think you should head a detective Agency!; after all your thought could be the true facts".

Seshadri: "Mr. Rao, yes with you as my adviser, let us open a detective agency to help other needy poor people in similar distress situations!". And went on to add:

"By the way, I strongly feel the above suggested manipulations are a reality because the Hon'ble NCDRC has pronounced all OPs: OPI- the hospital institution ; OP2- the great "Nobel" laureate Dr. Adimanov who performed the butchery Act; OP3- the invisible Dr. Neurosurgeon ; OP4- the great Professor in Internal Medicine perhaps from some < celestial university!!>; OP5-the great Director of the Institution of Medical Sciences – ALL grossly negligent and deficient in service. This Court Order is a Directive and has bearing on the reputation of all OPs. Together with their legal adviser they must have hatched plan to delay, indefinitely delay the Judgment Order reaching our hands far beyond the one month permitted time frame".

Seshadri continued: "I cannot think of ,Mr. Rao, any other possibility because my telephonic talks with the registrar of NCDRC, my series of fax messages , my letters sent to them duly registered have all proved futile".

Rao: "I am fully in tune with your thoughts; a criminal conspiracy by the OPs in these delaying tactics seemed certain."

Seshadri: "Let us explain to the Higher court, namely, the Hon'ble Supreme Court of India, the whole episode by bringing out clearly how we are not at all responsible for the inordinate delay; how we got certified copy of the Land mark Judgment Order finally in September 1999 (a full 7 months later) after requesting for the registrar.

Losing no time, the duo (father and legal adviser) sat through several rounds of discussions extending into late midnight hours and finally brought out "the Land Mark Petition" before the Hon'ble Supreme Court of India.

The Appeal, as required under the law, **had also to, crystal clearly, bring out how the compensation offered is trivial compared to the astronomically huge enforced expenses; whether they are just and reasonable**. There was no scope for raising any new issues or presenting any new and fresh witnesses. Our learned counsel being a senior Advocate practicing in the very same Apex court had no difficulty in drafting the Appeal Petition.

After several day and night efforts, < A 300 page Appeal> was filed before the Hon'ble Apex Court under section 23 of the Consumer Protection Act (as arising from the Order of the National Consumers Disputes Redressal Commission New Delhi in OP 124/93)

The mile stone that went on to become a < Land mark> was anchored in October 1999!.

Minutes appeared to be days and days appeared to be months. Prashant, his parents kith and kin and their legal counsel were all charged with anxiety as to when and how the Apex court would receive our Appeal which was filed belatedly, albeit for no fault of ours. Finally Rao received the famous letter from the registrar of the Apex Court of our land. It brought the gladdest, on the earth for us, tiding that our case is < posted for admission or otherwise in December 1999>.

Prashant's father and their legal counsel planned the historic visit to Delhi Apex Court.

Once in the Court room, the Hon'ble Bench consisting of 3 eminent Justices directed the Appellant/ Petitioners to explain as to why their time barred Appeal should not be rejected outright.

The learned counsel for the Petitioner began his averments: "Your Honour, as a practicing senior Advocate of the Apex court, I would not have entertained the complaint at my end itself before approaching the Hon'ble Apex court; but here I am standing before the Hon'ble Bench to prove that the OPs have left <no stone unturned> to make sure that the NCDRC's Judgment Order did not reach the Appellants' hands even 6 months after the Order was pronounced in Feb 1999; the cat was out of the bag when the father of the Complainant requested the registrar of NCDRC to furnish them with a copy of the postal acknowledgment of the Judgment Order which, they claim to have dispatched to legal counsel's address as far back as Feb 1999!

They could not produce the same; further hectic enquiries through telephonic talks , registered letters, fax messages sent by Prashant's father to NCDRC registrar's office at Delhi, brought only standard stereo type replies "we have dispatched the certified copy of the Judgment Order in Feb 1999 itself !".

Finally we suggested to the concerned registrar to warn the Opposite Parties of a possible magistrate level enquiry into the apparent underhand intervention by them to wantonly, indefinitely delay 1) either in dispatching from Delhi NCDR Court order letter, 2) or in delivering the promptly dispatched post at the receiving end Bangalore city .The registrar finally sent, by registered post ,a certified copy of the < land mark Judgment Order> in September 1999, which was received promptly within 4 days of dispatching from Delhi.

The Hon'ble Bench at the Apex court were shown all these witnesses of our efforts to possess the certified copy!!

Convinced beyond shadow of doubt, our Appeal was finally admitted by the Hon'ble Bench and posted for further hearing. This must have undoubtedly sent shock waves into the OPs' camp!

Our Appeal before the Hon'ble Apex court did carry enough ammunition to blast < none –the- less arrogant> & <we are not negligent> asserting OPs.

Came Jan 2000! Dear Prashant, his parents, our legal Adviser, were all at Delhi to partake in the first hearing by the Apex court. The Court room was overflowing with enthusiastic public including host of highly enthusiastic advocates to hear the proceedings in this LANDMARK case. The public were also aware that the NCDRC court had held the doctors and the hospital institution <grossly negligent, grossly deficient in service to the hale and hearty Petitioner > because, it did take into cognizance that the Petitioner had only gone to the OP 1 Institution for diagnostic investigations but rendered the litigant paraplegic for life.

Promptly the OPs had filed their "Counter"/Objections/ Denials to our main complaint and pleaded not guilty of any disservice or deficiency in service or negligence!. In fact their counter was loaded with self praise, self accolades claiming that the incident of permanent damage was only the < rarest of rare cases in medical history>, that they have followed only <standard practices followed everywhere on the globe in getting rid of the ailment>, blob –blob and so on and so forth!!

Petitioner's Legal Adviser: "Your Honour, we have carefully gone through the Counter by the OPs Para by Para. They deserve to be outrightly rebuffed and rejected. However, we are seeking Your Leave to file our Rejoinder as Para by Para reply to their counter to expose the hollowness in their submissions in the counter.

Hon'ble Bench: "Rejoinder accepted; make sure you give copy of the same to the OPs also".

Petitioner's legal advisor: "Yes Your Honour, here are the requisite number of copies for the OPs".

Unfortunately at this crucial juncture fate took away our learned Counsel ; he died of heart failure.

When the Hon'ble Court met for the next hearing , it was

the Petitioner alone without his legal counsel in the court

Hon'ble Bench: "why don't you engage the services of a legal counsel to put forward your arguments?"

Petitioner's father: "Your Lordships!; we are seeking the Leave of the Hon'ble Court to present our case "in person" (IP) for these justful reasons :-

1) Firstly, because of the clarity of presenting the case can come more emphatically, more pronouncedly from the recipients of the ghastly tragedy namely family members

2) Secondly, because we just have no means to bear the huge / astronomical legal fees for engaging their services as we are already economically strangulated: with me having retired from service on reaching the age of superannuation (and without Pension facility); with my wife having given up the teaching job for obvious reasons of necessity of round the clock care to young Prashant; with his younger brother only recently starting to earn modestly".

Hon'ble Bench: "we will give you legal adviser who will guide you and conduct you through litigation, free of any financial burden".

Prashant's father: "we are indeed obliged, Your Honour!. For a third person to <enter our shoes> to feel the pain and suffering, it would demand round the clock living in our midst at least for a few weeks. Our late adviser during our litigation at the NCDRC level did exactly that, your Honour, for days on end. We therefore humbly appeal before the Hon'ble Bench to grant us Leave for appearing <in person>

Hon'ble Bench: "We may not permit the father of the affected person. However we have no objection for the Complainant himself appearing in person".

Prashant's father: "we are indeed obliged, Your Honour!

Hon'ble Bench: "Permitted; OPs to note the Directive".

;

Father returned to Bangalore from Delhi: Anxious mother of Prashant ran to the door to greet her spouse and Lo!, questions galore hurled at him in succession!

"Tell me what happened; so has the court permitted you to argue in person as was allowed in the previous NCDRC commission court?".

"Dear, the Apex court has permitted non engagement of any legal adviser and to argue the case in person. But......": so responded Seshadri to his better half's anxious enquiries.

"But, why this <but> is coming in between?": Another salvo from Prashant's mother!.

"You see dear, Apex court wants only the affected person to present his case of medical tragedy and medical negligence."

Hearing this, she expressed her apprehensions as to how Prashant could find time to prepare for arguing his case in the midst of heavy office work besides his compulsions

All the same she went on: "I have confidence in our dear son. Let us wait for him to return from office"

Prashant promptly arrived; mother took the lead: "Dear how was your day at office? I am sure You have had no inconveniences in movements within office premises, canteen, lecture hall? What about your light exercising schedule before lunch break? Did your attendant cum driver attend to your calls in time?"

Prashant smiling, replied all her questions: "Mummy, everything went well at office. I did not miss out on light exercising either"..

Mother feeling relieved: "Thank God, you are best looked after".

Prashant turning his attention to his father: "Daddy, what is the result of visit to the Apex court? Did you raise the issue of yourself arguing our case in person without engaging any legal counsel? And how did the Hon'ble Bench respond?".

Father:"Yes darling, the question did come up; but the Hon'ble Apex Court ruled that I, as father, the one not directly affected by medical negligence, cannot be permitted to argue the case in person; instead the Authorities have no objection if you, the direct victim of alleged negligence, argue your case or else you must engage the services of legal counsel only".

"I did opt for your arguing the case in person being pretty sure you are game for all challenges!".

Prashant: "yes you are right daddy. I am prepared for the onerous responsibility."

All in the family heaved a great sigh of relief at his gallant decision.

LANDMARK decision taken to appear before the Apex court in person, preparations began in right earnest. Both the concerned (father and son) were aware that they have to be thorough in their arguments in the Court, justful and without any bias; the Balance of Law does tilt, but only under the weight of Absolute Justice ; no room for anger, despair. But only the truth and nothing but Absolute Truth .

Whereas Prashant's father's extra ordinary efforts in studying all medico-legal aspects in the company of learned counsel had come good for the NCDRC case and for the preliminaries of the Apex court admission stage; Now it was the turn for <Father and son> to be closeted together for exchange of medical and legal points; the latter being busy with his professional work schedule, **his father had to find ways out for discussions**!

Prashant utilized the journey time to office for exchanging, with his father, all the medico-legal arguments and he went on noting down all arguments in his lap top computer.

The return journey from office to home was also utilized for the legal battle preparation with his father. Yet another hour was culled out for this task on returning home!. Poor Prashant would have logged already a full 10 hours on duty alone; and these 4 hours to legal battle preparations; yet another 3-4 hours for the mandatory medical attentions needs. During whatever time that was left over from the < 24 hours per day kitty >, he slept comfortably, soundly and got up fresh always!. What an enforcement on a human being!; And what for this torture?

The author wishes to leave it to the readers to gauge the depth of tragedy enforced by the lack of simple common sense of Dr.Vaidya & butchery deeds of Dr. Adimanov.

Finally the day dawned when we received the much awaited Notices from the registrar of the Hon'ble Supreme Court for the first hearing.

Prashant, accompanied by his mother, flew into the country's capital; father took the journey by rail two days earlier so as to be in time at Delhi to receive the VIP wheel chaired dignitary!

All went well and we all promptly reported in the Court hall for the hearing. Being the Complainant cum Petitioner, Prashant was called in to start the proceedings.

Lo! It was a tense moment for everybody.

There was hushed silence among the audience; the Court hall had been packed to capacity and people even standing. Unruffled, ever calm, cool and collected Prashant began: "Your Revered and Honoured Lordships, I would like to begin with statement that my hands automatically clasp together to offer our motherland's traditional <Namaste> to all majority of doctor-brethren and sister-doctors who undoubtedly belong to the most noble profession on the globe ,by dint of their highly and deeply thought over medical service they all render to humanity, (and the veterinary doctors to animal kingdom) to mitigate their sufferings, ailments- either acquired by or enforced on them".

"But here, I am going to unfold, before the Divine Hon'ble Bench, how thoughtlessness and arrogance; how half knowledge and self-pride displayed by a minority few black sheep from amongst the vast majority (in white coat and   stethoscope) could destroy peaceful living ; causing severe irreversible damage to this patient they have attempted to treat; and claimed to be the best treatment practiced all over the globe!. Pain clearly discernible on his face he continued: "Whereas it was not at all <UNAVOIDABLE>, by any yardstick on earth because: I was <hale and hearty> as certified by these very doctors themselves; although huge lobulated tumor masses had grown in the posterior mediastinum region of my thorax (as indicated by pre-operative X-ray of chest & pre-operaive CT scans), there were no outward symptoms of any ailment/ suffering except for <on and off fever>; taken inside for a simple surgical biopsy, the operating CT surgeon opened out 21 inches of my left hemi thorax…..".

The Hon'ble Bench instantly intervened to say "we did not find the <21 inches of my left hemi…> notings in the records available with us and directed not to deviate from the records available in this court".

The Petitioner took note of the directive, vowed again to speak only the truth; quoting only from the documents taken <on records> by the earlier NCDRC copy of which he was having with them.

Then he went on further with his averments stating: "Your Lordships, I seek the Leave of the Hon'ble Bench to state, I and my parents had consented only and only for a minor surgical procedure as a biopsy first, biopsy next procedure only for taking out a micro sized (grain sized) sample of the tumor masses......"

Again the Hon'ble Bench was quick to interrupt him and went on to warn him:"You are simply wasting the time of the Hon'ble Court with averments not at all to be found in the records/ files available with us. The Bench went on further, to suggest and directed Prashant's father: "you take these records from us into your hands and go on flagging or book-marking every point you want to elaborate in the court's file firstly and only then the proceedings can be continued and not otherwise": so stating the Hon'ble Bench gave time up to reassembling after lunch break; took up another case up to lunch time and adjourned for lunch.

Prashant and his father immediately thanked the Bench for the directions and feeling <obliged > set about the task of comparing each and every page from the court custody file and the petitioner's file. As the two- some (father & son) went deeper and deeper into the two files, mystery after mystery went on unfolding!!.

Guess what? The Court had only bits and pieces, as compared to the whole and genuine < taken on records> points which Prashant had relied on and had started making his averments in pre-lunch hearing session.

Soon <the cat was out of the bag>. We the two- some

(father & son) waited with abated breath for the Hon'ble Court to reassemble post lunch break.

The Hon'ble Bench did permit us to resume and wanted to know, introducing some humor, whether Prashant's father could <use up all the book marks given to him by the court master>.

Prashant submitted: "Your Lordships, the <court file> clearly and evidently appeared to have been tampered with and that many of the authentic witnesses < taken on records > by the previous NCDRC court did not find their place in the Hon'ble Apex Court's file".

The Bench instantly sought the Petitioner's reference file and carefully scrutinized the same. To their surprise the Hon'ble Bench did find the discrepancies between the two files. They could easily conclude from the scrutiny that somebody, somewhere, sometime during the records' journey from the NCDRC court to the Apex court, important evidences have either been not sent at all or made to <disappear >. The Bench immediately smelt the conspiracy and came to the rescue of the Petitioner firstly, by addressing a letter to the NCDRC court directing them to forthwith send each and every bit of paper forming part of the case under review in the Apex Court and secondly and simultaneously, permitting the Petitioner "to file any and all papers as his witness/ evidence" and posted the case for continued hearing the subsequent month.

It was a great moment for all in the Petitioner's camp. The Apex Court did find foul play by the OPs. The path of righteousness strictly followed by Prashant, the bold and the brave, was rendered totally <obstacles free> by The highly Jurisprudential pronouncements of the Hon'ble Bench.

The learned counsel for the OPs was questioned as to why this Apex court should not hesitate to order a magistrate level enquiry to find out the truth of missing evidence in the court's file.

Prashant in all had to appear before the Hon'ble Bench up to and excluding the final arguments stage, six times. At no point of time he lost his nerve; he was sure he was treading the path of absolute truth. The highly understanding Bench went on, at every stage, to appreciate the clarity and weight of his arguments; he never ever swerved from the path of truth and equally importantly , he never ever displayed any bitterness towards the medical men who had certainly damaged him lifelong.

However much the Opposite Parties tried to defend themselves, their arguments were exposed before the Hon'ble Bench as simply hollow and unsubstantiated by medical publications. It was made clear to them (the OPs) that their statements justifying their negligent acts must be substantiated/ evidenced from medical text books, publications from luminaries in the medical knowledge field. It was argued by the Petitioner that the <balance of law> does not favour one party against the other; nor does it disfavour either of the two parties. If a non medical man is pitted against a medical man in a legal battle, Jurisprudence dictated that both speak the same language from the same parental knowledge source.

The Petitioner submitted that he will be producing evidences from the sacred medical Quaran, sacred Granth Saheb, sacred Bible and sacred Bhagavad-Gita and the OPs cannot get away by simply making self serving statements from out of their brains before the Hon'ble Bench .They must, mandatorily, substantiate their arguments /averments quoting from the same sacred route namely –medical publications, medical journals, medical text books.

This appeal/objection by the Complainants was upheld/ sustained and the OPs were directed to support whatever arguments they make with references to medical publications. Such a Directive from the Hon'ble Bench to OPs could only shake their confidence in trying to escape their responsibility by uttering whatever that occurred in their brains and expecting them to be taken on records!. The Hon'ble Court by such a Directive had put brakes on their unreasonable, illogical and unsubstantiated averments and half the battle had been won for Justice.

A definite first victory for the Complainants!.

"You OPs can now continue": so directed the Hon'ble Bench.

Legal counsel for the OPs: "Your Honour, my client, the CT surgeon OP 2 in the case, has clearly averred that "I did not, at all, touch the spinal cord during surgery and the paraplegia deficit that had occurred was only the <rarest of rare cases perhaps even one in a million>".

Quick on his "feet" instantly, the petitioner submitted: "Your Lordships, I seek the Leave of the Hon'ble Bench to expose the OPs' explanations as only bundle of lies; I hereby produce this document, filed as Annexure to our complaint; this is an extract from <Dr. Gray's Anatomy>, a text book having the honour of being prescribed by scores of Universities across the globe, for recognized medical courses. The< splanchnology> chapter on vasculature of the spinal cord, clearly held out that damages could be caused to the spinal cord even remotely, without physically encountering it, by thoughtlessly meddling with supplementary blood supply arrangement through intercostals space by damaging arteries".

"And precisely Your Honour, the OPs THEMSELVES, have admitted in their OWN signed treatment records/patient discharge summary, that they have ligated two intercostals arteries as they were found feeding the extra grown tumor masses in the mediastinum posteriorly.

"There cannot be any greater and more transparent suicidal self-destroying evidences, Your Lordships": gleefully averred Prashant the Petitioner. And he went on further: "Your Honour, the OPs have averred in their statements that it is the rarest of rare case that paraplegia has occurred".

"This, my lord, is a futile attempt by the OPs to self-serving themselves and they are duty bound to explain how anything on earth can happen whether rare, rarer or rarest of rare or for that matter frequent , more frequent or most frequent without any induced /applied activity". And the Petitioner went on further:"I never ever entered the OT as a paraplegic!; How come I am paraplegic in the OT when once the CT surgeon started to drive his scalpel into my thorax!. The operating surgeon himself has admitted that he had to ligate the arteries as they were found feeding the tumor"; our Prosecuting medical witness has clearly stated that,< if intercostal arteries are ligated after branching off to spinal cord supply route there should be no problem. But if they are ligated before branching off i, e before teeing off then it is obvious that spinal blood supply is certainly tampered with>. Obviously baffled by the detailed analysis coming from a non-medical person, the OPs did not seem to be comfortable within themselves;

The legal counsel for the OPs rose from his seat uttering:"Your Honor ,the complainant is assuming that he is the Doctorate of doctors by stating that the arteries giving off branches to provide supplementary blood supply to the spinal cord have been ligated but..."

Grabbing this opportune moment, Prashant sitting in wheel chair, sought the Leave of the Hon'ble Bench to further clarify his point.

"Leave granted you may proceed to clear the anxiety in the OPs' minds": so directed the Hon'ble Bench.

Petitioner submitted: "Our learned counsel for OPs would probably have total clarity with my giving a down to earth parallel example!.The Grand Trunk Rail

Road Express proceeding from south to northwards (to Delhi), approached Itarsi junction. But the engine driver noticed rail track is grossly disturbed. He immediately applied brakes and brought the train to a complete halt- thereby avoiding a big catastrophe. Had he not been alert, he would have taken the train neither towards Delhi nor towards Allahabad but only derailment before the Tee off (branching off); it would have been a great tragedy".

"But here , My Lordships ,the great "Nobel laureate" CT surgeon OP2, by cutting off blood supply before the junction itself, has caused <Ischemia>(the lack of blood supply) not only to spinal cord but also to the other branches/adjacent organs of the human body".

The Hon'ble Bench after hearing these vivid explanations of the calamity of loss of/reduction of, blood supply to spinal cord from the most challenging Petitioner, intervened to signal the OPs:"Do you still need any further clarification. We are totally made aware of the ghostly crime and are convinced with the graphic explanation coming from the damaged person-that is, the Complainant himself"

Prashant sought Leave of the Hon'ble Bench to submit further: "Your Honor, consent was given by us including myself and my parents only for a biopsy procedure through a mini surgery only to take out a small grain sized sample of the unwanted extra-grown tumour masses; for histopathological examination in the hospital laboratory during the tenure of surgery itself. OPs own averments and declarations, in this context, clearly state: "before the surgery parents were explained about the plan of management, viz thoracotomy will be done and a piece from the mass will be taken and sent for histopathological examination and further management will be based on the report and the local pathology"

"Your Lordships", I would like to add further, "at the pre- diagnostic stage itself, it was known to one and all, that the tumour masses were huge, extensive spanning three consecutive (2nd, 3rd and 4th) ribs in the posterior mediastinum; had, most evidently, eroded, thinned these 3 ribs in continuous succession as crystal clearly displayed in the pre-operative X rays and CT scans!! And yet the "Nobel" Laureate –CT surgeon removed the whole of the tumor masses in one go!; Without even discussing with neuro specialist. Your Lordships, What procedure is this? It can only be barbarism, arrogance displayed when he came to know in the OT itself that they are benign and neurofibroma in nature"..

"We do not need a Mch –Post Doctorate qualified Doctor to explain this butchery act .It is a serious charge from us the aggrieved Petitioners; what right, he, a cardio thoracic surgeon, had to operate on neurofibroma and that too having clear cut extension into adjacent spinal cord through the anatomical hole called the < intervertebrate foramina > (in medical parlance) and when further management will be based only on the report and the local pathology".

"Even at this belated stage, he the butcher surgeon, could have consulted with the 'most apt' *professionals namely* the neurosurgeon/ neurologist/ neuro-pathologist all available under the same hospital roof at just an announcement on the inter- com- distance away from OT".

"Can there, Your Lordships, be any more glaring example of arrogance, overconfidence and most relevantly, deficiency in medical service and attention? To what low level the barbaric surgeon has stooped to come to Court and aver that he has not touched the spinal cord, that the paraplegia that has occurred is simply the < rarest of rare cases > in medical history, that he has followed the procedure followed all over the world !".

I strongly object to these OPs coming to Hon'ble Courts of Justice and uttering whatever that occurred in their brains as their sacred valuable statements. Under all circumstances both the litigant parties are to be jurisprudentially bound to produce witnesses / evidences duly substantiated by medical literature/ medical publications/medical journals written by luminaries in that field   . OPs' actions at the diagnostic stage as also at the surgical stage   cannot be found in the medical literature read across the globe!.**Their mal/ mis/non/ill actions, if at all to be qualified, ARE ONLY CRIMINAL".**

"OPs' actions, post operatively, are equally ghastly and criminal. These barbaric actions coming from minority few of the vast majority of noble men have brought disgrace to that unquestionably noble profession".

"I wonder, Your Honour, how the Indian Medical Council –a statutory Authority overseeing the smooth treatment procedures; encouraging advancements in medical sciences and scores of such noble acts, have turned a blind eye on such dastardly criminal acts coming although from a minority few in this noble profession".

"I have definitely not come to Courts of law, Your Honour, to seek the scalp and other physical punishments to the butchers. I want to live life gracefully, meticulously and purposefully without financial strangulations. I have sought reasonable monetary compensation from the criminals **to meet each and every expenditure enforced on me solely due to their negligence; which would not have been there, if this medical tragedy had not been forced on me. And by all standards this tragedy was avoidable; would never have taken place IF only the OPs had** resorted:-

a)   To total diagnoses

b)   To consultations with neuro specialists much before applying the scalpel on my dorsal spinal area

c)   To establishing through total knowledge and further diagnoses ,the risk benefit ratio of the intended procedure

d)   And if they had clearly realized that there was no emergency whatever

On the contrary they have:-

a)   Carried out half diagnosis

b) Failed to correlate the wear out/ erosion of 3 consecutive ribs and that too posteriorly with possible extension of these extra grown masses into the spinal cord through the anatomical hole called < inter vertebrate foramina>

c) Failed to establish where the intercostal arteries are going further supplying blood to which organs beyond the unwanted extra grown masses. (the doctors have themselves voluntarily admitted that two inter costal arteries were feeding these extra grown masses and therefore they were ligated!!)

d) Failed to carry out further tests/diagnoses to rule in / rule out involvement of other organs with a view to preventing damages to them during surgery!

e) Failed to map blood supply routes in the instant region in order to understand   which are all the organs that these intercostal arteries are supplying blood to, apart from the apparent masses".

"What more descriptions are required, My Lordships, to explain, to prove the ghostly inhuman action by these doctors in human shape".

"Physically shattered and battered apart, are the dreams of my life:-

a) To become a Ph.D. holder in the US in order to pursue the academics as Professor

b) To contribute to human society in the form of some useful product/ service.

Now I am reduced to the state of living vegetable needing

round the clock support and help to perform EVEN simple day to day activities.

If these helps do not come readily, then I am left without fulfilling even these petty and routine activities. My parents, younger brother and hosts of well wishers are always around me to boost my morale. This apart, I have been compelled to engage the services of

1)   A helper

2)   A physio therapist

3)   A nurse

4)   And certainly the most important help -a driver to keep me on the go to take me places including offices.

All these activities need money not simply in coins and rupee notes but in tens of thousands of rupees month on month, quarter-on-quarter, year on year till I bid good bye to this earth.

There certainly, is no hope of any semblance of recovery in the immediate decades to come, as clear from various publications on medical advancements <currently and in near future>

Under the circumstances, I appeal to the Hon'ble Court to dismiss all defense arguments of the OPs as simply hollow and without an iota of truth but only brought out for the sake of self- defence, without substance, and award the most reasonable and humble compensation of Rs 5.80 crores to cover all mandatory and enforced expenses. I seek the Leave of the Hon'ble Court to further emphatically state that each penny of the compensation sought is only to meet the enforced expenses, not at all applicable to all normal humans without any handicaps enforced!

"I entered the hospital on 19th Oct 1990 as a highly active youth of 20 +years of age driving a two wheeler (scooter) myself and rendered paraplegic for life; confined to wheel chair for life and enforced to seek help to get on in life hour to hour without which I would remain a living vegetable!"

"Your Lordships! The negligences by the OPs are so huge and lifelong damaging that no punishment is too big for the magnitude of the damage inflicted.

But nevertheless, I do not choose to seek any life term sentence for these singular most minority butchers in white coat and stethoscope only because I cannot get back my walking faculties simply by these OPs going to the gallows. However they, the OPs, deserve to be censured, black marked in their careers and ordered to compensate me monetarily for each and every enforced life activity, which I have already detailed earlier.

"Your honour, I can go on and on highlighting the ghastly damages caused to my body and mind; with all their- OPs' , qualifications; there is just no explanation on the globe except of course to attribute to their arrogance and lack of thought".

Even a good tailor would have <measured ten times before cutting the cloth once>, whereas this arrogant surgeon with half knowledge, with half diagnosed findings went ahead with <cutting arteries and removing ribs> at his free will"

"What justification, Your Lordships, this butcher had to remove organs left and right when his primary mission as permitted and consented to, was only to take out a tiny grain sized sample for histopathological investigations in the same hospital's laboratory?"

"My Lords!

"How did he think he could remove the tumor masses in their entirety without knowing the pathological nature -whether non malignant or malignant?"

"No sane patient or his attendants would have permitted removal of a malignant tumour, so huge and extensive!; Without detailed investigations by oncologists and that too in a hospital/institution totally dedicated to treatment of this dreaded disease".

"And If it were to be benign there, certainly, was no emergency; the excision procedures could have been easily deferred to future dates giving importance to the immediate need of completion of my education first".

"Further, Your Lordships, **the malignancy findings of the tumours, if any, would have dictated the necessity of ascertaining the stage of cancer:**

1) **whether in its initial stages**

2) **Or advanced stages**

And if in advanced stage, whether justified in removing them when the adjacent anatomical structures including the ribs are definitely involved ?!, **without any benefit of allowing the patient to die a peaceful imminent**

death instead of torturing him with needless surgery of such a highly advanced case.

And if it were only in initial stages, the oncologist would have certainly tried out cure with chemotherapy and or oral medicines".

"All such thoughts have been, Your Honour, thrown into the winds and **foolishly, the butcher surgeon decided to <excise out> even before <laboratory findings> Ah! What a decision making by a super qualified surgeon?!**

Ah! What a brainless creature the other criminal, investigating and damage initiating Internal Medicine Professor turned out to be!.

Kudos! To their brains,! Worthy of recommending their cases to the creator- Lord Almighty, for deputing them as Professor- Emeritus and Professor- Noble and Royal to the Celestial Universities deemed much superior than this earthly globe!!. Prashant ended his arguments by expressing his profound thanks to the Hon'ble Court thus: "I am very much thankful to the Hon'ble Court for having given me full opportunity to express my thoughts in the matter freely and without allowing any interruptions by the Opposite Parties".

The Hon'ble Court responded through a filial, parental and highly affectionate gesture when the 3 Hon'ble Justices rose from their seats and expressed their wonder and awe: "The way you conducted yourself so behavedly; your argument were so crystal clear and soothing. Even if you had argued another two days we would have gladly continued to hear you; they were simply so much arresting and compelling".

"We rarely come across such emphatic but soothing arguments". The Presiding Judge looked at the other two Member Judges and remarked: "Prashant had you been a member of the bar, we would not have had any hesitation in recommending you to the seat of an Hon'ble Judge of the Apex court. Am I right?" The entire audience filled with multitude of learned advocates (who had specially gathered to see how a non legal complainant himself presented and defended his case with dignity and clarity) rose and sang in one voice:

"Yes he is as good, for the coveted Honour"

These fine gestures brought uncontrollable tears of joy to the proud parents of the gallant Prashant, and readily hugged him spontaneously. Even in this scenario the proud parents could see their ever smiling, never- given- to- emotions and highly balanced son.

The Hon'ble Bench profusely thanked the complainant for bringing out his case with total clarity, duly substantiated with clinching impartial evidences from medical literature and publications, beyond any favours; And finally directed :< "The case is closed and reserved for Judgment Orders">.

Soon the entire audience of eager legal luminaries descended on the eloquent Petitioner to shower their overjoyed blessings on him. Most notable in this audience was no other than the highly respected & honoured Sri Arun Jetley–a very Senior practicing advocate, in the Apex Court of our motherland. He walked to the wheel-chair seated Prashant and congratulated him & his father for masterly arguing his own case In Person. He was overwhelmed with joy and blessed both son & father for land mark Judgement & success to follow soon. The young Petitioner felt highly honoured with his blessings so received.

Note: Sri Arun Jetley continued to serve the country as an Outstanding Leading Member of our country's Parliament and Central Cabinet handling the coveted portfolios as senior cabinet minister-Finance; Corporate Affairs; Defence; Information&Broadcasting; Law&Justice during the period 2009 to 2019

Both the parties had to < await judgment orders with fingers crossed > and < abated breath>. And finally, on the 14th day of May2009, the Hon'ble Apex Court of our motherland **pronounced its Judgment, a Land Mark at that**. It had taken into cognizance the inexplicable tragedy enforced on a hapless engineering student, the serious setback to normal living with the Complainant driven to a vegetative state with no possibility of , any semblance of decent living if left to himself.

A Land mark Judgment where the case was argued <In Person > by the complainant himself sitting in wheel chair all through the proceedings.

A Landmark Judgment pronounced after elaborate references to past medico- legal cases both within and outside the country.

A Land mark Judgment thoughtfully arrived at, after the Hon'ble Court itself went into various authentic medical literature including those produced as evidences by both the Complainant and the Respondents themselves. Interestingly, the OPs had themselves quoted extensively from a medical publication entitled <Glenn's Thoracic and cardio- Vascular surgery > [edited by Arthur B et all ;Sixth edition volume 2] to submit "that needle biopsy could miss a neuro fibroma; so excision biopsy (as in this case) should be resorted to"; "neurofibromas can occur as isolated lesions---; when these tumours occur near the vertical body, the presence of < dumb bell > tumor with extension into the spinal cord must be documented by CT or MRI scan". "If present, NEUROLOGICAL consultation is needed for combined resection".

The Land mark Judgment read: "These observations do undoubtedly justify an excision biopsy but equally support the case of the Complainant in as much that his case too was that had an MRI been performed, the extent of the tumor mass and its extension into the spinal Cord would have been revealed ;**we have therefore no hesitation in holding that the complete investigations prior to the actual operation had not been carried out".**

The Hon'ble Court had displayed exemplary inquisitiveness to get at the truth of the matter. In the process the Hon'ble Bench had < left no stone unturned> whether it be reading and rereading the complainant's version of the case and come out/ churn out from them the truth of the matter!!

OPs had averred: < it is submitted in addition, that as tumor though initially benign can cause several medical complications endangering the patient life and can also turn malignant at a later stage; it had been thought fit to remove the tumor along with the involvement ribs and that all care expected of doctors had been taken and that it was only a CT surgeon who had the skill to perform such a surgery and that help of a neurosurgeon would have been taken <if the tumor had any intra spinal extension and as in this particularly case there was no <such> extension the presence of a neurosurgeon was not required.>

The Hon'ble Bench has also dealt into intricate interpretations of <consent>. They have gone into cases in UK courts, in American courts and come out clearly on <informed consent>; on <real consent>; on <implied consent>; and come out empathetically: "consent that is given by a person after receipt of the following information:-1) The nature and purpose of the proposed procedure or treatment,2) the expected outcome and the likelihood of success; 3) the risks and the alternatives to the procedure and supporting information regarding those alternatives;4) and the effect of no treatment or procedure, including the effect on the prognosis and the material risks associated with no treatment.5)**Also included are instructions concerning what should be done if the procedure turns out to be harmful and unsuccessful.**

Armed with these clarities on <informed consent!>, the Hon'ble Bench has gone deeper into questions whether in an action for negligence/ battery for performance of an unauthorized surgical procedure, the doctor can put forward/ forth as defence, the consent given for a particular operative procedure as consent for any additional or further operative procedures/ performance in the interests of the patient and to provide absolute insight; in the case on hand the Hon'ble Court has studied into utmost details of past cases. The Judgment Order quoted: "Murray vs Mc Murchy, (1949) DLR 442 (1941) I WWR 989, the Supreme Court of British Columbia, Canada which pronounced the Judgment against the doctor who additionally removed fibroid tumor in the patient's uterus during the course of pre-planned caesarean section. The doctor did caesarean section alright for which he had consent from the patient. But to perform the removable of fibroid tumor without consent for this additional procedure from the patient even if it meant to wait for the patient to recover from the GA because sterilization was no any urgent situation and the doctor was duty bound to have waited to take informed consent from the patient herself.

****

CHAPTER- XXIII

PATIENT HEARING BY THE HON'BLE SUPREME COURT OF INDIA CONTD:-

Performing the sterilization operation without consent merely because the patient was already under general anesthesia was held by the Hon'ble Supreme Court of British Columbia Canada, to be not a valid defense.

Perhaps to strengthen their clarity further, this Hon'ble Bench in the instant case, has gone deep into yet another case:< Court of Appeal in England in the F,Inre, (1933) 3 DLR 260:60ccc136>. It was <held> that <the additional or further treatment which can be given (outside the consented procedure) should be confined to only such treatment as is necessary to meet the emergency, and as such, needs to be carried out at once and before the patient is likely to be in a position to make a decision for himself. Lord Geoff observed (ALL ER p566 g..j) "where, for example, a surgeon performs an operation without his consent on a patient temporarily rendered unconscious in an accident, he should do no more than is reasonably required in the best interests of the patient before he recovers consciousness. I can see no practical arising from this requirement which derives from the

fact that the patient is expected before long, to regain consciousness and can then, be consulted about longer term measures"

The Hon'ble Bench went on in its Judgment Order: "what is relevant and of importance is the INVIOLABLE NATURE OF THE PATIENT'S RIGHT in regard to his body and his right to decide whether he should undergo the particular treatments or surgery or not. Therefore at the risk of repetition, We may add that unless the unauthorized additional or further procedure is necessary in order to save the life or preserve the health of the patient and it would be unreasonable (as contrasted from being merely inconvenient) to delay the further procedure **until the patient regains consciousness and takes a decision, a doctor cannot perform such procedure without the consent of the patient"**

"It is clear from the evidence in the case before us, that there was no urgency in the matter as the record shows that discussions for the deferment of the proposed excision biopsy had taken place between the complainant, his parents and Dr. Adimanov (name changed) in the OPD (Out Patient Department) and the consent for the procedure had been obtained. Also in the light of the observations in the cited case any implied consent for the excision of the tumor cannot be inferred. even the medical publications brought before them, as evidences by both the parties,clearly bring out the necessity of thorough diagnoses before even inking, on paper any prescription The seventy pages of the Judgment Order are replete with such highly **Jurisprudential unbiased study with open minded scrutiny of all the evidences put forward before them (the Hon'ble Bench) by both the litigants. And the Hon'ble Bench has left no stone unturned to go into greater depths to dispassionately, study several medical negligence cases brought before the Apex courts of British Columbia Canada, the USA; Courts of Appeal in England besides going through:**

Whether it is on the aspects of total complete diagnosis before surgery; whether on the aspects of additional surgery far in excess of the simple surgical biopsy procedure contemplated to start with; Whether it is on the aspects of consent for a simple biopsy procedure through minor surgery or implied or taken for granted consent unilaterally decided by the operating surgeon as the helpless patient lay on the Operating Table duly generally anaesthetized; The Hon'ble Court did not hesitate to go into all aspects thoroughly so as to establish negligence or non negligence beyond shadow of any doubt most clinchingly..

Whether there was any urgency or emergency to go ahead with additional surgical procedure without the express consent of the grown up patient without waiting for the patient to come out of general anesthesia.

Whether it is a case of occupational negligence or professional negligence or no negligence at all, keeping in view a simple lack of care, an error of judgment or an accident cannot be considered as proof of negligence on part of a medical professional.

Further a case where the doctor has followed a practice acceptable to the medical profession of that day cannot be held liable for negligence merely because a better alternative course or method of treatment was also available or simply because a more skilled doctor would not have chosen to follow or resort to that practice or procedure which the accused followed.

The Hon'ble court has evaluated ALL the evidences in the background of the above discussed observations and has gone on to accept the arguments of the Complainant who did not question the skill or competence of the operating surgeon but who charged him for the lack of care and caution and the neglect on the part of the attending doctors and Dr. Adimanov in particular, to make the necessary pre-operative investigation that had led to the complications at the time of the operation and thereafter.

We now come to the allegation with regard to the negligence shown at the stage of the operation itself. "The record shows that the tumor mass 4cm x 4cm dimension was located on the left upper chest side of the thorax and there had been erosion of the 2nd, 3rd, and 4th ribs"; "The discharge record pertaining to the operation also reveals that there was a 1cm opening in the vertebral body sexposing spinal cord at the thorax level and that the tumor <had been excised along with the 4th rib>.

"The record also shows that the tumor was not only Confined to the thorax but had extended into the

Posterior mediastinum also, showing that it had some connection with the spinal cord".

" It is in this background, the Hon'ble Court recorded in its Judgment, that the Complainant has argued that whereas a cardio thoracic surgeon was undoubtedly competent to perform the surgery for the excision of the tumor, but as the tumor had extended into the posterior meditational column containing intercostals blood vessels and nerves, the involvement of a neurosurgeon was essential and as this procedure had not been adopted a case of negligence or indifference on the part of the attending doctors has been proved.

"It has also been highlighted", by the Complainants "that the information that the the tumour had extended into the mediastinal zone and 2nd, 3rd and in particular 4th ribs had been eroded, was available with the doctors long before the operation and thus the fact that the tumour had extended into mediastinal zone (column) was a clear possibility".

The Hon'ble Court in its final study of past cases with a view to coming to clinching decision as Judgment has referred to yet another past case; <we are also cognizant of the fact that, in a case involving medical negligence, once the initial burden has been discharged by the complainant by making out a case of negligence on the part of the hospital or the doctors concerned, the onus then shifts on to the hospital or to the attending doctors and it is for the hospital to satisfy the court that there was no lack of care or diligence as in <Savita Garg (smt) vs

Director National Heart Institute (2004) 8, SCC 56> and goes on further to rely on the Judgment: "if the hospitals fail to discharge their duties through their doctor being employed on job basis, employed on contract basis, it is the hospital which has to justify and not impleading a particular doctor will not absolve the hospital of its responsibilities".

And finally, this instant Land mark Judgment Order concluded as below:

"In the light of the above facts, we have no option but to hold <that the attending doctors were seriously remiss in the conduct of the operation and it was on account of this that the paraplegia has set in. We accordingly confirm the findings of the National Commission (the previous court of litigation) on this (negligence) score as well".

As for compensation enhancement the Apex Court has This to say in its Final Judgment Order:

"Concededly, the Complainant is a highly qualified individual and is gainfully employed as an IT engineer. The very nature of his work requires him to travel to different locations but as he is confined to a wheel chair he is unable to do so on his own. His need for a driver cum attendant is, therefore made out.

The complainant has also sought compensation towards nursing care as he is unable to perform even his daily ablutions without assistance. We grant expenses on this Score

Likewise the complainant has sought compensation towards physiotherapy etc. We grant these expenses as well.

Further Judgment Order goes on: "keeping in view the need for continuous medical aid which would involve expensive medicines and other materials and the loss towards future earnings etc, we direct a lumpsum payment"

In addition we direct a payment towards the <pain and Suffering> that the appellant has undergone.

The Hon'ble Court concluded its Judgment Order thus:

"Before we end a word of appreciation for the complainant who, assisted by his father had argued his matter. We must record that though a sense of deep injury was discernible throughout the protracted submissions made while confined to a wheel chair, he remained unruffled and with behaved quiet dignity, pleaded his case bereft of any rancor or invective for those who, in his perception, had harmed him"

<SUCCESS NEVER EVER DISAPPOINTS THE BOLD & THE GALLANT>

The writers of this biography- PRASHANT's parents will feel honoured if all our brothers and sisters, unfortunately driven to similar physical compulsions take heart from this real life story and develop steel will to fight and come up in life. Ten out of ten such attempts will surely meet with success and rise in society and social order and service perhaps far above millions of normal people, who are otherwise blessed with sound health credentials.

Likewise the authors wish to appeal to one and all, to browse the internet, acquire fairly deep knowledge so as to explain their case before doctors most powerfully and forcefully to avoid pit falls in diagnoses and treatment; so as to insist on SECOND OPINION; and to insist on RISK BENEFIT RATIOS of proposed treatment to be undergone or refused. (for whatever reasons such as no urgency, time required for funds arrangements, or more importantly, for continuing education right up to Doctorate Level as in the instant case).

A word for the Medical Authorities too. Majority most doctors do approach their patients very cautiously and treat them carefully. Such men and women in white coat are definitely second Gods to society and humanity. They deserve unreservedly, reverence and admiration even though, in stray cases the diseases may not be cured for no fault of theirs.

But unlike the above dealt Prashant's case, abundant care, caution have to be mandatorily imposed on all treatment procedures. Towards this end, the Medical Councils and such other State Authorities must mandate <Dos and Don'ts> for each and every procedure, on each and every human patient (not permitting any generalization) **and for that matter on all other living beings existing on this globe.**

ONLY THEN TENS OF THOUSANDS OF PRASHANTS CAN RETURN SAFELY AFTER DIAGNOSTIC INVESTIGATIONS.

OTHERWISE BE PREPARED LIKE this book's HERO PRASHANT: - FIGHT he did, BRAVELY and BOLDLY;

OVERCOME he did, HIMALAYAN ROAD BLOCKS;

SMILE he did, all through STRESSES & STRAINS;

SKY ROCKED he, to NAME & FAME;

BUT had to bid GOOD –BYE to MOTHER EARTH

DECADES EARLIER at his YOUTHFUL age of 41 Years only (28th June 2011)

NATIONS OF THIS GLOBE LET US ALL REMAIN UNITED FOR ALL SUCH NOBLE CAUSES OF UPHOLDING JUSTICE IN ALL ASPECTS OF LIFE ON EARTH FOR ALL LIVING BEINGS INCLUDING HUMANS.

+ Bibliography

This Author wishes to gratefully acknowledge with million thanks to the enlightened Authors, for their transmitting clinching medical Knowledge **eve**n to a non medical man: to understand how the paraplegia damage has been caused AND MORE IMPORTANTLY **to understand as to how it could have been avoided in all cases like that of our Dear Prashant, who was hale and hearty without any pre-existing ailments**.

1)	Extracts from Text book on General Thoracic Surgery	Thomas Shields
2)	Spinal Vasculature neurology: Chapter 7 ,Anatomy	Dr Grey
3)	Central Neurogenic Tumors of the Thoracic region	Med-Line Data Base ; National Library of Medicine ,USA Farid.M.Shamji ;Thomas. R. Shields & Others

4)	Diagnostic &Treatment Options for Neuro-fibromas	Robert.R.Chase ;Stephen Bosacco ; Richard Levenberg
5)	Extracts from Text Book on < Radiology &Imaging >	David Sutton ;Jeremy P R Jenkins & Others
6)	Extracts from Text Book on < The Biological Bases for Modern Surgical Practices >	David Sebaston
7)	Study of Tumours in Text book < Pathologic Basis of Diseases >	Stanley .L.Robins
8)	Extracts from Text Book on < Current Surgical Practices >	Michel Hobsley &Others ; Published by The Royal College Of Surgeons
9)	Extracts from Text Book On < Principles Of Surgery >	Seymour .I. Schwarts; G .Tam Shives.
10)	Ionising Radiation Permissible Levels Regulations ICRP 1984-92	International Council for Radiological Protection
11)	The <WHO > manual on Radiation PROTECTION in Hospitals &General Practices ; AND The Atomic Energy Regulation Board	ICPR 1984-92

12) Carcinogenic Agents and their Cellular Reactions	Dr. Robbins ;3 rd Edition
13) International Protocol for Treatment of Acute Spinal Cord Injuries	Displayed in all hospitals' Emergency Treatment Wards as First –Aid Guide lines
14) Diagnostic Cytology and its Histo-pathological Bases	Leopold .G. Koss
15) The Principles of Surgical Management in Dumbbell tumours	PUB- MED ,National Library of Medicines (NLM) Yuksel.M ; Pamir .N ; Ozer. F ; Batirel H.F. ; Ercan.S
16) VATS resection of mediastinal neurogenic dumbbell Tumours	Mc Kenna R.J ; Maline D ; Pratt G
17) Dumbbell Neurogenic Tumours of the mediastinum – their Diagnosis & Management	Mayo Clinic Proc-1978 ; PUB-MED NLM ; Akwari O.E; Payne Y.S
18) Combined Approach to dumbbell intra-thoracic & intra spinal neurogenic tumours	Grillo H.C ; Ojemann R.G and Ors

19) A COMBINED method of removing Hour-glass shaped neurogenic Mediastinal –intra vertebral tumours	Irger I.M ; Koroleva N.S ; Stolypin S. V
20) Diagnosis & Surgical Management of Mediastinal neurogenic tumours	Zhang Z ; Zhou Y ; Cui Y and Ors
21) Diagnosis Imaging and surgical treatment of dumbbell tumours of the mediastinum	Ricci C ; Gagliardi ; and Ors
22) Dangers to spinal cord arterial Vascularisa-tion during surgery for neurogenic tu-mours of the posterior mediastinum (**Article in French; duly trans-lated**)	Guidicelli R ; Pellet W ; Fuen-tes P ; Huevt P
23) Anesthesiologic prob-lems in unsuspected extra-adrenal Pheo-chromocytoma	PUB-MED NLM ; 17 , Anesthesist 1985 ; Lenz ; Lampl L ; Hug J

24) Laparoscopic Approach ; Department of Minimal Access Surgery	Sir GangaRam Hospital (New-Delhi, India) ;Choubey P K ;Vashishta A Khullar R ; Sharma A ; Soni V ; Baijal M; Dhir A ; Dewan A October 1989
25) Combined posterior & postero-lateral ONE-STAGE removal of giant cervical dumbbell Schwannomas	Orukaptan 1111 ; Gurcay O ; Department of Neurosurgery
26) Current Status of Surgery for mediastinal tumours ,duly **(Article in Japanese; duly translated)** 27) Pre-operative embolization in surgical treatment of spinal thoracic dumbbell Schwannomas	PUB-MED (NLM) 1989 October Nakahara K A Case Report 1996 June ; PUB-MED (NLM) Neuro-Surgical Science ; Fiumara E ; D' Angelo V ; Florio Fo ; Nardella M ; Bisceglin M

Acknowledgments

Through this book i would like to take the opportunity to acknowledge and thank all our dear friends and family members, some of whom don't find a mention in the different episodes in the book but have supported us all through the difficult phase of our life and we will be ever indebted to them.

Family -
Jayaprada, H.P Krishna Murthy & Family
G.D Sharma and Family
G. Nagaraj, Indira & Family
Chimma Baabu and Pedda Baabu
H.P Ananda Murthy
H.P Vasudev Murthy
Anand Rao & Family
Madhava Rao & Family
Prasan Kumar, Dr. Vandana & Family
Rajendra, Vijayalakshmi & Family
Uday Simha, Dr.Aparna & Family
Gurucharan & Family

Friends -
Nirmala, P.V Bhat & Family
Saroja, Narasimhamurthy & Family
Mohan Rao & Family
B.S Roopa & Family

Acknowledgments

P.K Bhat & Family
Jayalakshmi, Narayan Rao & Family
Biksham & Family
Rajesh Shivanna & Family
Sudha Rajamani & Family
Kishor Dutt & Family
Sunil Dutt Jha, Poornima & Family
K. Subrahmaniam
Sriram Jutturi
Shalabh Singh
Shivesh Kumar
Chagla S.M.C
Rajiv Bijjal
Wing commander Krishnan
Niranjan Nerlige
Mahalinga

Prashant, rayonnant as the sun,
Every battle you won,
Your endurance
a source of inspiration,
You, our dear,
with the everlasting smile,
Will make us walk for miles.
Smt. & Shri M.R. Seshadri & Family
In memory of Prashanth Seshadri Dhananka 28-09-1969 to 28-06-2011

9 789390 040186